Cracking Gilles Deleuze's Crystal

This book is dedicated to the memory of my French teacher,
Noël Kirrane (1955–2008)

Cracking Gilles Deleuze's Crystal

Narrative Space-time in the Films of Jean Renoir

Barry Nevin

EDINBURGH
University Press

Edinburgh University Press is one of the leading university presses in the UK. We publish academic books and journals in our selected subject areas across the humanities and social sciences, combining cutting-edge scholarship with high editorial and production values to produce academic works of lasting importance. For more information visit our website: edinburghuniversitypress.com

Edinburgh University Press Ltd
The Tun – Holyrood Road
12 (2f) Jackson's Entry
Edinburgh EH8 8PJ

First published in hardback by Edinburgh University Press 2018

Typeset in Monotype Ehrhardt by
Servis Filmsetting Ltd, Stockport, Cheshire

A CIP record for this book is available from the British Library

ISBN 978 1 4744 2629 9 (hardback)
ISBN 978 1 4744 2632 9 (paperback)
ISBN 978 1 4744 2630 5 (webready PDF)
ISBN 978 1 4744 2631 2 (epub)

Contents

Figures

Notes on Style

By and large, I have cited French texts in their original French editions rather than opting for their translated editions. As aspects of this book may appeal to readers without a command of French, English translations appear in the body of the text and the original French is included in endnotes. Certain key terms developed by Deleuze remain in the French language in order to retain nuance and aid syntax. I have chosen to retain the French-language titles of films made in France. Conversely, titles of Renoir's American productions are given in their original English-language versions. British spelling norms have been respected, but cited texts respecting American norms remain unchanged. All typographical errors are my own.

Acknowledgements

In 2009, with one hour to spare and nothing to read, I viewed Jean Renoir's *Partie de campagne* (1936) for the very first time. I was enthralled by the image of Rodolphe (Jacques Brunius) opening the shutters of a provincial restaurant to reveal Henriette (Sylvia Bataille) swinging on a tree, bathed in natural light. Although the same moment continues to move me after innumerable viewings, such rewards alone are not always enough to sustain four years of research. I would like to take this opportunity to thank a number of colleagues and friends, without whom this book could not have been envisaged, let alone completed.

This book has been developed from my PhD thesis for which the research was funded by a Galway Doctoral Research Scholarship from the College of Arts, Social Sciences, and Celtic Studies at the National University of Ireland, Galway. L'Association des Études Françaises et Francophone d'Irlande (ADEFFI), in association with the Swiss Embassy in Ireland, also provided generous financial support for my research trip to the University of California, Los Angeles. Travel to important research events was facilitated by bursaries from the Association for Studies in French Cinema (ASFC) and the Society for French Studies (SFS). Without the generous funding offered by each, it would not have been possible for me to acquire the full range of necessary research materials, or to attend numerous conferences that provided helpful feedback.

Essential research at the Jean Renoir archives at UCLA was assisted by many members of academic staff. Brian Clarke processed much paperwork over a number of months to secure my registration at the university. The entire library staff worked efficiently to locate key documents in a timely manner. I particularly wish to thank Julie Grahame, who provided me with library training at very short notice upon my arrival at the university, and regularly offered practical advice on archival research. Janet Bergstrom acted as temporary faculty adviser during my research trip and generously allowed me to attend her insightful seminar on Renoir's work.

Jenny Romero, of the Margaret Herrick Library in Los Angeles, permitted me to view important production files regarding Renoir's post-war work, allowing me to maximise the potential results of my trip.

I have been fortunate to receive support from a number of colleagues over the course of this study, who share my fascination with Renoir's work. Katie Golsan spoke to me of her interviews with the cast of *The River* (1951), and provided encouraging feedback on my archival research. Martin O'Shaughnessy personally provided copies of *Chotard et cie* (1933) and *Madame Bovary* (1934), each of which was otherwise unavailable. Keith Reader provided me with encouraging support and valuable contextual knowledge for my research on *Le Crime de Monsieur Lange* (1936) at a number of conferences. I am particularly grateful to Susan Hayward, who read a previous draft of this work, generously offered extensive feedback, and provided a much appreciated source of encouragement and support as I prepared to tailor the book for publication. Gillian Leslie, Richard Strachan, and Eliza Wright of Edinburgh University Press patiently provided steady support and helpful information throughout the publication process.

I have received consistent support from the library staff, the Huston School of Film and Digital Media, and members of the French department at NUI, Galway. I wish to thank Rosie Dunne, who offered essential advice regarding formatting and referencing. I particularly wish to express my gratitude to Geraldine Curtin, who patiently processed innumerable requests for inter-library loans, including many essential books and articles on Renoir, and passed on helpful suggestions from her own experience of research. I am especially grateful to all the members of the French department, who have provided a supportive environment since I began my undergraduate degree in 2006. Maria Scott strongly encouraged this project when it was merely a vague idea. Aoife Connelly, Maura Stewart, and Jennifer Martyn patiently listened to my many rants. The members of my graduate research committee provided essential feedback throughout the completion of this study. Máire Áine ní Mhainnín provided frequent encouragement and valuable suggestions. Sylvie Lannegrand, who has guided my learning since my very first French lecture at NUI Galway in 2006, continued to provide incisive comments and feedback on my research throughout my four years of research. Philip Dine introduced me to Renoir's *La Grande Illusion* (1937) and *La Bête humaine* (1938) over the course of my undergraduate degree, and I was privileged to have his generous and enthusiastic support as my director of studies. As co-supervisor of my doctoral research, Conn Holohan offered essential feedback throughout my research, particularly on my methodology. Conn's enthusiastic approach to film theory and philosophy encouraged me to penetrate the more difficult aspects of Deleuze's work.

Of the many colleagues who aided my project, I must reserve my greatest thanks for Catherine Emerson, the second of my two PhD co-supervisors, who provided me with my first opportunity to create a presentation on French film during my final undergraduate year, and introduced me to the subjectivity of history, which profoundly influenced my approach to Renoir's body of work. Catherine frequently set aside her own work throughout my four years of research, including a significant portion of her much deserved sabbatical year, to read countless drafts and make essential suggestions, all of which have moulded my perspective on the relationship between Renoir's life and work. Thanks to her unwavering support, endless patience, and contagious enthusiasm for both teaching and research, Catherine turned the potentially isolating task of conducting this research into a productive, ongoing dialogue which, I am glad to say, did not end with the completion of this work. Catherine's snarling contempt towards *The River* still pains me deeply, but I am willing to forgive her.

Fiona, Aisling, Sherida, Carlotta, and LD made certain that there was always tea and chocolate in the house. Most of all, I wish to take this opportunity to thank my sisters, Laura and Kate, and my parents, James and Margaret, who have consistently helped me to keep a practical perspective on my studies, and who all ensured that I never starved. I must add a special word for my father, who explained deep focus technology to me and casually bought me *The Maltese Falcon* (Huston, 1941), *The Third Man* (Reed, 1949), *Sunset Boulevard* (Wilder, 1951), and *Rebel Without a Cause* (Ray, 1955) a number of years ago, accidentally igniting a passion that I have been fortunate enough to channel into this project.

An earlier version of some of the material in Chapter 1 appeared in the *Journal of Urban Cultural Studies*. Portions of Chapters 2 and 3 previously featured in different volumes of *Studies in French Cinema*. Material has been reprinted by kind permission of Intellect and Routledge respectively.

Preface

This book does not aim to provide a comprehensive account of Jean Renoir's entire body of work. It represents a conjuncture of two growing interests: first, an admiration for Renoir's portrayal of class in a number of films, especially *La Chienne* (1931), *Le Crime de Monsieur Lange* (1936), and *The Golden Coach* (1952); second, a growing enthusiasm for Gilles Deleuze's film philosophy, which provided me with a liberating foundation for a revised approach to the innovative narrative styles pioneered by the quintessential French *auteur*. Deleuze convinced me that previous studies of Renoir's films, despite their careful attention to Renoir's distinctive narrative style at each stage of his career, had not done justice to the importance of temporality to Renoir's portrayal of societal hierarchies. Remedying this oversight and building on current knowledge of Renoir's technical achievements, political engagement, and close attention to class structures, this book examines the relationship between time and space in Renoir's films, examining key aesthetic turning points, political influences, and stylistic motifs over the course of Renoir's career, among them Renoir's public commitment to the Front populaire, his post-war costume dramas, and his *mise en scène* of the country and the city. In each case, this book argues for the importance of Deleuze's film philosophy towards a deeper understanding of the core components of Renoir's distinctive narrative style, whilst also assessing and amending the critical limits of Deleuze's insights.

The present study insists that it is impossible to adequately consider Renoir's temporal representation of societal hierarchies by isolating them from spatiality, hence the space-time of the title. The term, defined by Russell West-Pavlov as 'a hybrid dimension in which both space and time as relational variables together form a variable composite', has continued to be used in physics since Albert Einstein's theories of relativity punctured the illusion of the independence of space and time.[1]

The value of recognising the integral relationship between space and in Renoir's work is indirectly indicated by scholars of literature and film alike. Drawing on Einstein's Theory of Relativity and concurring that time is inseparable from space, Mikhaïl M. Bakhtin develops the concept of the chronotope (literally 'time-space' in Greek) to emphasise the 'intrinsic connectedness of temporal and spatial relationships' in literature.[2] Bahktin remarks that:

> In the literary artistic chronotope, spatial and temporal indicators are fused into one carefully thought-out, concrete whole. Time, as it were, thickens, takes on flesh, becomes artistically visible; likewise, space becomes charged and responsive to the movements of time, plot and history.[3]

Although Bahktin is addressing the specific case of the novel, his theories are equally amenable to cinema studies. Jean Epstein, arguably the most insightful early theorist of time in cinema, argued that film, unlike human perception, is not hampered by a 'physiological inability to master the notion of space-time and to escape this atemporal section of the world, which we call the present and of which we are almost exclusively conscious'.[4] For Epstein, 'if [. . .] the cinema inscribes a dimension of time in a dimension of space, it also demonstrates that there is nothing absolute or fixed about these relations'.[5] Epstein further argues that the mutual implication of space and time operates as a register 'of the variance of all relations in space and time, of the relativity of every measurement, of the instability of all markers [*repères*], of the fluidity of the universe', evoking Bakhtin's description of the chronotope as 'the place where the knots of narrative are tied and untied'.[6]

This book aims to explore the meaning and implications of these claims, firstly by relating Deleuze's film philosophy to a body of spatial theory (the texts of Henri Lefebvre, Michel de Certeau, Doreen Massey, Deleuze and Félix Guattari among others) and to the spatial and temporal preoccupations of film theorists, a number of whom are contemporaneous to the periods analysed, such as Epstein and Éric Rohmer; secondly, through interpretations of a variety of films directed by Renoir.

The Introduction situates Deleuze's insights in relation to previous scholarship on Renoir and Deleuzian readings of Renoir's work in order to produce a flexible methodological framework that may be further modified by the readings it generates. Subsequent chapters closely engage with the relationship between space and time in a diverse range of films directed by Renoir during the silent era, the conversion to sound, his famous affiliation with the Front populaire, the eve of war, his stint as an émigré director in Hollywood, and his post-war 'transnational' period.

Introduction

It is Renoir who had an acute awareness of the identity of liberty with a collective or individual future, with a surge towards the future, an opening of the future.[1]

– Gilles Deleuze

The space presented to the spectator is as movable as the spectator [. . .]. Not only do solid bodies move in space, but space itself moves, changing, turning, dissolving and recrystallizing.[2]

– Erwin Panofsky

Jean Renoir: *l'exception glorieuse*

André Bazin's landmark article, 'L'Évolution du langage cinématographique' ('The Evolution of the Language of Cinema', first published in 1958), retrospectively argues that Renoir alone held 'the secret of a cinematographic narrative capable of expressing everything without chopping the world up, of revealing the hidden meanings of people and things without interfering with their natural unity'.[3] For Bazin, Renoir's tendency to avoid montage in favour of deploying a mobile camera, deep space, and an ongoing dialectic between on-screen and off-screen space, elevated the cinema towards a closer ontological engagement with reality and, by extension, fulfilled what Bazin perceived as the seventh art's core vocation.

Renoir's work exemplifies Bazin's criteria to the extent that the theorist consecrated an entire book, *Jean Renoir* (published posthumously in 1971), to the director's body of work. Although Bazin's texts continue to exert a salient influence on studies of Renoir's narrative style, scholars are still catching up with Bazin's vision of the 'hidden things' revealed by Renoir's preservation of continuity in space and time. This concern constitutes the core question posed by this book. A comprehensive examination of the relationship between space and time in Renoir's films demands an analysis of two key facets of Renoir's work that have proven crucial, either individually or in combination, to virtually all critical studies of Renoir's oeuvre to date.

The first of these is Renoir's lucid dissection of social hierarchies, most notably class barriers, through a variety of motifs including costume design, speech, décor, and theatrical etiquette. Renoir writes in his autobiography:

> When a French farmer finds himself eating at the same table as a French financier, these two Frenchmen have nothing to say to each other. One is entirely indifferent to what interests the other. But if we imagine a meeting between our French farmer and a Chinese farmer, they will have lots to tell one another. This theme of the grouping of men through jobs or shared interests has pursued me throughout my entire life and continues to do so. It is the theme of *La Grande Illusion* [1937]. It features in every one of my works, more or less.[4]

One could certainly argue that this outlook was instilled in Renoir long before he even began his career as a director. It is worth remembering that Renoir's mother, Aline Charigot, was of peasant origin, and that the Montmartre residence within which his father, Impressionist painter Pierre-Auguste Renoir, secured his family's privileges contrasted strongly with Montmartre itself, which, as Martin O'Shaughnessy notes, was 'indicative of a degree of marginality, for the area was classically associated with prostitution, crime, artists and the entertainment industry, all a far cry from bourgeois respectability'.[5] Furthermore, Pierre-Auguste, for whom 'money already held little appeal' as a teenager according to Jean, rejected bourgeois decorum throughout his life, preferring to present himself, in Jean's words, as 'a worker of the painting profession' rather than as an artist.[6] Thanks to Renoir *père*'s success, Jean's family was privileged with servants and the Renoir family divided its time between Montmartre, Essoyes (his mother's homeplace), and Les Collettes in Provence, where Pierre-Auguste spent his twilight years.[7] Furthermore, Renoir was exposed to the exclusionary nature of class barriers and the final breath of Europe's pre-war aristocracy whilst serving as a cavalry officer and pilot during the Great War, an experience which famously laid a foundation for *La Grande Illusion*.

As Renoir himself suggests, his penetrating investigation of hierarchised societies lends consistency to a career that spanned over four decades, brought the director from Europe to Africa, Hollywood, and Asia, and which saw Renoir develop from a silent filmmaker into one of the most audacious innovators of the early sound era, the French Left's famous filmmaker during the 1930s, and a leading international filmmaker of the post-war period. A small number of Renoir's silent films (*Nana*, 1926; *Le Tournoi dans la cité*, 1928; *Le Bled*, 1929) took societal divisions such as class, religion, and colonialism as their core focus but, as O'Shaughnessy observes, it was not until the advent of sound that Renoir's films developed a 'greater thematic consistency and a new-found critical edge' through their often satirical 'portraits of sectors of French society, usually the bourgeoisie'.[8] Renoir's films during the transition to sound explored class tensions in the heart of Paris (*La Chienne*, 1931; *Boudu sauvé des eaux*, 1932) and Martigues (*Toni*, 1935). His attention to class and other social structures was unquestionably conditioned by his affiliation with numerous left-wing artistic figures including the *groupe octobre* and Louis Aragon during the rise of the Front populaire. Between 1936 and 1938, he directed a cycle of films including *Le Crime de Monsieur Lange* (1936), *Les Bas-fonds* (1936), and *La Marseillaise* (1938), which examined themes such as liberty, upper-class corruption, and the potentially transformative capacity of working-class enterprises. The dark, naturalistic portrayal of working-class railway labourers in *La Bête humaine* (1938) and the scathing satire of France's *haute bourgeoisie* in *La Règle du jeu* (1939) foreshadowed the inevitable advent of the Second World War. After abandoning a production of *La Tosca* in fascist Italy, Renoir emigrated to Hollywood. Although issues regarding social class continued to provide an important element of his films, his projects were either challenged by on-set interference from producers (*Swamp Water*, 1941), hampered by budgetary constraints (*The Southerner*, 1945; *Diary of a Chambermaid*, 1946), or wrested from his hands and recut (*Woman on the Beach*, 1947). Following a mid-career slump, Renoir re-established himself as a leading international filmmaker with *The River* (1951), *The Golden Coach* (1952), and *French Cancan* (1954), respectively shot in India, Italy, and Paris. After the lukewarm reception of *Eléna et les hommes* (1956), Renoir divided his attention between films including *Le Déjeuner sur l'herbe* (1959) and *Le Caporal épinglé* (1962) and two television productions, *Le Testament du Docteur Cordelier* (1959) and *Le Petit Théâtre de Jean Renoir* (1970).

Across these films, individuals or groups belonging to different social classes clash in public and private spheres, alternately eroding and bolstering ideological values, and implementing traumatic social upheaval on a local, national, or even international scale. Renoir's exploration of class barriers is doubly fascinating because of the range of periods in which they are addressed throughout his work. Viewed collectively, Renoir's films chronicle intractable social tensions in eighteenth-century Peru (*The Golden Coach*), the French conquest of Algeria (*Le Bled*), Franco-Prussian tensions in the *belle époque* (*French Cancan*; *Eléna et les hommes*), the Great War (*La Grande Illusion*), the rise of the Front populaire (*La Vie est à nous*, 1936), the eve of the Second World War (*La Règle du jeu*), the Occupation (*This Land is Mine*, 1943), life in Second World War prison camps (*Le Caporal épinglé*), and colonial life in British India (*The River*). Even those that unfold within their contemporary production contexts – such as *La Chienne*, *Boudu sauvé des eaux*, and *Les Bas-fonds* – bear witness to Renoir's acute attention to everyday interactions amongst diverse social strata in modern France.

The second hallmark of Renoir's work is his audacious preservation of continuity in space and time through deep staging, elaborate lateral camera mobility, and extended takes. Inspired by autocratic mavericks such as D. W. Griffith (*Intolerance: Love's Struggle Throughout the Ages*, 1916), Erich von Stroheim (*Foolish Wives*, 1922), and F. W. Murnau (*Sunrise: A Song of Two Humans*, 1927), Renoir developed a fierce determination to pioneer a modern cinematographic style during his formative years. By 1928, Renoir was constructing his own lighting equipment in collaboration with cinematographer Jean Bachelet to employ panchromatic film in interiors for *La Petite Marchande d'allumettes* (1928).[9] During this period, Renoir also went to great lengths to exercise camera mobility. To this end, he employed purpose-built mobile platforms to navigate the interior sets of *Le Tournoi dans la cité* – a device which he would later employ on the set of *Les Bas-fonds* – and relied on planks to construct pathways for travelling shots whilst shooting *Le Bled* in Algeria's rural landscapes.[10]

The advent of sound in France during 1928–9 imposed new filmmaking conditions that threatened to exclude deeply composed images and location-shooting from film practice: improved arc lights that had previously proven conducive to composition in depth were virtually abandoned and the silence required for filmmaking confined most cameras to enclosed containers in studio-sets.[11] More broadly, as Colin Crisp notes, the French cinema 'quite rapidly reject[ed] nine-tenths of the aesthetic possibilities open to it and regularly practiced in the twenties', a move that caused most films of the period to revert, in Susan Hayward's analysis, 'to their earlier prototype of filmed theatre'.[12] Nonetheless, Renoir continued to innovate, recording direct sound in the streets of Montmartre in *La Chienne*, his first feature-length sound film. Throughout the remainder of the 1930s, Renoir made a set of audacious aesthetic choices representing deviations from standard film practice, even exploiting technology considered obsolete in order to reintroduce the flexible cinematographic language developed during the silent period. By 1934, he was deploying a SuperParvo camera (a more recent model of the 1908 Parvo silent camera) and the Caméréclair-Radio that allowed him to record sound and image onto two separate reels of film. Both cameras permitted Renoir to record sound at greater distances and, by extension, proved conducive to location-shooting.[13] Renoir's determination to exploit and further refine techniques deployed during the silent era only strengthened as the decade progressed. Writing on the making of *Partie de campagne* (1936), actor Jacques Brunius recollected that 'it was only with great effort that we were able to procure old lenses, considered fossils', whose ability to register multiple planes of the image allowed Renoir 'to get ahead of the alleged innovators by almost ten years'.[14] In a 1938 article, Renoir stated his conviction that

> the longer I work in my profession, the more I am led to compose images in depth relative to the screen. The more I do that, the more I avoid confrontations between two actors placed soberly before the camera as though they were having their photograph taken.[15]

In an interview granted to the critics of *Cahiers du Cinéma* in 1966, Renoir acknowledged that he and Bachelet ordered lenses for *La Règle du jeu* that lent 'a certain depth in such a way that we could retain our backgrounds in almost any circumstances'.[16] Certain aspects of Renoir's style were altered permanently during Renoir's adaptation to Hollywood's unfamiliar studio infrastructure and socio-economic context: for example, his average shot length in *Swamp Water* is almost half that of *La Règle du jeu*, and Renoir would never again employ long takes to the same degree as in his films of the 1930s.[17] Despite a notoriously challenging adjustment to the Hollywood mode of production, he continued to develop his signature style on subsequent projects during his wartime exile in California: as Renoir himself remarked regarding *The Southerner*, which was shot for an independent producer within strict budgetary constraints, 'I proceeded largely with very small apertures that granted a great depth of field so that I would never lose sight of the fields behind my characters.'[18] Renoir continued to expand his arsenal of techniques during the post-war period, most notably on the production of *The River*, for which he used Technicolor cameras for the first time in his career and exploited a magnetic tape sound system based on technology captured from the Germans during the Second World War, even though no Hollywood studio had yet used the system and many in the film industry had expressed doubts regarding its practicality.[19] As is clear from all of the examples above, even when certain techniques pioneered by Renoir were no longer considered technical innovations in themselves, he continued to develop and refine visual and aural aspects of cinematographic language. These elements of Renoir's narrative style continue to challenge casual critics, theorists, philosophers, and casual viewers alike to consider the relationship between space and time in the cinema and the world that surrounds us.

To date, analyses of Renoir's films have primarily focused on the director's lucid portrayal of social class or on how his signature techniques preserve continuity in space and time. Conversely, considerably less attention has been lent to how Renoir's stratified societies structure the relationship between space and time at each stage of his career. A comprehensive understanding of the dynamic relationship between space and time must be integrated into our interpretation of the relationship between Renoir's distinctive narrative style and the unstable social barriers that he portrays. Otherwise, the very centrality of class to Renoir's films risks becoming an explanatory convenience for his *mise en scène*, and obscures the relationship between Renoir's techniques and the vulnerable social hierarchies that his films portray.

Anthony Giddens defines social class broadly as 'a large-scale grouping of people who share common economic resources, which strongly influence the type of lifestyle they are able to lead', and differentiates class from other forms of stratification in capitalist society such as caste, estates, and slavery through the lack of clear-cut boundaries between classes and the high possibility for mobility across them.[20] Giddens further asserts that understanding of the distribution of social practices in time and space 'is fundamental to analysing encounters, and also to understanding social life in general', indirectly indicating the importance of class to our study of the relationship between space and time in Renoir's work.[21] Similarly, Pierre Bourdieu reminds us that a class 'is defined not only by its position in the relations of production, as identified through indices such as occupation, income or even educational level, but also by [. . .] a certain distribution in geographic space', suggesting that how members of a given class interact with their surroundings plays a crucial role in the continuity of their echelon.[22] Furthermore, Bourdieu asserts that social classes may 'resist the forces of the field with their specific inertia, that is, their properties, which may exist in embodied form, as dispositions, or in objectified form, in goods, qualifications etc.', hinting towards the temporal tensions inherent to social space.[23] The permeability of social class should constitute a core avenue of enquiry towards the textual richness of Renoir's narratives at each stage of his career since, as Jonathan Murdoch astutely reminds us, 'class should be considered not as a primary determinant of multiple processes but as a general characterisation of social *outcomes*', which continuously modify social space over time.[24] To this end, the following section shifts our focus from how social configurations stratify space in film to how these configurations are (re)produced in a fictional composite of space-time that constantly remains open to the ineffaceable uncertainties of the future.

Theorising Renoir's Narrative Style: Bazin, Faulkner, and Braudy

Present understandings of Renoir's narrative style are largely informed by Bazin's major critical reappraisal of Renoir in *Cahiers du Cinéma* (especially 'Renoir français'[25]), *Qu'est-ce que le cinéma?* (an anthology of Bazin's major texts, first published 1958–62), and his posthumous *Jean Renoir*. Considering Renoir's pioneering exploitation of deep space, lateral camera mobility, and extended takes, Bazin proposes that Renoir, Orson Welles, the Italian neorealists, and a select number of their predecessors such as Robert Flaherty (*Nanook of the North*, 1922), von Stroheim (*Greed*, 1924), and Murnau (*Sunrise: A Song of Two Humans*, 1927), pioneered shooting styles that 'are based on a respect for the continuity of dramatic space and, of course, for its duration'.[26] Because Bazin emphasises the interconnectedness of time and space and their shared importance to the cinema with reference to Renoir's films, Bazin's views remain a crucial foundation to this (and arguably any) study of Renoir's narrative style.[27] However, because Bazin's project derives from a primarily ontological understanding of realism, he depoliticises Renoir's narrative style, even in the case of the director's most socially engaged works of the 1930s.

Building on earlier auteurist textual studies conducted by Raymond Durgnat (1974) and Alexander Sesonske (1980), Christopher Faulkner's *The Social Cinema of Jean Renoir* (1986) remedies Bazin's interpretation on two counts: first, by judiciously interpreting Renoir's films as products both of their director's vision and of contemporary political and socio-economic contexts; second, by foregrounding the social concerns embedded in Renoir's narrative style. Drawing on Eric Rhode's observation that Renoir's signature style 'has the effect of socializing space', Faulkner asserts that Renoir's techniques perform an 'active social analysis rather than merely passive observation'.[28] Faulkner illustrates his argument with reference to Renoir's *Toni*, a story examining Spanish and Italian immigrants whose daily lives revolve around a quarry and farmland in Provence. For Faulkner, the deep staging of a shot in which the eponymous protagonist speaks to his co-worker, Fernand, whilst labourers work in a quarry located in the background implies that 'Toni's social condition is coextensive with the condition of other workers included by the shot', and that 'what [Toni] says and feels during the scene is determined by the space in which we see him'.[29] Thus, seemingly inconsequential scenes situating labourers in a quarry in the film 'allow for the development of his narrative in space as well as through time'.[30] Faulkner's detailed examination of *Toni* points to how aural and visual elements such as characterisation, landscape, and dialogue collectively emphasise the dual social and physical aspects of the space occupied by Renoir's characters. However, Faulkner emphasises the formal qualities of Renoir's narrative style to the exclusion of how these techniques dynamise the relationship between individuals and their surroundings, and consequently neglects the temporal aspect of Renoir's narratives.

Leo Braudy's earlier analysis of Renoir's work in *The World in a Frame* (first published in 1976) points to a range of thematic and formal elements that contribute to Renoir's *mise en scène* of social space. Braudy counterposes Renoir's 'open' worlds with the 'closed' style of Fritz Lang's work (*Metropolis*, 1927; *Fury*, 1936), arguing that these styles represent the two major ways in which film imposes 'structures of perception' on the viewer.[31] The following table outlines the core characteristics of each category.[32]

The 'open' / Renoir style	*The 'closed' / Lang style*
Realistic and theatrical origins	Expressionistic and novelistic origins
Pictorial	Architectural
Frame as window to ongoing reality	Screen defines the world
Importance of character	Importance of architecture
Reflexive references to filmmaking	Illusion of sufficiency of film
Camera explores scene	Camera orders scene
Impartial camera	Camera is omniscient or identifies with character
Audience as invitee	Audience as victim
Irresolvable relationships and stories	False summary or 'happy ending'
Frame within narrative as refuge	Emphasis on inescapable limits of world

Braudy's categories are intended as a series of observations on stylistically opposed tendencies rather than theoretical frameworks for systematic analysis, but they nonetheless open our perspective to a diverse range of elements that potentially inscribe the ongoing process of becoming in our experience of viewing Renoir's films. Most interestingly, Braudy's description of Renoir's 'open' style draws our attention to the camera's transposition of incoherent social relations within a fundamentally incomplete vision of the world, each of which should be considered when interpreting Renoir through Bazin and Faulkner. The core remaining question posed by this Introduction regards how the relationship between Bazin's theorisation of the relationship between space and time in Renoir's narratives, Faulkner's emphasis on the 'socialization' effected by this analytical narrative style, and Braudy's observations on how Renoir's camera functions as a window to a heterogeneous world may be coherently integrated into an understanding of how Renoir's *mise en scène* of societal hierarchies inscribes the passage of time in film. In this context, the film philosophy of Gilles Deleuze provides an invaluable point of reference.

Deleuze's *Cinéma*(s) and Renoir's Image of the Future

Film theorist Béla Balázs distinguishes between three different concepts of time implied by the cinema, respectively pertaining to projection (the chronological duration of the projected film), action (the duration incorporated within the diegesis), and perception (the spectator's subjective experience of time whilst viewing a film).[33] It is the latter that primarily interests Deleuze. Deleuze provides an essential point of reference, not only because his film philosophy remains a canonical examination of how film represents temporality, but also because he lends Renoir a privileged status within his landmark *Cinéma* volumes, respectively entitled *Cinéma 1: L'Image-mouvement* (1983) and *Cinéma 2: L'Image-temps* (1985), in accordance with the two primary structures that Deleuze associates with the cinematographic image. Corresponding with the sensori-motor schema, the *image-mouvement* (movement-image) incorporates perception, affection, and action within a unity of movement, providing the spectator with a range of narrative signs that readily conform to everyday spatio-temporal coordinates. Such signs are located by Deleuze in classical Hollywood narratives and a variety of national pre- and post-Second World War schools including French Impressionism, Soviet montage, and German Expressionism. According to Deleuze, the *image-mouvement* presents us with 'a successive present in an extrinsic relation of before and after' and implies that the cinematographic image unfolds in the present, whereas the purely visual and sonic signs which distinguish the *image-temps* (time-image) from the *image-mouvement* preclude the creation of a coherent narrative by foregrounding simultaneous non-chronological temporalities.[34] The *image-temps* no more implies an absence of movement than the *image-mouvement* implies an absence of time. However, in the case of the *image-temps*, 'it is no longer time which is subordinate to movement; it is movement which subordinates itself to time'.[35]

Deleuze's approach to the *image-temps* and the particular temporal texture that he associates with Renoir's *mise en scène* derives from Deleuze's own understanding of Henri Bergson's conceptualisation of time as *durée*. Bergson employs this term to resolve tensions between notions of duration and succession that tend to be invoked by chronological, cause-and-effect understandings of time, which plot a frozen past and project an inevitable future. As Deleuze clarifies in *Le Bergsonisme* (1966),

> the past and the present do not designate two successive moments, but two elements that coexist, one of which is the present, which ceaselessly passes, the other of which is the past, which does not cease to be, but through which all presents pass.[36]

By virtue of this inextricable relationship between the past and the present, *durée* is essentially indeterminate, and constantly introduces qualitative change to both the present and the embodied past.

Deleuze asserts that because the past is formed at the same time as the present, time (taken to mean Deleuze's understanding of Bergson's *durée*) must ceaselessly split into two dissymmetrical jets, one of which is oriented towards the future and continuously allows the present to pass, the other of which falls ceaselessly into the past, where it is permanently stored in a region of memory. This eternal scission constitutes 'the most fundamental operation of time' and informs Deleuze's categorisation of virtual and actual images in the *image-temps*.[37] As Deleuze surmises, 'the present is the actual image, and *its* contemporaneous past is the virtual image'.[38] The actual and virtual enter into dialectic in the *image-souvenir* (memory-image) and the *image-rêve* (dream-image), which respectively refer to flashback structures such as those that feature in the films of Marcel Carné (*Le Jour se lève*, 1939) and Joseph L. Mankiewicz (*All About Eve*, 1950), and to the dreamlike worlds of Vincente Minnelli (*The Pirate*, 1948) that affect the real worlds within which fictional characters project their dreams.

Whereas virtual *images-souvenir* and *images-rêve* enter into broad, dilated circuits with actual images, this actual–virtual circuit is contracted within the *image-cristal* (crystal-image), which presents us with 'the bifaced image, actual and virtual at the same time'.[39] According to Deleuze, a perfect crystal of time eternally juxtaposes the actual image (the present image) with the virtual (a potentially coexisting image located in the past). This irreducible circuit produces a vision of the world as a concatenation of interpenetrating reflections: Deleuze remarks that Renoir's *La Règle du jeu* frames correspondences between servants and their masters, living beings and automata, theatricality and reality, which collectively juxtapose the actual and the virtual.[40] For Deleuze, the visible inextricability of the actual and the virtual also has the effect of conditioning the spectator's vision of the passage of time, specifically the tension between the embodied past and the ongoing present, and their joint influence on the openness of the future: by virtue of the crystal's ability to depict the scission of time, the present is portrayed as an ongoing construction, but one that is invariably dictated by the past. A perfectly crafted crystal therefore precludes the emergence of a new future within the world viewed.[41] Deleuze likens Renoir's entire oeuvre to a single metaphorical crystal, but observes that

Renoir's crystal 'is never pure and perfect. There is a fault, a point of flight, a "flaw".'[42] Because the crystal is 'always cracked', time can escape and, in doing so, 'gives itself a future'.[43]

Thus, on the one hand, Deleuze describes Renoir's crystal as a theatre of 'frozen, fixed, ready-made, too conformative roles', referring to La Colinière (a rural château that houses the *haute bourgeoisie*'s murderous antics on the eve of war in *La Règle du jeu*) and Wintersborn (where the European aristocracy's antiquated officers serve the remainder of their military careers during the First World War in *La Grande Illusion*), each of which imposes roles that are 'already doomed to become memories'.[44] On the other hand, he asserts that one role among these may allow a character to enter 'a decanted reality'.[45] Central to Renoir's ability to frame this fissuring of time is deep staging[46] – a hallmark of Renoir's visual style – which 'makes it clear that the crystal is there so that something can escape from it, in the background, through the background'.[47]

Asserting that Renoir is the director who came closest to understanding time 'in terms of a dimension of the future'.[48] Deleuze proceeds to relate the temporal texture of Renoir's *mise en scène* to the director's own engagement with the Front populaire during the 1930s:

> It is Renoir who had an acute awareness of the identity of liberty with a future, be it collective or individual, with an impulse towards the future, an opening of the future. It is Renoir's very political awareness, the manner in which he conceives the French Revolution or the Front populaire.[49]

Deleuze's film philosophy valuably foregrounds the import of Renoir's signature style from a perspective that is not circumscribed by Bazin's purely ontological understanding of realism. In particular, Deleuze usefully emphasises Renoir's ability to weave what Malcolm Bowie calls a 'pattern of cross-stitching between times and tenses that ordinary usage often seems intent on keeping apart' whilst lending temporal texture to familiar Renoirian thematic and stylistic attributes such as theatricality and deep space.[50] Deleuze's reading of Renoir represents a particularly interesting case study because of the four crystalline oeuvres examined by Deleuze (each of which will be discussed over the course of this book where relevant), only Renoir's allows us to consider the ongoing present in a potentially positive way, specifically as a realm that is open to the creation of genuinely new realities rather than as a prohibited virtual dimension (Deleuze provides the example of Max Ophüls's perfect crystal [*Lola Montès*, 1955]), or as an inevitably tragic social regression (represented, according to Deleuze, by Luchino Visconti's crystal in dissolution [*Ludwig*, 1973]).

However, a number of basic methodological inconsistencies within Deleuze's analysis are immediately evident. First of all, even though Deleuze alleges that Renoir's entire oeuvre is characterised by the cracked crystalline state, the extent to which Renoir's images consistently portray the bifurcation of time is open to dispute. Although Deleuze specifies that Renoir's crystal is always cracked, he observes that the crack is not always apparent, notably 'during his pessimistic moments', as when aviator André Jurieux (Roland Toutain) is accidentally shot by the *haute bourgeoisie*'s gamekeeper, Schumacher (Gaston Modot) in *La Règle du jeu*.[51] Deleuze nonetheless argues that 'something forms within the crystal which will manage to escape through the crack and spread freely'.[52] The veracity of Deleuze's assumption demands further elaboration within the context of Renoir's rich and varied output. Secondly, detailed textual analysis is largely absent from Deleuze's prescriptive philosophy when it would seem essential to support his case. Even though Deleuze states in the introduction to *L'Image-mouvement* that the goal of his two volumes is 'a taxonomy, an attempt to classify images and signs', his discussion of Renoir's crystal relies heavily on plot details of *Boudu sauvé des eaux* and *The River* without analysing the specific cinematographic qualities that distinguish such moments from a written text.[53] This is a major failing in the case of a film such as *The River*, which was originally published as a novella. Thirdly, Deleuze's discussion of Renoir in *Cinéma 2* elides key works such as *La Chienne* and *Toni* as well as Renoir's entire Hollywood output. Colin Davis rightly asserts that Deleuze 'chooses the corpus that suits his reading'.[54] Yet Deleuze even ignores films such as *Le Crime de Monsieur Lange* and *Eléna et les hommes*, which could bolster his proposals regarding Renoir's attitude towards the Front populaire and theatricality respectively.

It should be noted that Deleuze adamantly refused to categorise himself as an interpreter of films and that his primary concern was to elucidate the ways in which moving pictures could be analysed through 'concepts proper to the cinema' rather than 'concepts brought from outside'[55] (a claim which has been contested by Davis and Alain Badiou[56]). Rather than criticising the shortcomings of Deleuze's film philosophy and obscuring its relevance to a potentially richer understanding of Renoir's films, we can place Deleuze's conceptualisation of time in a mutually respectful dialectic with other theories of time and space in order to integrate temporality into a suitable interpretation of Renoir's complex *mise en scène* of space.

If we are to systematically and constructively integrate Deleuze's conceptualisation of Renoir's work into an analysis of how visual and aural components of Renoir's distinctive narrative style frame the dynamic relationship between space and time, three specific methodological issues concerning Deleuze's understanding of Renoir's metaphorical crystal of time demand further interrogation. These issues relate to the constitution of Renoir's filmic environments, shifts in his ideological outlook, and developments in his arsenal of techniques. Because these three matters inform the structure and central questions of this book, it is important to address them here in detail. First of all, Deleuze reduces the many environments of Renoir's films to theatres. In Deleuze's analysis, Renoir's crystal is '[a] collection of roles' and the crystal itself is a theatre that 'is only valuable as a search for an art of living'.[57] It is true that theatricality repeatedly forms a crucial point of reference in Renoir's work, either as an aspect of set design or a signifier of artifice. However, Deleuze thereby reduces settings as diverse as Lestingois's bookshop in *Boudu sauvé des eaux* and the Hindu environment in *The River* to imprisoning theatrical structures. The only exception to this generalisation is the river, which provides Boudu (played by Michel Simon in *Boudu sauvé des eaux*) and Harriet (played by Patricia Walters in *The River*) with an escape from the stultifying influence of dead roles through the *point de fuite* that characterises Renoir's crystal.

Beyond the example of the river, Deleuze avoids distinguishing between the temporal rhythms articulated by Renoir's *mise en scène* of urban Paris (*La Chienne*; *Le Crime de Monsieur Lange*), the rural landscapes of la Sologne (*La Règle du jeu*) and Texas (*The Southerner*), and the emphatically theatrical settings of Renoir's trilogy of spectacle (*The Golden Coach*; *French Cancan*; *Eléna et les hommes*), and broadly fails to elaborate the import of place towards the production of a new future. More specifically, Deleuze's primarily philosophical approach stops short of considering the social contexts that produce the theatrical regimes that stratify society and stultify time. Deleuze readily acknowledges that 'the visual image shows the structure of a society, its situation, its places and functions, the attitudes and roles, the actions and reactions of the individuals, in short the form and the contents' within his discussion of silent cinema in *Cinéma 2*.[58] However, if Deleuze's overall project is, as Felicity Colman writes, 'to engage [the cinema] as *the* political media [sic] of the twentieth century', the fact remains that he is conspicuously evasive regarding the ways in which these socio-political elements are incorporated within Renoir's *mise en scène*.[59] As this book will demonstrate, the theatres within Renoir's work are produced by pre-existing hierarchical social frameworks such as capitalism and colonialism, which are imbricated in issues regarding gender, sexuality, and ethnicity.

Applying Deleuze's comments on the relationship between temporality and Renoir's theatres as a tool for systematic analysis rather than a reductive unifying perspective necessitates a careful consideration of the impact of these social structures on the settings that potentially offer freedom to Renoir's characters. Such an avenue of enquiry is particularly pertinent as Deleuze's delineation of the factors that liberate characters is essentially ambiguous. On the one hand, Deleuze suggests that characters may orchestrate their own exit from the crystal: Boudu (in *Boudu sauvé des eaux*) simply 'finds the water's current by leaving the intimate and closed-up theatre of the bookseller where he has tried many roles'.[60] Similarly, Harriet is liberated from the crystal because she sacrifices her juvenile infatuation with Captain John (Thomas Breen) in *The River*.[61] On the other hand, Deleuze notes that characters may escape the influence of the past 'without the need for violence and through the development of experimentation', and even leave 'imperceptibly'.[62] However, this perspective is partly contested by Deleuze's assertion that 'the trying of roles is indispensable' in his discussion of *The Golden Coach*.[63] Moreover, the precise visual and aural elements capable of portraying the range of roles and their availability within the world viewed remains open to question.

Secondly, Deleuze undermines the intellectual rigour of his own philosophical treatise by valorising Renoir's exploitation of deep space to the exclusion of the other classical and non-classical techniques – among them camera movement and off-screen space – that are integral to Renoir's style. As O'Shaughnessy astutely notes, Deleuze 'makes depth staging stand in for Renoir's compositional style as a whole, without discussion of other important elements such as lateral camera mobility'.[64] In doing so, Deleuze implies that Renoir's use of deep space differs from that of other directors such as John Ford, William Wyler, or Orson Welles, who all composed images in depth as part of their respective shooting styles. Deleuze's remarks are particularly dubious since he also relates the visual depth of Welles's images to the temporal texture of *images-souvenir* in *Citizen Kane* elsewhere in *Cinéma 2*.[65] Each of Deleuze's two technical oversights – the omission of camera movement and off-screen space – is particularly surprising. Deleuze himself observes the importance of camera mobility to Renoir's shooting style in *Cinéma 1*, in which he describes the *plan-séquence* (sequence shot/extended take) as 'an extended fixed or mobile shot [. . .] with *profondeur de champ*', considering the interaction of these two Renoirian techniques in a fashion that is absent from Deleuze's discussion of Renoir in *Cinéma 2*.[66] Deleuze's failure to address off-screen space in *Cinéma 2* is little short of bewildering: in *Cinéma 1*, Deleuze himself singles out Renoir and Alfred Hitchcock as the directors who most notably forged a dialectic between on-screen and off-screen space.[67] In fact, Deleuze specifically remarks that the camera can serve as

'Bazin's alternative of concealer or frame'[68] (a concept developed by Bazin most famously in his essay, 'Renoir français'[69]) and refers to Noël Burch's case study of off-screen space in Renoir's *Nana*,[70] in which Burch argues that Renoir was one of the first to constructively harness the 'intermittent or, rather, fluctuating existence' of off-screen space, and was one of relatively few directors to 'have used this implicit dialectic as an explicit means of structuring a whole film'.[71]

Deleuze also dismisses the manner in which Renoir's appropriation of classical narrative techniques enters into dialectic with Renoir's signature techniques over the course of his cinematographic narratives to produce an image of time. Classical narrative style incorporates a variety of elements including, among other elements, a linear chain of events structured through the motivations and actions of characters, and the masking of spatial and temporal ellipses between shots through continuity editing.[72] Just as Bazin counterposes continuity editing with the deep compositions developed by Renoir, Deleuze largely relegates classical narrative techniques to the regime of the *image-mouvement*.[73] However, Kristin Thompson's neoformalist analysis of *La Règle du jeu* (the film that Deleuze draws on most frequently to support his views regarding *profondeur de champ*) reminds us that a 'juxtaposition of classical and non-classical devices' is embedded in 'the spatial and temporal layout of the whole', which modifies the narrative functions of classical techniques considered antithetic to Renoir's style.[74] Interestingly, Deleuze's analysis of Welles and Alain Resnais's portrayals of memory cautiously observes that 'there are time-images which are formed through suppression of depth' and asserts that the fissuring of time, if 'less visible', also operates in 'flat images [*l'image plane*], as in *The Golden Coach*'.[75] In doing so, Deleuze hints towards the importance of situating 'flat' images (that is to say, images incorporating a shallow spatial depth) within the broader temporal context of Renoir's narratives rather than focusing exclusively on deeply staged images or travelling shots. Furthermore, his philosophy usefully supports Ronald Bogue's suggestion that entire films (rather than isolated individual shots and sequences) function as crystals, which implies that the cumulative interconnections between various shots contribute to Renoir's unique image of time.[76]

The third issue that inhibits a constructive application of Deleuze's framework to Renoir's films is the philosopher's approach to the relationship between ideology and Renoir's *mise en scène* of temporality. More specifically, Deleuze draws on sweeping presumptions regarding Renoir's public commitment to the Front populaire and vague acknowledgements of the importance of class to Renoir's stratified societies. By implying that Renoir was confident in the Front populaire's agenda and that *La Règle du jeu*, in which an invitee is murdered and swiftly forgotten by a shooting party, is merely uncharacteristically pessimistic,[77] Deleuze suggests that Renoir's alleged ideological perspective informs his post-1938 corpus despite Renoir's notorious disenchantment with the French Left following the outbreak of war and his subsequent exile in Hollywood.

Closer attention to Renoir's evolving ideological outlook is essential to any study of Renoir's work because his arsenal of visual and aural techniques evolved in various ways over the course of his career in Europe, Africa, America, and Asia. Christopher Williams has convincingly argued that economic and ideological factors, alongside technological, aesthetic, and economic ones affected the emergence of deep focus technology, and the broader implications of his arguments could well be applied to any of the aforementioned techniques.[78] Conversely, Deleuze's approach is exemplary of Jean-Louis Comolli's criticism of Bazin and Jean Mitry's erroneous emphasis on technical progress at the expense of ideological influences, whereby 'the question of its utility [. . .] (what is it used for?) was completely obscured by that of its utilisation (how is it used?)'.[79] Without a pre-existing understanding of Renoir's mobilisation of deep space informed by theories of space and historical contextualisation, spectators will, like Deleuze, remain narrowly confined by the empirical notion of film style.

With these issues in mind, the next section addresses the ways in which Deleuze's own spatial thought usefully complements our understanding of crystallisation and the *point de fuite*, which provide our key points of access towards the temporal texture of Renoir's *mise en scène*.

The Future Beyond the *point de fuite*: Opening the *image-temps* to Space

Within the context of the analysis of space-time advanced by this book, the most flagrant obstacle posed by Deleuze's analysis of Renoir's work is arguably its elision of any coherent spatial framework in favour of emphasising film's capacity to generate conceptualisations of temporality. Deleuze's discussion of Renoir's realist aesthetic is particularly revealing in this regard. In *Cinéma 1*, Deleuze states that realism is a quality of the *image-action* (action-image) and that realism itself 'is simply this: milieux and modes of behaviour, milieux which actualise, and modes of behaviour which embody'.[80] Such would seem an accurate description of how Renoir entrenches his characters in their physical and social context through the realist techniques lauded by Bazin and Faulkner among others. However,

Deleuze esoterically dissociates Renoir's mobilisation of deep space from the realist school, arguably in order to justify his focus on films directed by Renoir, whose most stylistically influential works were filmed a number of years before the post-war emergence of the *image-temps* and even longer before the materialisation of the *image-temps* in French cinema (1958, according to Deleuze[81]); as Deleuze writes:

> One would be hesitant to give it the role intended by Bazin, namely a pure function of reality. The function of depth is rather [. . .] to absorb the real which thus passes as much into the virtual as into the actual.[82]

In fact, the elusiveness of any clear treatise on cinematographic space within Deleuze's reading of Renoir is endemic to the entirety of Deleuze's *Cinéma* volumes. From the opening pages of *Cinéma 1*, it is clear that Deleuze's film philosophy is less concerned with space than the movements that unfold within it. Deleuze does state that 'the shot of *images-mouvement* is a bloc of space-time', but only with a view to asserting that the *image-mouvement* implies 'a temporal perspective' that is subjugated to movement.[83] Where Deleuze does mention space in relation to film style within *Cinéma 1*, it is through descriptive labels such as the 'empty spaces' of Yasujirō Ozu (*Tôkyô monogatari*, 1953) and 'disconnected spaces' of Robert Bresson (*Pickpocket*, 1959).[84] Deleuze's most consistent reference to space is incorporated within his understanding of the *espace quelconque* (an 'anyspace-whatever'), described by Deleuze as a space of immeasurable non-rational links which displays 'only pure Powers and Qualities, independently of the states of things or milieux that actualise them', as in the films of Bresson, Carl Th. Dreyer (*La Passion de Jeanne d'Arc*, 1928), Agnès Varda (*Le Bonheur*, 1965), Michelangelo Antonioni (*Il deserto rosso*, 1964), and in the neorealist city (Roberto Rossellini's *Roma città aperta*, 1945; Vittorio de Sica's *Ladri di biciclette*, 1948).[85]

The closest Deleuze comes to lending spatial texture to his conceptualisation of temporality in the *image-temps* is his dichotomisation of perceived reality and manifestations of emphatic falsity in the cinema. To this end, drawing on Kurt Lewin's terminology, Deleuze distinguishes between a lived hodological space defined by fields of dynamic opposing forces and a homogeneous Euclidean space structured by centralising spatial forces which subjugate the tensions and spontaneity inherent to hodological space.[86] Deleuze interestingly remarks that spaces in the *image-temps* cease to be Euclidean, and that 'their nature cannot be explained in an exclusively spatial way', because they incorporate non-localisable relations.[87] In light of this, Deleuze tantalisingly refers to the existence of 'empty and amorphous spaces which lose their Euclidean coordinates' (alluding to

Ozu [*Banshun*, 1949] and Antonioni [*L'Avventura*, 1960]) and to 'crystallised spaces', where 'landscapes become hallucinatory in a setting which retains nothing other than crystalline seeds and crystallisable materials'.[88] However, Deleuze merely employs these references to space and scientific terminology as a prelude to his discussion of the realms of truth and falsity constructed by crystalline regimes in the cinema, leaving the active role of space in either its physical or social aspects undiscussed.

Interestingly, despite the elusiveness of any clear conceptualisation of space in either of the *Cinéma* volumes, Deleuze's 1980 collaboration with Félix Guattari, *Capitalisme et schizophrénie 2: Mille Plateaux*, grants us a greater insight into what Deleuze understands as the fundamental qualities of space and lends consistent spatial texture to Deleuze's analysis of Renoir's work through its similar terminology and social scope. Discussing the formation of social strata, Deleuze and Guattari provide a useful distinction between smooth and striated space, each of which is respectively defined through nomadic molecular movements and sedentary molar deposits. Whereas smooth space incorporates an amorphous realm occupied by nomads exercising free action, striated space identifies the inherent homogeneity of multiplicities which are potentially translated into systems for organising space.[89] Deleuze and Guattari further distinguish between molar tree-like structures that striate space by incorporating hierarchical organisations within centralised points, and molecular rhizomes which subvert these structures by conducting spatial elements along lines towards interleaving multiplicities of space. By exploiting smooth space, the rhizome subverts the stultifying influence of origin, genealogy, and history, rendering the most apparently impenetrable hierarchies permeable, as when Jurieux, modern hero of the skies, secures an invitation to the anachronistic realm of La Colinière. In the words of Deleuze and Guattari, 'the world has lost its pivot'.[90] Deleuze and Guattari's terms are deliberately polarised, but they admit that neither brand of space exists in its purest state. Rather, the striated and the smooth 'only exist, in fact, in mixture with one another'.[91] Therefore, although molar segments 'never cease to seal, plug, block the lines of flight', they remain inherently vulnerable to ruptures engendered through molecular flux, resulting in an ongoing tension between opposing processes of fragmentation.[92] As a result, any given social field (*champ social*) 'never ceases to be animated by all sorts of movements of decoding and deterritorialisation which affect "masses", operating at different speeds. These are not contradictions, but escapes [*des fuites*].'[93]

Deleuze and Guattari's conceptualisation of *lignes de fuite* usefully allows us to investigate the relationship between social forces and the temporal *point de fuite* made manifest by Renoir's *mise en scène*. Such a prism of analysis is important to films as diverse as *Le Bled* and *La Chienne*: in the former, the future of *l'Algérie française* is put into question by shots of established French-born landowners discussing France's duty to his indifferent next of kin in Sidi Ferruch; in the latter, wide shots frame a chance encounter between a *petit bourgeois* bank clerk and a world-weary prostitute in the unregulated public space of Paris, revealing the fallibility of social barriers erected between different social classes in the French capital.

Most interestingly, Deleuze and Guattari illustrate their treatise on space with reference to the process of crystallisation, the metaphor which informs Deleuze's interpretation of Renoir's *images-temps*:

> One may make a rupture, draw a *ligne de fuite* but there is still a danger that one will re-encounter organizations that re-stratify everything, formations that restore power to a signifier, attributions that reconstitute a subject – everything you like, from Oedipal resurgences to fascist concretions. Groups and individuals contain micro-fascisms simply waiting to crystallise.[94]

Gregory Flaxman rightly remarks that Deleuze's writing on space remains elusive, primarily because Deleuze's theories elide any traditional definition of space, developing spatial modalities (the striated/the smooth; the molar/the molecular) which 'only serve to confuse any more general sense of space'.[95] However, these intersections among metaphors featuring in Deleuze's reading of Renoir and Deleuze and Guattari's spatial thought allow us to formulate three proposals regarding the relationship between temporality and Renoir's rigorously hierarchised (albeit inherently porous) societies: firstly, space itself, whether it incorporates the bustling streets of Paris in *Boudu sauvé des eaux* or the rural Texan fields of *The Southerner*, may feature in film as a contested site for the actualisation of a genuinely new future in ways that are overlooked by Deleuze's film philosophy; secondly, Renoir's theatres, which are by-products of the stultifying force of social regimes that pre-exist them (as in the case of the emphatically theatrical setting of the Spanish court's colonial palace in *The Golden Coach*), operate as resistant molar lines rather than as mere signifiers of the embodied past; finally, the *ligne de fuite* that brings characters beyond the *point de fuite* (such as Rosenthal [Marcel Dalio] and Maréchal's [Jean Gabin] escape from a German prison camp across the Swiss border during the First World War in *La Grande Illusion*) potentially represents little more than a pyrrhic victory. As Marcus A. Doel remarks, Deleuze's vision of space is not constituted by discernible points but by 'conjunctives, intervals and bonds' that challenge stratification engendered by a given social force within 'a fractal world of infinite disadjustment, destabilization, and disjointure'.[96] How the *point de fuite* and *ligne de fuite* may be related to precise physical and social aspects of space framed by Renoir's camera is the core concern of the next section.

Open Spaces/Open Futures: Filming Spatial Politics

Without disregarding other key theorists of space (among them Gaston Bachelard, Michel de Certeau, and Michel Foucault) whose ideas contribute to this book's analysis of particular films, Doreen Massey's human geography consistently informs this book's understanding of the joint import of space and time towards the crystalline state of Renoir's films, primarily because her work usefully links formal issues of space and time to cultural questions of politics. Massey's work is clearly indebted in part to Henri Lefebvre, who proposes that 'every society (and hence every mode of production [. . .]) produces a space, its own space', which involves both human and non-human components: for Lefebvre, space is a social relationship, albeit one that is 'inherent to property relationships (especially the ownership of the earth, of land) and is also closely bound up with the forces of production (which impose a form on that earth or land)'.[97]

Massey builds on Lefebvre's conceptualisation of space as a physical and social construct with a view to addressing the intrinsic relationship between space and time. Recalling Lefebvre's understanding of space as an extensive sphere that 'subsumes things produced [and] encompasses their interrelationships in their coexistence and simultaneity', Massey argues that the coevalness of such relationships constitutes a 'dynamic sphere of simultaneity'.[98] Echoing Deleuze and Guattari's assertion that molar lines established by centralised power structures may be subverted by the molecular rhizomes, Massey emphasises that the restructuring of cartographies of power can only be achieved through 'the construction of (temporary, provisional) stabilisations' and that much spatial politics is concerned with 'how such chaos might be ordered, how juxtapositions may be regulated, how space might be coded, how the terms of connectivity might be negotiated'.[99] The creative relationship between the human and the non-human results in the creation of a space that, no matter how apparently enclosed, 'is neither a container for always-already constituted identities nor a completed closure of holism' but, rather, is composed of 'loose ends and missing links'.[100]

Crucially, Massey argues that the vast multiplicities hosted by space are themselves 'a precondition for the temporal' and that 'the multiplicities of the two together [space and time] can be a condition for the openness of the future'.[101] As Massey succinctly remarks, 'for time to be open, space must be in some sense open too'.[102] Her emphasis on the ineffaceable temporal inflection of social forces valuably provokes us to consider how the unstable, oscillatory class barriers (and the variety of capitalist and colonialist models through which class structures are established) that provide a core concern of Renoir's *mise en scène* are recognisably imbricated in what Deleuze describes as 'the gushing forth of time as doubling, as scission'.[103]

Massey, by virtue of her propositions, prefers to refer to 'open space' or 'space-time'. Therefore, at this point, it is important to distinguish between the implications of the term 'space-time' regarding cinematographic space on the one hand and, on the other, the spectator's lived experience of social space: for example, our experience of the relationship between space and the scission of time in Paris in our everyday lives will inevitably differ from our aural and visual experience of this relationship in the filmed city (take Renoir's portrayals of the French capital in *La Chienne*, *Boudu*, or *La Règle du jeu*), which is reproduced from a series of juxtaposed vantage points of varying duration. Although Bergson's theses on time refer to the constant possibility of a genuinely new present, Deleuze suggests that the scission of time in the *image-temps* does not necessarily imply the emergence of the truly new. As noted earlier, the emergence of a new reality beyond predetermining elements is impossible within what Deleuze calls the 'perfect' crystal (best exemplified in his view by Ophüls's work): in *Lola Montès*, the eponymous protagonist's memory and the circus spectacle in which she performs ceaselessly mirror one another to the exclusion of any event that could rupture the petrifying impact of her past on the present moment. Conversely, the world represented in Renoir's cracked crystal does not solely provide what Massey would call 'a precondition for the temporal', in which time passes (as in the case of the perfect crystal).[104] Through its inherent *point de fuite*, the cracked crystal further accommodates the very openness of any process of becoming, even in a film like *The River* which, like *Lola Montès*, recounts a female protagonist's introspective reflection on the transient joys and tragedies that have punctuated her life. If time and space are mutually implicated within cinematographic space, then Deleuze's valorisation of Renoir's ability to frame time 'in terms of a dimension of the future' necessarily invokes the question of open space-time.[105] By referring to open space-time (rather than space-time or crystalline space-time), this book addresses a combination of visual and aural elements present in Renoir's oeuvre which collectively register the perpetual disembeddedness of molar strata and portray the rhizomatic *lignes de fuite* that threaten to disintegrate such strata (and sometimes succeed in doing so) within a geographical setting that is composed of mutually affective physical and social elements.

Reading Deleuze on Renoir: Critical Opinions

It is important to outline the particular aspects of this study that intersect with previous analyses of Renoir's work. In an invaluable survey of scholarship on Renoir, O'Shaughnessy notes that such criticism 'has been dominated by *auteurists* and critics of the left and the quarrel between the two', the former mythologising Renoir by transforming an uneven body of work into a coherent oeuvre, the latter relinking Renoir to these contexts and interpreting his films as responses to contemporary political and ideological issues.[106] Critics at *Cahiers du Cinéma* perceived Renoir as a benign humanist and the quintessential *auteur*, and tended to efface the political statements embedded in his innovative narrative style in favour of providing moral readings of his work. These views have since been met with a variety of auteurist studies that have examined Renoir's films as personal expressions of his moral, political, aesthetic, or philosophical vision, including book-length studies by Raymond Durgnat, Alexander Sesonske, Maurice Bessy and Claude Beylie, and Irving Singer. Such auteurist interpretations are supported by Renoir himself, who described himself to Hollywood agents as 'much more author of films than a director' and remarked in a 1964 interview:[107]

> I have essentially shot one film, I have continued to shoot one film since I began, and it is the same one. I add things to it, I see things that I had not said previously and which I have to say.[108]

On the other hand, a number of left-wing critics (most notably Faulkner, O'Shaughnessy, and Keith Reader) have focused on the manifold ways in which Renoir's films reflect or refract the sociological, political, and economic contexts in which he worked, though it is important to note that these critics also consider the import of Renoir's own vision without allowing their interpretations to be dictated by it.

Philosophical frameworks have become increasingly important avenues of enquiry towards Renoir's films in recent years. Drawing on Freudian theory, existential philosophy and Dionysian vitalism, Serceau's *Jean Renoir, l'insurgé* (1981) and *Jean Renoir: la sagesse du plaisir* (1985) collectively analyse recurring themes including love, liberty, and class domination, and elucidate underlying philosophical explorations of pleasurable contact with the physical world in Renoir's work which reach full maturity in Renoir's post-war output. Irving Singer's *Three*

Philosophical Filmmakers (2004) compares the teachings of Plato, Aristotle, and Christian tradition with Renoir's consistently discernible insights into the human condition, situating the latter in relation to Renoir's realism, naturalism, and humanism. More recently, Davis (2009) has advocated a move towards philosophically informed frameworks that grant a greater degree of intellectual respectability to interpretations of film 'as the expression of something unique or someone external to it and giving to the medium itself a degree of reflective autonomy'.[109] To this end, Davis fruitfully draws on philosophers including Stanley Cavell, Deleuze, and Slavoj Žižek to illuminate recurring philosophical enquiries such as murderous desire, friendship, and community in Renoir's films of the 1930s.

With the exception of Davis, scholars have largely failed to consider the rich possibilities for film analysis proposed by Deleuze's examination of Renoir's films. However, it is important to note that two perceptive Deleuzian interpretations of Renoir's work have been provided to date by O'Shaughnessy and Richard Rushton. Rushton (2011) discusses Renoir's work with a view to demonstrating that Deleuze's film philosophy, unlike frameworks advanced by film theorists of the 1970s and 1980s (such as Jean-Louis Baudry and Stephen Heath), allows us to conceive of the imaginary in the cinema in a positive way, specifically as an apparatus which opens up new expressions of the real. Rushton's analysis centres on the tension between reality, portrayed by Renoir as an inadequate 'show of decrepitude and social stagnation', and the imaginary, which offers the potential reinvention of the real beyond predetermining elements.[110] Rushton's interpretation valuably focuses on the entry of Renoir's characters to a transcendental field where non-subjective, pre-conscious impulses emerge, potentially opening the characters to cracks in the crystal, at which point the challenge for Renoir's characters is to keep discovering new realities in the hope of escaping the crystal.[111] However, the focus of Rushton's insightful emphasis on the liberating potential of Renoir's characters results in three key oversights: first, Rushton's argument unjustly supplants the import of the characters' social and physical space towards the introduction of cracks to the crystal; second, Rushton's assertion that the crack can be 'sealed up and the inadequacies of the real re-established' is an oversimplification of the social and physical factors that constantly catalyse the ongoing construction of the crystal;[112] third, Rushton fails to sufficiently address the import of Renoir's *mise en scène* towards the spectator's perception of the *point de fuite*. As a result, Rushton's approach ultimately succeeds far more in contrasting Deleuzian thought with alternative psychoanalytical approaches to Renoir's work than in assessing the validity of Deleuze's sub-arguments or engaging with Renoir's texts in depth.

O'Shaughnessy (2013) interprets Deleuze's reading of Renoir's cracked crystal in ways that are significantly more grounded in both Renoir's political engagement and signature techniques than Rushton's study. Furthermore, whereas Davis, Singer, and Rushton address different philosophical doctrines and use Renoir's films to illustrate these, O'Shaughnessy employs a sustained philosophical methodology in order to develop an argument regarding Renoir's films of the 1930s. According to O'Shaughnessy, whereas the unconventional visual depth of Renoir's early films of the 1930s (such as *Boudu sauvé des eaux*) allows the spectator to interpret the social stratification of Renoir's societies, Renoir's later films of the decade (*La Grande Illusion*, *La Bête humaine*, and *La Règle du jeu*) incorporate a 'chronological depth' that encourages us to read their *mise en scène* in both historical and social terms.[113] Thus, whereas Boudu's physical nonconformity disputes the rigid, deeply composed frames of the Lestingois' bourgeois residence within the world of the film, the interplay between the camera's frame and other aspects of *mise en scène* including set design and characterisation in Renoir's Front populaire output portrays worlds that are 'uneven and in flux', and results in history being 'opened up to collective intervention' in certain scenes.[114] In O'Shaughnessy's view, Renoir's films of the late 1930s retain this 'chronological depth' but mark a definitive rupture with the 'solidarity between the camera and human figures' that features in *Le Crime de Monsieur Lange* and *La Marseillaise*:[115] *La Bête humaine* and *La Règle du jeu* both portray a 'closing down of possibilities' where the frame is no longer open to intervention by the characters and 'the future is already charted'.[116]

O'Shaughnessy perceptively demonstrates that characters and objects may negotiate the parameters of the screen to depict the flow of a specifically non-chronological time in a manner unique to the cinema, and avoids Bazin, Faulkner, and Deleuze's formalist tendencies. Most importantly, O'Shaughnessy argues that history features in these films as 'an uncertainty driven by the co-presence of competing possibilities' in a fictional universe devoid of fixity, and that escape from the crystal is never guaranteed.[117] Thus, the circular courtyard of *Le Crime de Monsieur Lange* signals both utopian possibilities and their potential limits, and the feudal-era castle of *La Grande Illusion* holds both 'a potentially authoritarian future' and 'a progressive, egalitarian history [that] may still be rescued' in tension.[118]

Although O'Shaughnessy offers several enlightening avenues of enquiry towards inscriptions of temporality in Renoir's work, the limited scope of his analysis results in one key oversight: O'Shaughnessy's decision to read Renoir's *mise en scène* through significant events, such as the First and

Second World Wars, limits our understanding of the term 'history'. For O'Shaughnessy, when Boudu abandons the Lestingois' bourgeois circle on the day of his arranged wedding, the tramp 'is returning to an earlier asocial state, not changing society or moving history on', whereas *La Règle du jeu*, through its evocations of the First World War and its prescient commentary on the war that will inevitably come to pass, incorporates a 'much greater social density'.[119]

O'Shaughnessy confines his interpretation of the cracked crystal to the possibilities of major historical advance or regression and, by neglecting the relationship between space and time across Renoir's work, tends to overlook the import of both major events and quotidian narratives (a duality that comes closer to the French *histoire*) to the inscription of temporality in Renoir's work even though both Boudu's passage through Paris and the *haute bourgeoisie*'s *bal masqué* in *La Règle du jeu* are lent equal dramatic scope by Renoir's narratives. It is important to note, however, that O'Shaughnessy's lucid reading valuably fulfils the aims clearly proposed by his own analysis. Both Rushton's and O'Shaughnessy's discussions provide useful points of reference that will be discussed over the course of this book.

Discursive Positioning: Renoir *auteur*

Any discussion of Renoir's work raises the question of the extent to which his *mise en scène* may be traced back to Renoir himself. However, Renoir repeatedly collaborated with a number of artists including screenwriter Charles Spaak (*Les Bas-fonds*; *La Grande Illusion*), set designer Eugène Lourié (*La Règle du jeu*; *The Southerner*; *The River*), and his nephew, cameraman Claude Renoir (*La Grande Illusion*; *The River*; *The Golden Coach*), to say nothing of the actors, producers, and budgets involved in each of his projects.[120] Furthermore, although most Renoir scholars would rightly maintain that Renoir's creative imprint is beyond dispute in each of these examples, Renoir's evolution as a director was also conditioned by contemporary social, political, and economic conditions. As Dudley Andrew notes in his study of Renoir's canonical films of the 1930s, 'history, even more than genius, ran through his camera and his pen'.[121] Thus, although this book occasionally draws on his production materials curated within the Jean Renoir archive at the University of California, Los Angeles, it does so in order to lend credence to unorthodox interpretations of Renoir's work rather than to enforce his status as an *auteur* or to argue that Renoir envisioned the meanings elucidated by this study. This book's approach to auteurism is most concisely encapsulated by Peter Wollen's structuralist understanding of how a director inadvertently introduces stylistic continuity to his or her work:

> The structure is associated with a single director, an individual, not because he has played the role of artist, expressing himself or his own vision in the film, but because it is through the force of his preoccupations that an unconscious, unintended meaning can be decoded in the film, usually to the surprise of the individual involved. The film is not a communication, but an artefact which is retracing a film to its origins, to its creative source. It consists of tracing a structure (not a message) within the work, which can then *post factum* be assigned to an individual, the director, on empirical grounds.[122]

When referring to Renoir, this book is therefore implicitly addressing the various combinations of personnel that contributed in varying measure to the production of each film.

Given both Renoir's status as a key *auteur* and the importance of Deleuze's discussion of Renoir's work to the methodology, it should be emphasised in advance that Deleuze never blatantly asserts that the cracked crystal was conceived by Renoir – the terminology remains Deleuze's own – but Deleuze's corpus implies that it is consistently produced by Renoir's works, from *La Petite Marchande d'allumettes* (1928) to *Le Petit Théâtre de Jean Renoir* (TV, 1970). Deleuze specifically argues that the crystal is enacted by the director's frame: the actual–virtual circuit 'is the objective characteristic of certain existing images which are by nature double'.[123] Although the exchange between the virtual and actual within the crystal of time 'is produced solely "in someone's head"', crystalline description remains 'an objective illusion' constructed by the filmmaker.[124] In short, open space-time in Renoir's work is embedded partly in Renoir's *mise en scène* and partly, as Bazin might have put it, 'in the shadow of the image projected by montage onto the spectator's field of consciousness'.[125]

Chapter Breakdown

As a comprehensive analysis of Renoir's entire oeuvre could not have been accommodated by this book, a number of films have been deliberately set aside in favour of a representative sample of canonised landmarks and underdiscussed works that respond to the core questions that structure this investigation. By this, I mean a selection of films which investigate narrative settings frequently portrayed by Renoir's camera, the impact of his famous engagement with the Front populaire on his *mise en scène*, and post-war developments in Renoir's narrative style. Due to the centrality of Deleuze's arguments to the present analysis, it is worth noting that six of the twelve films selected are directly addressed by Deleuze's *Cinéma* volumes.

Renoir's works sustain analysis through a variety of structures: thematic, in terms of the milieu or period in which they were made, and either as separate films or as groups. This book draws on three aspects of Renoir's work which, in Deleuze's tantalisingly underdeveloped analysis, condition Renoir's framing of temporality. The first two chapters, which respectively engage with Renoir's Paris and rural landscapes, examine the import of setting to Renoir's portrayal of space-time. The last two chapters respectively examine Renoir's Front populaire output and the impact of his post-war aesthetic development on his *mise en scène* of open space-time. Each chapter examines three films in chronological order with a view to discerning evolutions within Renoir's methods of framing open space-time.

The first chapter analyses *La Chienne*, *Boudu sauvé des eaux*, and *La Règle du jeu*. Each was filmed during the 1930s as French society underwent traumatic social change, and the topography of Paris in each is informed by the social, economic, and political crosswinds that buffeted the city over the course of the decade. Through Renoir's mobilisation of urban monuments and theatrical motifs, all three films establish a counterpoint between the fluctuating Parisian cityscape and the *rôles morts* conceptualised by Deleuze, illustrating the characters' abilities to actualise select conditions of possibility presented by the very act of walking in the city.

The second chapter examines rural space in *Le Bled*, *The Southerner*, and *The River*. The conditions of engagement with the natural landscape in all three of these films vary chronologically and geographically: whereas the first two constitute thoughtful responses to the contemporary social, political, and economic circumstances in which they were produced, *The River* relegates spatial politics in favour of portraying space itself as a recollected realm. In all three, the deceptively inert landscape becomes a site for the actualisation of a genuinely new present, either through the production of new social hierarchies or the discarding of the embodied past from the deepest layers of human memory.

This entirety of the third chapter elucidates the impact of Renoir's affiliation with the French Left on his portrayal of open space-time. Drawing on previously unpublished production materials, this chapter argues that Renoir's *mise en scène* of open space-time in *Le Crime de Monsieur Lange* and *Les Bas-fonds* is informed by Renoir's own pessimism regarding the rise of the Front populaire, and proposes that *La Grande Illusion* mobilises motifs associated by Deleuze with the cracked crystal in ways that are highly uncharacteristic of Renoir's work and which interestingly challenge Deleuze's own interpretation of Renoir's work in constructive ways.

The fourth chapter examines the impact of Renoir's post-war *crises anti-réalistes* on the spectator's perception of open space-time in *Diary of a Chambermaid*, *The Golden Coach*, and *Eléna et les hommes*. In all three of these films, geographical place-names are secondary to theatricality, which is foregrounded by different combinations of set design, costume design, camerawork, music, and performance. How this newfound emphasis on spectacle enriches potential interpretations of Deleuze's conceptualisation of crystalline imagery in ways that Renoir's previous works do not provides an underlying concern of this chapter.

All four chapters consider the relationship between temporal texture of theatricality, deep space, and other motifs that structure Deleuze's analysis in order to restore a greater sense of the complexity and diversity of Renoir's *mise en scène* of space-time in each. The Conclusion briefly summarises the findings of each chapter, and relates them to the overarching importance of addressing space and time in equal measure within any analysis of Renoir's work, and to new ways in which we may usefully reconceptualise Deleuze's metaphor of the cracked crystal.

CHAPTER 1

Theatrum Mundi: Framing Urban Dynamics in Renoir's Paris

> Old Paris is no more (the form of a city
> Changes more quickly, alas! Than the human heart . . .[1]
>
> – Baudelaire, 'Le Cygne', in *Les Fleurs du mal*

> It [. . .] happens that, if you move along Marozia's compact walls, when you least expect it, you see a crack open and a different city appear. Then, an instant later, it has already vanished.[2]
>
> – Italo Calvino, *Invisible Cities*

Introduction: Renoir, Cinema, and the City

Building on Deleuze's association of the theatre with the force of the past in Renoir's work, this chapter argues that Renoir's *surcroît de théâtralité* enters into dialectic with urban dynamics in Paris to produce an image of open space-time in *La Chienne* (1931), *Boudu sauvé des eaux* (1932), and *La Règle du jeu* (1939). To say that Renoir was well acquainted with Paris by 1931 would be an understatement. Renoir himself was born in Montmartre at 13 rue Girardon. The Renoir family divided its time between Montmartre, Essoyes (Aline's homeplace), and *Les Collettes* in Provence, where Pierre-Auguste spent his final years. Renoir *fils* nostalgically recounts a number of memorable excursions to various locations in the city in his autobiography, *Ma vie et mes films*: visits to les Grands Magasins Dufayel where he experienced his first (and ironically forgettable) encounter with the cinema; the Café des Amis where his father frequently met with neighbours; the Guignol at the Tuileries; and plays on the Boulevard du Crime.[3] Furthermore, by the time Renoir was transposing Georges de la Fouchardière's *La Chienne* to the screen, he had already filmed *Nana* (1926) in reconstructed *belle époque* Paris and *Sur un air de Charleston* (1927) in a post-apocalyptic vision of the city.

Renoir would continue to revisit Paris throughout the remainder of his career: *Boudu sauvé des eaux* and *Le Crime de Monsieur Lange* (1936) all take Paris as their primary setting; although *La Règle du jeu* is better remembered for its photography of la Sologne, the first twenty minutes are set in Paris; *French Cancan* (1954) and *Eléna et les hommes* (1956) each celebrated life in the French capital after his Hollywood exile; *Le Testament du docteur Cordelier* (TV, 1959) was partly shot on location in Paris; and even *Le Caporal épinglé* (1962), a prisoner-of-war story set largely within a prison camp during the Second World War, ends with the protagonist gazing wistfully from the pont de Tolbiac following his escape.

The relevance of separate examinations of urban and rural space-time has been challenged by certain social theorists. Raymond Williams's seminal *The Country and the City* (1973) determines that ideologically infused representations have blurred our real social experience, which 'is not only of the country and the city, in their most singular forms, but of many kinds of intermediate and new kinds of social and physical organisation'.[4] Similarly, Howard Newby succinctly asserts that 'what constitutes "rural" is wholly a matter of convenience [. . .] and of little utility'.[5] Echoing Williams and Newby, Doreen Massey emphasises that 'the unavoidable challenge of negotiating a here-and-now [. . .] must take place within and between both human and non human', but is reluctant to distinguish the city from other spatial forms.[6] Rather than elucidating a set of qualities unique to urban space, Massey writes that the spatial mobility of cities 'is a hyperversion of spatiality in general': the particularity of cities 'consists primarily in an intensification, a dramatic exaggeration, of characteristics [. . .] intrinsic to space more generally'.[7] Essential to this intensity are the 'weavings together, mutual indifferences and outright antagonisms' of a vast variety of trajectories that, in cities, have 'a spatial form which will further mould those differentiations and relations', challenging the negotiation of space in 'shockingly unequal' ways.[8]

It is with this aspect of the urban experience in mind that Michel de Certeau, in *L'Invention du quotidien* (1980), draws on the shifting social configurations and distinctive architecture of urban space to illustrate his Foucauldian distinction between strategies and tactics, the former postulating 'a mastery of time through the foundation of an autonomous place', the latter referring to 'calculated action' that can only exploit 'the terrain imposed upon it'.[9] These tactics extend to everyday practices (or, to use Certeau's term, 'manières de faire', literally 'ways of doing'[10]) that challenge the hegemonic powers that structure the city, manipulating the circuit of time and allowing for the creation of a new future (if only on a local scale).

The potential impact of such deceptively minute actions on the formation of strata in the city is increased by the proximity of varying social classes and the difficulty of accurately identifying class affiliations of individuals and groups. Discussing 'knowable communities' in fiction, Williams counterposes the 'essentially transparent' nature of rural communities to 'essentially opaque' urban communities. For Williams, the latter is made manifest by the increased complexity of labour and altered relations between and within social classes, which make 'assumption of a knowable community – a whole community, wholly knowable – [. . .] harder and harder'.[11] In doing so, Williams restores a distinction between experiences of urban and rural environments overlooked by strictly sociological perspectives and also signals the risk of encountering or misidentifying members of varying social strata in the city.

It is precisely this dense social tissue and its fluctuating relationship with urban architecture that have captured the attention of film theorists examining the specific historical affinity between the cinema and the city. Asserting that film is primarily concerned with 'actually existing physical reality – the transitory world we live in', Siegfried Kracauer devotes significant attention to the inherent rapport between cinema and the city:[12]

> The affinity of film for haphazard contingencies is most strikingly demonstrated by its unwavering susceptibility to the 'street' – a term designed to cover not only the street, particularly the city street, in the literal sense, but also its various extensions such as railway stations, dance and assembly halls, bars, hotel lobbies, airports, etc.[13]

Kracauer particularly emphasises the import of urban architecture towards the most banal narrative: 'a street serving as background to some quarrel or love affair may rush to the fore and produce an intoxicating effect'.[14] Geoffrey Nowell-Smith similarly remarks on a category of films in which 'the city becomes a protagonist, but unlike the human characters, it is not a fictional one', not only providing a topographical backdrop for the drama but catalysing the characters' individual trajectories within the narrative.[15]

Echoing Kracauer's vision of the world as an endlessly disintegrating substance, Susan Hayward describes the filmed city as 'a transubstantial virtual city of celluloid imaginings (a spectre, a ghost on screen)'.[16] For Hayward, the transitory nature of cities is evidenced by the inevitable erosion of the repressed Paris. Such permutations are denied through a series of binary oppositions such as male/female, self/other, public/private, familiar/unfamiliar, and present/absent that fulfil our desire for an illusory expulsion of the real.[17] However, as this chapter demonstrates, the real 'refuses to go away, always manages to penetrate through the rhetoric of the body politic that seeks to contain the threat of otherness'.[18]

The impact of the city on human perception has been further discussed by James Donald, who asserts that 'the city is not a place' but rather a historically specific 'structure of visibility'.[19] For Donald, the city is an ephemeral projection, a pluralistic entity at the intersection of geographically and historically specific relations that are constantly repatterned by acts of perception, participation, and transgression: 'ways of seeing and understanding the city inevitably inform ways of acting on the space of the city, with consequences which then in turn produce a modified city which is again seen, understood and acted on'.[20] How this constant recreation of urban space – in both its physical and social aspects – is transposed by the camera and juxtaposed with Renoir's theatrical motifs to create an image of open space-time is central to this chapter. Just as 'the multiplicities of [space and time] together can be a condition for the openness of the future', inherent fissures in the molar lines that stratify socialised urban space necessarily provide a '[a] condition of possibility' for tacticians who endeavour to exploit them.[21]

Two characteristics of Renoir's urban narratives are of immediate relevance to this chapter: first, the import of Renoir's framing towards the mapping of the mutually affective relationship between the social space and physical architecture of Paris, specifically the ways in which urban space catalyses spatio-temporal trajectories of characters belonging to different social strata and consolidates new relationships between different classes; second, the commonly recognisable landmarks that punctuate the topography of Paris. Such sites include the Moulin Rouge (which features in *La Chienne*), Notre Dame and the Louvre (which both feature in *Boudu*), and the Eiffel Tower and the Palais de Chaillot (each of which is visible in *La Règle du jeu*). Victor Burgin remarks that such landmarks allow spectators to project their own perceptions of the city onto the screen in an effort to lend coherence to the narrative: 'the city in our actual experience is *at the same time* an actually existing physical environment, *and* a city in a novel, a film, a photograph, a city seen on television, a city in a comic strip, a city in a pie chart, and so on', reminding us that the 'modified city' theorised by Donald is as much the product of cultural representations as the navigation of the physical and social space of the city.[22] As Chris Rojex observes, topographical sites form the spectator's 'index of representations; that is, a range of signs, images and symbols which make the sight familiar to us in ordinary culture'.[23] John Urry further notes that our gaze is 'signposted' towards a 'relatively small number of tourist nodes'.[24] The deployment of landmarks therefore affects the legibility of urban settings in two key ways: firstly, as Maureen Turim argues, the manipulation of physical and cultural associations engendered by monuments introduces 'a decentering, a complexly reordered space' that transforms architectural realms into a conceptual rather than a purely referential space, and potentially 'transform[s] these spaces as part of a project to disturb the spectator's placement';[25] secondly, as this chapter seeks to demonstrate, Renoir's characters also interact with such nodes in unconventional ways, lending credence to Margaret C. Flinn's observation that 'important cities have important monuments, but the permanent and temporary residents of a city may or may not relate to those monuments in the ways intended by their creators'.[26]

Renoir often uses these landmarks unconventionally, even counter-intuitively, consequently deceiving such signposting, rendering such indexes useless, and distorting the topographical relationship between these landmarks and the broader geographical space of Paris. This confronts the spectator with a textual space in which the coordinates of social and physical space are emphatically unfixed. The city itself emerges as both a factor and product of open space-time, constructed not only through physical architecture, but also through what Massey refers to as 'different resources, distinct dynamics [. . .] and temporalities, which have their own directions in space-time', recalling Donald's theorisation of the city as a constantly remoulded entity.[27] The incongruity and diversity associated by these urban theorists with the social tissue of the city are particularly pertinent to cultural representations of Paris and their proximity of these portrayals to the lived experience of the French capital: Andrew Hussey writes that 'Paris has been variously represented as a prison, a paradise and a vision of hell', and remarks that that such descriptions are 'not a refraction but an accurate reflection of daily life: Paris really is made up of radically different spaces and multiple personalities, always at odds with each other and often in noisy collision'.[28]

We cannot address the ways in which Renoir frames these transient social relations that continually restructure the city without considering the fluctuating qualities of the urban space that hosts them. Drawing on social theorists and film scholars, this chapter proposes a central two-fold argument: first of all, it is argued that the tension between shots of the French capital and theatrically defined upper-class societies discussed by Deleuze foregrounds the impact of urban space on the consolidation of new class relations in *La Chienne*, *Boudu sauvé des eaux*, and *La Règle du jeu*. Secondly, this chapter demonstrates that Renoir depicts walking as a tactical act which subverts social order and erodes the class values that stratify the city, consequently producing new class relations in the manifestly open space-time constituted by everyday Parisian life.

La Chienne (1931)

Theatrical frames vs urban identities

The tension between urban dynamics and theatrical stasis is manifest from the opening moments of *La Chienne*. Interestingly, the film initially appears to comply with Deleuze's interpretation of theatre in Renoir's work as a locus of predefined, imprisoning roles and genres: the narrative unfolds in modern Paris but is bookended by a Guignol proscenium arch within which puppets introduce the drama. This represents a departure from Georges de la Fouchardière's novel (published in 1930), in which the characters are introduced by an omniscient narrator, and André Mouézy-Éon's stage adaptation (first staged 12 December 1930), which entirely eliminates La Fouchardière's comments on the characters and the ensuing drama.[29] In Renoir's prologue, music plays from an unseen source and the curtain behind a proscenium arch rises. Three puppets enter in sequence. The first is a moralising puppet who informs us that the spectator is about to view 'a great social drama' that 'will prove to you that vice is always punished'.[30] A second puppet dressed as a policeman enters the stage and contradicts the other puppet, stating that 'we are about to have the honour of presenting a moralising comedy'.[31] Guignol subsequently enters and unceremoniously beats the puppets into submission before making his own announcement: 'Ladies and gentlemen, do not listen to these people. The play that we are going to show you is neither a drama nor a comedy. It carries no moral intentions and will prove absolutely nothing at all.'[32] Guignol may initially appear revolutionary in comparison with the other puppets. However, the roles available in Renoir's *petit théâtre* are invariably reductive and even the boisterous Guignol himself attempts to describe the characters through labels which, although helpful in some measure, are inexact inasmuch as incomplete: Maurice Legrand (Michel Simon), we are told, 'embodies an intellectual and sentimental culture above the milieu where he dwells, in such a way that he gives the impression of a perfect imbecile'.[33] Yet, as Colin Davis notes, Legrand has sufficient self-awareness to label himself an imbecile upon his final, brutal disillusionment in Lulu's (Janie Marèse) apartment prior to his act of murder.[34] Lulu's inconsistency similarly defies labels: 'She is always sincere: she lies all of the time', and must therefore be treated with caution, even when she is not deliberately deceptive.[35] Guignol avoids any definition of Dédé's (Georges Flamant) traits, identifying him as 'just the lad, Dédé, and nothing more'.[36]

The very lack of Renoir's signature techniques in this sequence further exemplifies Deleuze's conceptualisation of Renoir's theatre as a locus of imprisonment: the deep spaces lauded by Bazin, Christopher Faulkner, and Deleuze are nowhere to be seen, and the image is emphatically shallow. Nor does off-screen space play any notable role: the spectator is confronted with a stationary frame that circumscribes the parameters of the drama and whose contents bear no relation to the diegetic space beyond the frame until the images of the three main characters materialise. This is particularly surprising since Noël Burch argues that Renoir was one of the first to constructively harness the 'fluctuating existence' of off-screen space and is one of few directors to 'have used this implicit dialectic as an explicit means of structuring a whole film'.[37] Within the prologue, the parameters of the proscenium arch are not challenged by the puppets who enter from below and do not address left-hand or right-hand spaces adjacent to the theatre, the space behind the theatre set-piece, or the space behind the camera. Thus, the tension between the embodied past and the ongoing present is absent from the prologue.

Davis suggests that 'however separate the worlds of the audience, the puppets and the human actors may seem to be, the prologue encourages us to regard them as interpenetrating'.[38] Such a view is supported by Guignol's remark that 'the characters are neither heroes nor absolute traitors. They are poor people like me, like you.'[39] Yet the *mise en scène* of the introductions to the main characters of the drama emphasises the disparities between the space of the theatre and the space of the city rather than the relationship between the two that Davis, Deleuze, and Leo Braudy advocate as a fruitful avenue of enquiry.[40] Interestingly, the inability of the puppets to interpret the characters or the narrative without employing futile labels already suggests the incompatibility of narratives in the theatre and in the city. The irreconcilability of the theatre and the city is also signalled by the failure of the stage to contain the characters to whom Guignol refers: as he recites his description of each of the characters, images of Legrand, Lulu, and Dédé appear in sequence. The deployment of superimposition – a specifically cinematographic device – is aesthetically counterposed with the space of the theatre, which is incapable of enclosing Renoir's three primary characters, who transcend its rigid frame. The *mise en scène* of the introductions provides a metafilmic commentary on the impossibility of subsuming the fluctuating world of the city within the rigid world of the theatre and on the broader physical and metaphorical limits of the frame. This tension between the petrifying *surcroît de théâtralité* and the malleability of urban space structures our perception of space-time in the remainder of the narrative.

Marches dans la ville*: the production of class relations in everyday life*

Drawing on a framing technique pointedly dismissed by the Guignol sequence, the on-screen space of Renoir's Paris is constantly held in tension with the off-screen space beyond the camera's frame. This dialectic challenges any attempt to confine the fluctuating qualities of urban space to a proscenium arch. After the prologue, the screen fades from the frame of the Guignol stage to an innovative establishing shot of the celebrations unfolding in honour of la maison Henriot. The camera rises upwards through a food shaft whose window frames M. Henriot and his employees at their table. In the background, three windows provide additional frames leading to exterior space. The additional frames offer the first instance of frames within frames in the human drama. Crucially, these windows provide apertures to larger social spaces beyond the current view of the camera's frame. Thus, unlike the all-inclusive frame of the proscenium arch, this shot dispels any temptation to view any single frame (be it the frame of the camera or any single framing device) as a definitive container of life within the city. As Bazin notes, interior décor in *La Chienne* is designed to permit a deep field of vision and there is 'a systematic search for the effect of the frame as a concealer within each shot'.[41] A subsequent view of the men dining, shot from the vestibule, reveals both a physical space that hitherto remained off-screen (the vestibule itself) and two additional windows in the background which similarly remained off-screen in the shot viewed from the food shaft. The camera subsequently returns to a position behind the food shaft, framing the table of employees as it did in the opening shot of this scene. By now, the evocations of the manifest limits of the camera's own frame have granted us an awareness of the fundamental impossibility of viewing the characters as a coherent set of elements within a single shot (be they framed by a food shaft, a window, or the camera itself), isolated from the wider society. On-screen space thus enters into a dialectic with the '*specific* existence' and '*primordial* importance' that Burch associates with Renoir's brand of off-screen space.[42] The reflexive critique of the limits of the camera's frame created by the *mise en scène* of this sequence, particularly through deep staging and off-screen space, provides a spatial blueprint for our exploration of the city.

Our first exterior view of Paris is granted after the celebrations honouring M. Henriot. During this sequence the camera frames the affective role of urban architecture, allowing the spectator to perceive crystalline space-time as the paths of the three major characters implicated in the drama converge for the first time. The scene opens with a wide shot of an area recognised by Alexander Sesonske as the steps near the church of St Jean

Figure 1.1 Legrand (right) encounters Dédé (left) and Lulu (lying on steps)

de Montmartre.[43] Dédé, an abusive pimp, and Lulu, a prostitute, descend a stone staircase. The camera briefly cuts to a medium shot of Dédé beating Lulu before cutting back to its original vantage point. Legrand subsequently enters the scene from the foreground and accosts Dédé (Figure 1.1). The camera cuts to a close shot of Lulu's face as Legrand beholds her features for the first time, and to another close shot of Lulu and Dédé as she nurses the latter's head. Once again, the camera returns to its wide view of the street as Legrand proceeds towards the background of the image to find a taxi to escort Lulu and Dédé home. The camera cuts briefly to show Dédé petulantly slapping Lulu's leg before returning yet again to a similar shot of the street, revealing Legrand emerging from the shadows of a road in the background, followed by a taxi. The camera cuts to a medium shot of the characters entering the car before returning to a wide shot similar to the one that opened this scene, as the taxi proceeds towards a road that leads towards the background of the image.

Sesonske notes two significant aspects of this meeting. First of all, their meeting is pure happenstance: 'Lulu and Legrand meet by accident [. . .] with no background to provide identity for each other, no time to prepare for the encounter.'[44] Secondly, the characters are 'from wholly different worlds'.[45] O'Shaughnessy views Lulu and Dédé as 'instantly recognisable urban types, walking clichés, preening pimp and subservient whore'.[46] Even the characters' clothes emphasise the social resonance of this meeting: Legrand's fedora, glasses, and discreet gestures immediately signal his *petit bourgeois* background. Lulu's brazen make-up and the garish flowers that adorn her hat recall Hayward's assertion that the circulation of sexual bodies 'allows us to see space and time performing in the city'.[47] It becomes immediately apparent that the shared public space of the city provides a locus for the intersection of diverse trajectories plotted by characters belonging to diverse social strata. Furthermore, the wide shot of Legrand, Lulu, and Dédé's convergence at these steps evokes Certeau's theorisation of walking as a tactical act whose footsteps 'privilege, transform or neglect spatial elements' and necessarily establish 'a conjunctive and disjunctive articulation of places' that creates polymorphous cities, devoid of fixed identities.[48] This encounter results in the partial disintegration of *petit bourgeois* society and the creation of a new social configuration that offers all of the characters new roles that efface the 'borders [. . .] of alterity' that structure the city.[49]

Renoir's *mise en scène* of the city, specifically the interaction between off-screen and deeply composed on-screen space in this shot, foregrounds the role of the city as an active social catalyst, recalling Richard Sennett's definition of the city as 'a human settlement in which strangers are likely to meet', and Geraldine Pratt and Rose Marie San Juan's assertion that urban streets filmed on location constitute 'a likely site of the fragmentary and the unexpected'.[50] Because the space photographed marks the confluence of at least three roads, each of which extends beyond the scope of the camera's frame, the spectator remains constantly aware of the possibility for the introduction of new elements from the off-screen spaces that pre-exist the encounter. Dédé physically assaults Lulu in the midground, Legrand arrives from behind the camera and finds a taxi on a road leading off-screen from the left-hand side of the image, and all three characters depart through a road that leads towards the background of the image. The roads leading off-screen evoke the subjective space beyond the frame, challenging us to consider the import of the city's architecture towards what Massey describes as 'juxtapositions yet to flower into interaction [. . .], relations which may or may not be accomplished'.[51] By framing the physical space of Montmartre as a social catalyst that produces *points de fuite* in the class hierarchy that structures the city, Renoir renders the potential creation of a genuinely new future limpid (to appropriate Deleuze's terminology).

Renoir's *mise en scène* of Paris arguably stems from the sharp contrast between Renoir's bourgeois upbringing and the diverse social groups that inhabited Montmartre, where his father secured his family's privileges. Nicholas Hewitt has described how Montmartre's growing *lieux de plaisir* fostered bohemianism and high cultural production in the twentieth century whilst Paris itself held these elements together in 'a complex and delicate ecology [. . .], highly vulnerable to urban trends beyond their control', creating what Louis Chevalier memorably described as Montmartre *du plaisir et du crime*.[52] It is also worth remembering that George-Eugène Haussmann's attempt to rigorously demarcate and homogenise the Paris metropole under the auspices of Napoléon III were begun between 1853 and 1870, but were only completed upon the renovation of the Boulevard Haussmann in 1927, four years before the release of *La Chienne*.

In a mobile character-oriented extended take that follows Legrand's meeting with Lulu, the camera continues to emphasise the interconnectedness of the physical subsections of Paris, further suggesting that if there are other parts of the city that appear exclusively lower class, the physical mobility of human beings within the city permeates the city's ultimately arbitrary social borders. After the taxi has arrived in front of Dédé's hotel, Dédé and Lulu proceed on foot to the latter's lodgings. Throughout this sequence, captured largely though a travelling shot, the camera refuses to fragment its view of the city, cutting only to situate the characters' shared trajectory in relation to their changing physical and social surroundings at Lulu's local metro station and outside her dilapidated lodgings. Tellingly, the average shot length of *La Chienne* is actually double that of the contemporaneous national norm.[53] This calculated alternation between stationary wide shots and deeply composed space photographed by a mobile camera reminds us that Lulu's residence, although worlds apart from the middle-class party that opened Legrand's narrative and even the cheap hotel where Dédé lives, is part of a single, physically unified urban environment that indiscriminately permits people of all class rankings to navigate and reconstruct the social space of the city. It also demonstrates that montage need not preclude spatial or temporal continuity, allowing us rather to view multiple technically disjointed shots within a single consistent vision of open space-time.

The narrative's refusal to situate Legrand and Lulu's trajectory in relation to any instantly recognisable urban landmarks that correspond with our pre-established 'index of representations' emphasises the progressive destabilisation of the coordinates of Legrand's social space: whereas the illuminated Moulin Rouge was visible through a window during the celebrations held by la maison Henriot, such urban landmarks are conspicuously absent from this scene, thus drawing the spectator's attention to the deceptive banality of everyday *pratiques d'espace*. Although Legrand is situated within a topographically specific site and Lulu has mentioned that she lives in the Barbès area, none of the events following their meeting feature any notable landmarks that allow us to readily clarify his precise location beyond the vague area of Montmartre. By producing an ontologically specific reality that deviates from popular images, Renoir defamiliarises the viewer, creating a textual space within which the relationship between class and urban navigation amidst the open space-time of Paris can be clearly assessed.

It is important to reiterate that Deleuze's emphasis on the petrifying influence of theatricality, insofar as this film (which is absent from his analysis) is concerned, is far from redundant. Like the puppets, Legrand is unable to elucidate the polymorphous identities embodied by Lulu and Dédé during their first perfunctory encounter. Zygmunt Bauman indirectly asserts that a '*mis*-meeting' such as that between the three characters generally precludes the creation of a socialised space:[54]

> The meeting of strangers is *an event without a past*. More often than not, it is also *an event without a future* (it is expected to be, hoped to be, free of a future), a story most certainly '*not* to be continued', a one-off chance, to be consummated in full while it lasts and on the spot, without delay and without putting the unfinished business off to another occasion.[55]

Bauman notes elsewhere that such social intercourse is 'always pregnant with the danger of false steps and costly blunders' that 'arise from the ignorance of rules, and the strangeness of strangers is, at bottom, our ignorance'.[56] This ignorance, in Legrand's case, stems from a limited knowledge of the various roles available amongst the lower strata occupying urban space. As Bauman remarks, 'I may know of the stranger so little that I cannot be even sure that she "fits" any of the types I am familiar with.'[57] Legrand proceeds one step further, misidentifying Lulu as a friend. Lulu's true character-type (which partly incorporates the *chienne* of the title) is not recognised by Legrand until the moments that directly precede his act of murder. Her exploitation of Legrand epitomises Bauman's figure of 'the stranger "sitting across the barricade", blurring the boundaries which ought to be kept watertight, and thus sapping the securely "typified" world'.[58] By pursuing the *ligne de fuite* introduced by Lulu, Legrand willingly undermines the porous social stratification of the city's public space. Their relationship, which O'Shaughnessy describes as a sign of 'fallen urban order', is itself indicative of the fact that this order was only ever a provisional social construct.[59]

'An event without a future' (?): from mis-meeting to murder

Much like the initial meeting between Legrand and Lulu, the climactic murder scene alternates between the two characters enmeshed in the drama and the wider urban space within which their dispute is unfolding, constantly situating the private world of Lulu's apartment in relation to the public space of the city street.[60] Inside the apartment, Legrand apologises profusely for failing to realise that Lulu was perhaps subjugated to another against her will. As they argue over Lulu's exploitation of Legrand and his painting, the music from the streets continues to play, uninterrupted by the camera's transition to the interior space, and a man outside begins singing 'La sérénade du pavé'. As tensions continue to mount between Legrand and Lulu, the camera repeatedly alternates between the street and the apartment. The camera cuts to a close-up of the envelope-cutter and, rapidly, to a shot of the street singers. As the camera rises, we see a boy staring out of his first-floor window onto the singers down below, blithely unaware of the stabbing being committed mere floors above him. By the time the camera has risen to the window of Lulu's apartment, she is already dead, lying horizontally across her bed whilst Legrand apologetically kisses her lifeless hand. Even at this intimate moment, the music continues to play outside and the camera displaces our attention once more towards the street singers outside, creating, in Christopher Faulkner's analysis, 'a fairly obvious synecdoche whereby the environment in which the murder takes place is larger than Lulu's room – by implication it is the whole of French society'.[61]

The role of the city as a 'structure of visibility' (and sonority, if we consider the soundscape produced by the singers) is interpolated as Legrand leaves the apartment and in the scenes of Dédé's trial. The audience gathered around the singer passes no remarks on Legrand as he departs from the scene of the crime. Dédé, however, imposes on both the performers and the bystanders by honking his horn and obstinately parking his car right in the middle of the crowd. Dédé enters the apartment building pursued by the concierge, who remarks that 'he could have said hello, especially since I have letters for Madame Pelletier'.[62] Dédé's obnoxiousness will cost him dearly. He walks out of the building a short time later in the presence of the concierge and the musicians and he drives away. The concierge subsequently decides to bring the letters to Lulu only to find her bloodied corpse. She is later among the people who unintentionally bear false witness against Dédé, even though they have not even seen him commit Lulu's murder. Faulkner accurately notes that Dédé 'is incriminated by the tell-tale Parisian argot of his class [. . .], by his arrogant manner, and by his past, rather than by actual proofs of his wrongdoing'.[63] However, Renoir's *mise en scène* of broader society and its limited gaze also implies that Dédé is as much the victim of the physical structure of urban space as of the society that condemns him: Dédé is incriminated not because he was found with the body in private, but because he flaunted his presence in public at the door to Lulu's building. Dédé's and Legrand's respective exits from the building occur in quick succession, and were it not for the musicians' presence outside the building, it is possible that the concierge would have remained inside and that Legrand would have been accused of the murder.

The stage-bound epilogue, like the film's prologue, satirises the representational limits of the theatre: life within Renoir's city is not limited to the theatre's stereotypical roles and morally informed genres, and thus 'mocks the order of art that is so totally separate from human anguish'.[64] Lulu's and Dédé's unwarranted deaths, much like the initial encounter between Legrand, Lulu, and Dédé, are hardly deliberate efforts to change their roles within the metaphorical crystal. Rather, these events are by-products of the topography of the urban landscape which effortlessly subsumes the traumatic personal impact of Lulu's murder on both Legrand and Dédé within the broader narrative of the city, and whose physical space and social order remain untarnished by this gross miscarriage of due legal process. Urban space prevents the law from offering a just resolution of conflicting claims, yet the very ocular shortcomings that sever Legrand's relationship with Lulu and Dédé also ensure that society's legal process is executed: by the end of the film, the impact of Dédé's death has long since dissipated and Legrand is a tramp, eking out a living by opening doors for cosmopolitan urban citizens. Legrand remains nonetheless open to prospective *lignes de fuite* in a city where a prostitute encounters his naïve benevolence as spontaneously as the discarded twenty franc note that greets his sight before a curtain falls in front of the camera, satirising the impossibility of confining the preceding drama to the theatre's rigid frame.

Boudu sauvé des eaux (1932)

Lestingois's theatre: screening the roles morts *of bourgeois fantasies*

In *Boudu sauvé des eaux*, Renoir's first film following *La Chienne*, the eponymous tramp (played by Michel Simon) is rescued from the waters of the Seine by Édouard Lestingois (Charles Granval), a bourgeois bookshop-owner. Over the course of the film, Boudu wreaks havoc on Lestingois's property and seduces Lestingois's wife, Emma (Marcelle Hainia). Boudu finally escapes the confines of Lestingois's bookshop when, on the day of his marriage to Lestingois's maid, Anne-Marie (Sévérine Lerczinska), he escapes on the current of the Seine.

As in *La Chienne*, the *surcroît de théâtralité* is a core element of the film's *mise en scène*. Deleuze usefully draws our attention to buildings whose theatrically informed etiquette and historically imbued décor make the coexistence of multiple temporalities tangible in the image:

> Everything that is past falls back into the crystal and remains there: it is the collection of frozen, fixed, ready-made, too-conforming roles that the characters try out one after another, dead roles or role of death, the *danse macabre* of memories of which Bergson speaks, as in the château of *La Règle du jeu* [. . .][65]

As this analysis aims to demonstrate, such is also the case of Lestingois's shop in *Boudu*. Deleuze specifically remarks that the eponymous tramp 'finds the water's current by leaving the intimate and enclosed theatre of the bookshop where he has tried numerous roles', whilst Perez rightly observes that the film displays 'a socialized rather than individualized point of view'.[66] Therefore, rather than simply view Lestingois's shop as a theatre, we should examine how Renoir frames its stultifying theatrical properties in relation to the fluctuating urban space of Paris to produce an image of open space-time.

Like *La Chienne*, the film opens with a scene set on a stage but proceeds to directly link the enclosedness of the stage with the social and semiotic stultification of the Lestingois' home. After the credits, the sound of a flute is heard. Two columns are located to the left-hand side of the screen on the stage, and a garden features on the visibly false backdrop. Anne-Marie, dressed as Chloë, skips across the screen. Lestingois dressed as Priapus, prances behind her, playing pan pipes. As Lestingois approaches Anne-Marie to embrace her, he pushes one of the columns, which bends flimsily. The artificiality of the prologue echoes the Guignol show that opens *La Chienne*, but differs crucially, in that the image of Priapus pursuing Chloë represents Lestingois's fantasy rather than a commentary provided by independent observers. The roles played by both Lestingois and Anne-Marie provide Lestingois with the only fantasies that distract him from the sterile routines that structure his world. However, the shoddy set creates a 'clumsy and farcical' fantasy,[67] and after the theatre has faded from view and Lestingois has sent Anne-Marie to prepare soup, he laments that 'my pipes are weary'.[68] Clearly, the productive capacity of the roles provided by mythology is diminishing.

This is primarily because, as evidenced by the Greek mythological imagery featuring in the prologue, the scope of Lestingois's dreams is moulded by his education and cultural interests, and is circumscribed by the *petit bourgeois* decorum that structures his domestic life. His statuettes, numerous portraits, and ornamental plates do not merely signify Lestingois's class, nor do the vertical columns and the doorways framed within doorways simply structure Lestingois's home. The prologue reveals that all of these elements of décor condition his ability to conjure fantasies. Numerous shots situate décor in the foreground to emphasise the narrow structure of the house, implying that Lestingois's imagination is stultified by his desires to ground his fantasies culturally. It is understandable that Deleuze likens Lestingois's shop (and, albeit indirectly, the roles within) to an enclosed theatre. However, whereas René Fauchois's source text is entirely set in Lestingois's bookshop, the shoddiness of the theatrical set-piece and the rigorous etiquette of the home are juxtaposed by Renoir with the spontaneity and diversity offered by the same city that remedies the drudgery of Legrand's everyday bourgeois life.

Individuals and institutions: appropriating the urban cultural landscape

As in *La Chienne*, deceptively irrelevant shots of urban landmarks play an important role in the *mise en scène* of urban space in flux. Renoir disperses these landmarks throughout the narrative to subjectivise Boudu's experience of walking in the city. Renoir's technique proceeds in two complementary ways. The first method is employed before Boudu dives into the Seine. Through a variety of wide shots and deeply composed shots, the spectator views a number of physically inert buildings that testify to France's historical, cultural, and intellectual legacy including the Louvre (located just across the Seine, which flows outside Lestingois's home), the Pont des Arts, and the Institut de France (both visible from Lestingois's first-floor window). Our views of these *répères* are purely incidental, occurring either during Lestingois's own views through his window or over the course of Boudu's indifferent navigation. At no point do they actively contribute to the dramatic thrust of the narrative.

Renoir's second method of subjectivising the urban experience involves montage, a technique whose *morcellement* of narrative space-time is rarely associated with his shooting style, unless we consider the hunting scene in *La Règle du jeu*. Although montage holds no place in Deleuze's conceptualisation of Renoir's *image-temps*, Deleuze usefully observes in *Cinéma 1* that shots contain two facets, framing being the facet turned towards objects, montage the facet turned towards the whole.[69] In *Boudu*, Renoir's images make the urban space of Paris (the whole) the specific subject of both framing and montage, dynamising both the frame and its interval, integrating temporality within its view of urban space by portraying the physically connected but socially disparate elements existing within open space-time.

Numerous images of Notre Dame are repeatedly edited into the narrative after Boudu's admission to the Lestingois household: the cathedral appears once after Lestingois's failed attempt to visit Anne-Marie's room during Boudu's first night at the residence; it features a second time after Lestingois has been decorated with a medal of bravery; and a third time in the film's final scene, its spire stretching into the sky as a procession of tramps sings 'Sur les bords de la Riviera'. As in the case of the previously discussed landmarks, these shots of Notre Dame relate to Boudu about as much as the relatively trivial shots of the cat prowling on the rooftop or Anne-Marie walking into the kitchen alone to eat a sweet. However, this is precisely the point of their inclusion. Renoir's use of montage emphatically detaches Notre Dame from Boudu's experience of walking and living in the city and provides a model of spectatorship for Boudu's wanderings in the city amidst the other aforementioned buildings. The separation implied by Renoir's use of montage emphasises Certeau's assertion that footsteps only appropriate particular spatial elements amidst a polymorphous urban space devoid of a fixed identity.[70] This quality of Renoir's cutting also intersects in enlightening ways with Deleuze's taxonomy of montage, specifically his understanding of D. W. Griffith's 'organic' montage (featuring in *The Birth of a Nation* [1915] and *Intolerance: Love's Struggle Throughout the Ages* [1916]) and Sergei Eisenstein's montage of attractions (Deleuze gives the examples of *Bronenosets Potemkin* [1925] and *Staroye i novoye* [1929]): as in the former, the spectator witnesses the editing of 'binary relationships which constitute a *parallel alternate montage*', and as in the latter, '*the interval, as well as the whole takes on a new meaning*'.[71] The buildings are emphatically relegated from Boudu's own narrative by means of montage, precisely because their intellectual and cultural values are not valued by the tramp.

Although the landmarks in *Boudu* correspond with the spectator's own 'index of representations' (to use Rojex's term), the narrative precludes the spectator's projection of any preconceptions regarding the monuments' ideological associations onto the screen by evoking the plurality of potential experiences of walking in the city. The range of characters viewed in the city by both Renoir's camera and Lestingois's telescope range from tramps like Boudu to middle-class women and a black woman who would doubtless find it difficult to appreciate urban sites such as the Exposition Coloniale, later advertised in the street outside Lestingois's bookshop. Given Boudu's own irreverence towards the landmarks that situate his trajectory, it is clear that the values that any of these buildings represent are only stable to the extent that they are recognised and appreciated by the populace (in Figure 1.2, the Louvre dominates

Figure 1.2 The public rush to the Seine as Lestingois comes to Boudu's rescue

the background, underscoring the indifference of the passers-by to the cultural legacy embodied by Paris, rushing instead to catch a glimpse of Boudu in the Seine). Even Lestingois, as he opens his windows for the first time in the narrative, employs his telescope in order to ogle a number of unwitting young women rather than to savour the cultural legacy embodied by these buildings. Just as Boudu cannot appreciate the bookshops that he passes on the quais as he shuffles towards the Pont des Arts (Boudu later tells Lestingois that he can only read 'large letters'[72]), these buildings represent one particular realm of the city which is unappreciated by certain citizens as we watch them navigate the city over the course of the narrative.

The relationship between urban society and the cityscape in these particular scenes produces the 'incessant flow of possibilities and near-intangible meanings' which Kracauer recognised as a core product of film's relationship with the city.[73] More specifically, Renoir's Paris coincides with Kracauer's theorisation of the spectator of the cinematographic city as Baudelairian *flâneur*, that is to say, one who is 'intoxicated with life in the street – life eternally dissolving the patterns which it is about to form'.[74] The selective appropriation of the city made manifest by the social diversity of Paris and the appearance of landmarks throughout the narrative subjectivises the urban experience, creating an image of open space-time in which social space dynamises values associated with physical space, repeatedly reminding us that space is, as Massey asserts, 'multiple, relational, unfinished and always becoming'.[75]

Dismantling domestic space

The ongoing dismantling of social values made manifest by the relationship between Boudu and the broader Parisian populace hints at the forces ranged against Lestingois's own home in the heart of the city. In *Le Sens pratique* (1980), Pierre Bourdieu theorises domestic space as a structure whose social code is not reducible to a single set of permanently inscribed rites, but which rather sustains a range of codes that alter depending upon the gender, social perspective, and physical position of the individual navigating within or outside the house.[76] The range of such perspectives is infinitely multiplied in the city, where any notion of home incorporating a stable identity is founded on 'fantasies of plenitude and security'.[77] The susceptibility of Lestingois's residence to social disruption is increased by the lower floor which, although private property, simultaneously operates as a shop that is open to the public. The shop's existence within a network of fundamentally open spaces is emphasised by the numerous shots that stage passers-by in depth beyond the glass window of the shop door throughout the narrative.

Defying the *rôle mort* imposed by Lestingois, Boudu's energetic physicality and complete disregard for bourgeois etiquette reveal that his benefactor's household is as fallible a social structure as the institutions dotted around Paris. He lurches and slides across a table on the shop floor after ungratefully consuming the sardines and bread offered by Mme Lestingois and precariously balances a tray of dishes on a carafe of wine with predictable results. Even indoors, he refuses to renounce his habit of spitting and wipes his freshly polished shoes with her bedsheets. Boudu rashly declares that he would be embarrassed to wear any of the clothes that his benefactor has to offer him. Boudu unhesitatingly employs the informal *tu* form as he eats his first meal at the house, a habit he later develops with Lestingois's wife before seducing her. Boudu also mockingly imitates Lestingois's assertion that that he must learn to change his behaviour and, moreover, proudly declares to Anne-Marie that he has never thanked anyone for anything in his life.

These dual interconnected aspects of Boudu's subversive behaviour – physical and social – converge in Boudu's manifest indifference towards Lestingois's books. Much of the house is cluttered with stacks of books, recalling Bourdieu's description of class as a cultural product capable of existing in objectified states including literature.[78] The shot that introduces Lestingois's home reveals books piled on multiple shelves that reach the ceiling of the room, creating what Flinn describes as a 'geometry of excess' by granting the impression of a domestic space that is secure in its intellectual ideas.[79] Lestingois's free distribution of Voltaire's work to a passing student further elevates these books from a mere professional commodity to symbols of the bookseller's passion for intellectual development. It is no surprise that Lestingois is tellingly indifferent towards Boudu's physical acts of subversion: he merely mutters tones of regret when a distraught Mme Lestingois expresses her shock over the dishevelled kitchen and immediately returns to reading his book. It is not until Lestingois subsequently discovers that Boudu has spat in a copy of Balzac's *La Physiologie du mariage* that the shopowner finally decides that Boudu truly merits 'a good kick in the rear' and 'is nothing to me'.[80] Boudu's act of spitting in Balzac's work is not merely a sign of the tramp's complete indifference to France's heritage. By disparaging the cultural products that provide Lestingois's home with its social function and physical structure, Boudu's act reveals a complete indifference to the Lestingois' personal domestic space, professional role and marital ties. Lestingois's main flaw lies in his belief that he can maintain the apparent integrity of the bourgeois codes that structure his home even though he is transplanting an element that is demonstrably antithetic to the physical structure, social values, and cultural history of Paris right into his bourgeois domestic interiors. Lestingois's home is, as Deleuze suggests, an imprisoning structure. However, this theatricality is a by-product of the household's own class values. Furthermore, Renoir's use of both framing and deep staging demonstrates that Boudu's defacement of Lestingois's *théâtre intime* is merely a microcosm of the Parisian populace's varying attitudes towards the cultural institutions dotted around their own city.

Considering Lestingois's vision of Boudu through a microscope early in the film, Perez rightly proposes that 'the narrative point of view [. . .], the limitation in our view of things, is not one character's perspective on the story but the way a whole social class sees the world'.[81] However, it is important to specify that Lestingois's perspective and that of his entire class are clearly held in tension with Boudu's own vision of the city. As in *La Chienne*, upper-class values, cultural assets, social mores, and historical memory are inevitably bolstered or eroded by the circulation of lower-class characters who alternately project, ignore, or dismantle them in cooperation with characters belonging to a higher social station than themselves. To this end, we must review *Boudu* repeatedly and consider aspects of Renoir's techniques that seemingly run contrary to general perceptions of his narrative style (particularly those articulated by Bazin, Faulkner, and Deleuze) in order to recognise open space-time in Renoir's Paris.

La Règle du jeu (1939)

The Trocadéro as lieu de mémoire*: l'Exposition Universelle de 1937*

Of the three films discussed within this chapter, the relationship between space and time is arguably most salient in *La Règle du jeu*. Such is Deleuze's admiration for the film that virtually all of his arguments regarding the range of elements that potentially inscribe temporality in the image – characters, buildings, and *profondeur de champ* to name some of his most accessible examples – stem from his reading of the film. However, Deleuze focuses exclusively on La Colinière and the characters within. Indeed, most textual analyses of *La Règle du jeu*, with the notable exceptions of Sesonske's and Keith Reader's comprehensive analyses, tend to focus on the hunting scenes in the marshes of la Sologne and the labyrinthine rural château to the exclusion of the geographical space lying beyond the Parisian residences viewed early in the film.[82] Critical neglect of the scenes set in Paris is understandable as urban life and landmarks are conspicuously relegated to off-screen space in most scenes set in the French capital: the majority of these scenes unfold in the insulated residence where the marquise and marquis de la Chesnaye – Christine (Nora Grégor) and Robert (Marcel Dalio) – first hear Jurieux's emotional denigration of Christine and where André Jurieux's (Roland Toutain) friend, Octave (played by Renoir), attempts to convince the la Chesnayes to invite Jurieux nonetheless to an upcoming retreat at La Colinière.

Interestingly, however, the narrative grants us one view of urban Paris: early in the film, as Robert tells Geneviève (Mila Parély), his mistress since the days before his marriage to Christine, that he desires to end their affair, the Eiffel Tower and Palais de Chaillot are visible in the background through a wide window, marking the narrative's sole view of the public space of Paris in a film whose first twenty minutes unfold in the capital (Figure 1.3). This shot is crucial to our understanding of Robert and Christine's flight to La Colinière and the continued presence of Paris as an affective off-screen realm that structures the open space-time of the world viewed.

The importance of the scene within the context of the entire narrative is suggested by the fact that the decision to set it in front of recognisable Parisian landmarks occurred relatively late in the production: originally, Geneviève's character was named Paula and only appeared at La Colinière. When Renoir eventually drafted the conversation between Geneviève and Robert, he intended to set it on a golfing green, and it was not until Renoir began to envisage the fully edited film that he set the scene in Geneviève's

Figure 1.3 A view of the Palais de Chaillot and the Eiffel Tower from Geneviève's apartment

apartment. Even then, Renoir provided no indication of décor or accessories. In Olivier Curchod and Christopher Faulkner's estimation, this afforded Renoir the possibility of filming the conversation in a wide range of environments.[83] They further deduce that this sequence was probably filmed after the sequences set at le Bourget and, by extension, provided the final note on which shooting wrapped.[84] Based on this information, the scene of Robert and Geneviève's conversation at the latter's apartment provides a potentially significant avenue of enquiry towards the overarching concerns of the film.

As in *La Chienne* and *Boudu*, urban landmarks play a crucial role in our interpretation of la Chesnaye's efforts to stabilise his social space. Unlike the main characters of either of these films, however, neither Geneviève nor Robert (nor any other character belonging to the *haute bourgeoisie*) ever walks in the city, preferring instead to remain insulated from mainstream society. The distance of the Palais de Chaillot and the Eiffel Tower from Geneviève's window suggests that Geneviève's apartment is probably located in the seventh *arrondissement*, one of the most upmarket areas of Paris.[85] These monuments also constitute registers of the social tensions that proliferated in contemporary France following the Exposition Universelle de 1937 and which motivate the *haute bourgeoisie*'s excursion to La Colinière. Prime Minister Léon Blum, whose government had brought hope to the working classes in the wake of the Depression and the 6 February 1934 riots, intended the exposition as a tool for national reconciliation.[86] However, strikes delayed the reconstruction of the palais,

France's key contribution to the exposition, far beyond the scheduled 1 May opening of the event and, ironically, Blum's own government had collapsed by the time the exhibition had actually opened. Furthermore, Blum's refusal to aid the Spanish subsequently put the Front's principles into question, and Sesonske suggests that by 1939, the sight of the palais recalled France's 'less than heroic role' in the Spanish Civil war since it displayed Picasso's *Guernica*.[87]

The second monument of relevance, the Eiffel Tower, recalls the pavilions designed by Europe's foremost ideological rivals, Nazi Germany and the Soviet Union, which directly opposed each other either side of the Eiffel Tower, transforming the Trocadéro into what Shanny Peer describes as 'contested [terrain] for the articulation of collective national identities'.[88] Hitler and Stalin each erected monuments that displayed the ideological iconography of their own countries, the German pavilion crowned with an eagle and swastika, and the Soviet pavilion featuring a worker and Kolkhoz woman, strategically homogenising popular perceptions of each country's national identity. Conversely, France's ethical diversity and conflicting interpretations of the Third Republic precluded state fetishism, resulting in a pavilion that was 'itself profoundly split'.[89] Indeed, the newly reformed palais displeased both right-wing and left-wing leagues: whereas the interior displays representing cultural métissage were labelled a 'jumble of exotica', commentators saw the architectural structure of the building as a 'rejection of foreign exoticism and a reaffirmation of classicism and Frenchness', resulting in an incoherent 'palimpsest of conflicting agendas and ideologies' which, rather than counter the propagandist displays of the dictatorships, 'showed the Republic in the midst of an identity crisis'.[90] France's fractured identity was further exposed during the making of *La Règle du jeu* following the signing of the Munich Agreement on 30 September 1938.

The view framed by Geneviève's window thus recalls Pierre Nora's theorisation of the development of *lieux de mémoire*, which he describes as material, symbolic, and functional sites 'where memory crystallizes and secretes itself'.[91] Nora proposes that interest in such sites emerges

> at a particular historical moment, a turning point where consciousness of a break with the past is bound up with the sense that memory has been torn [. . .] in such a way as to pose the problem of the embodiment of memory in certain sites where a sense of historical continuity persists.[92]

Framed after the fall of the Front populaire and the impending advent of war, the site beyond the apartment operates as a realm of embodied contradictory identities which France, due to its own fragmentary outlook, was helpless to resolve.

Renoir had previously expressed his malaise regarding the latest exhibition in 'Visite à l'Exposition', one of his many articles for *Ce Soir*, a left-wing newspaper to which he contributed articles from 1936 to 1938. Renoir's article opens with his own intention of attending a number of exhibits and events before realising that 'it was a guide for the 1900 *Exposition*, left in a corner of my library'.[93] Renoir does not pointedly attack the 1937 exhibition, but he is evidently nostalgic for an event that presents the musical talents of the late Camille Saint-Saëns (1825–1921) and places '*science within everybody's reach*', whereas Junyk's and Peer's analyses suggest that the prominent artistic and technological spheres had, by 1937, been largely supplanted by national propagandist efforts.[94] Interestingly, Renoir alluded to the exhibition in derogatory terms later in his career when, upon returning to Hollywood after a brief trip, he remarked that he was 'a little disappointed and saddened to find myself in the middle of this kind of 1937 *Exposition* that is the city of Hollywood'.[95]

The identity crisis embodied by this *lieu de mémoire* reflects major local, national, and international unrest that carries substantial potential ramifications for a class determined to guard its place in the uppermost echelons of contemporary society. However, the *mise en scène* of this shot leaves little doubt that the *haute bourgeoisie* is actively endeavouring to enforce fixed 'chains of meaning' which, in Massey's analysis 'embed [space] with closure and stasis'.[96] Much like their peers, Geneviève and Robert are not *promeneurs* and do not venture beyond the physical parameters of the apartment. Their physical insulation, much like Certeau's theorisation of the act of walking, 'has the function of locating the other relative to this "I"', with the effect of expressing interrelationships or divisions among places.[97] Geneviève's enclosure amidst her colonial décor physically isolates her private space from the fluctuating urban space beyond her window: a series of black figurines in the apartment hint at France's colonialist regime in Africa whilst her Buddha statues recall the French involvement in Indochina. The apparent stability of the home prompts Sesonske to note that 'no stir from the political storms that buffeted Paris during that decade reaches inside this quiet room' where Robert and Geneviève debate their personal affairs.[98]

However, their distance from the streets is an illusory bulwark against the social alterity that has installed itself within the very heart of the French capital. The *haute bourgeoisie* is no longer in a position to actively mediate the influence of these other cultures but can eliminate what Massey describes as 'that business of walking round a corner and bumping into alterity', a denial linked by Massey with 'a tendency to try to escape one of its most productive/disruptive elements – one's different neighbour'.[99] Thus, although lacking the location-shots of city streets that feature in *La Chienne* and *Boudu*, a pre-established awareness of the political, national, and ethical debates that problematise the *haute bourgeoisie*'s day-to-day existence allows us to simultaneously perceive both the ongoing present and, within the apartment, the stultifying influence of the past.

Christine and Robert: crystallising domestic space-time

The identity crisis made manifest by the embodied history of the Parisian metropolis underscores the *haute bourgeoisie*'s socially regressive conceptualisation of class, ethnicity, and nationality in contemporary France. Discussing conceptions of nationhood, Samir Amin praises the 'ideology of citizenship' that emerged in the wake of the French Revolution to include all of those who had participated in the Revolution, regardless of their ancestral blood ties or religion, and notes that *la laïcité* proceeds one step further than religious tolerance, 'attempting to rid the new nation of a reference to the past'.[100] Amin counterposes this model with the continuity of German states who proudly vaunted the old aristocracy, hereditary blood ties, and religious heritage.[101] Each of these tendencies, notes Amin, represents an extreme point in the potential trajectories available to nation-builders and neither is ultimately attainable in its purest form.

The *haute bourgeoisie* in *La Règle du jeu* is a case in point. France was not yet under Fascist control but, as Reader notes, 'elements of its ideology – authoritarianism, racial nationalism, vicious anti-Bolshevism – undoubtedly infected the French body politic'.[102] The members of Renoir's *haute bourgeoisie*, like the societies subject to Amin's analysis, 'still inherit cultural patterns that become reintegrated with new societal needs', in this case fascism.[103] The two focal points of these debates are Robert and Christine: whereas Geneviève's heritage is never questioned (she is white, upper-class, and readily recites Chamfort), the position of Robert in front of the window framing the Palais de Chaillot and the Eiffel Tower draws our attention to the complexity of 'the nation' as embodied by him and his wife. Each is an outsider in contemporary France in terms of either ethnicity or nationality, and both live in a residence that is conspicuously insulated from the Paris metropole. By 1939, the horizontal social barriers that formed the crux of Renoir's social portraits had entered into dialectic with increasingly virulent discourse surrounding Jewish and Germanic identity and problematised the relationship between the *haute bourgeoisie* and those of its members who belonged to such minorities in contemporary France.

The most flagrant slur against Jewishness in the film is uttered downstairs in La Colinière, where a butler snidely remarks that 'La Chesnaye's mother had a father named Rosenthal who came right out of Frankfurt.'[104] Most noteworthy is the fact that a servant may consider himself entitled to insult his master, simply because contemporary discourse has convinced him of his biological superiority over his master. Thus Sesonske, whilst discussing Robert's gestures as performance, accurately interprets la Chesnaye as a character who 'has been so absorbed by the life of style and yet remains so doubtful of his position in it [. . .]'.[105]

Christine, an Austrian immigrant, embodies contemporary issues pertaining to Germanic identity. As Durgnat states in his self-consciously right-wing interpretation of Christine, her Austrian heritage implies that she is 'not a French wife, but a woman whose loyalties must, like Marie-Antoinette's, remain half to France's hereditary enemy'.[106] This interpretation is echoed by the la Chesnayes' peers. Viewing Christine's life in France as a fundamentally extraneous existence, Saint-Aubin remarks, 'Poor Christine . . . I pity her because she is a foreigner', and recollects that she was 'forced to live here in Paris, in the middle of people who don't even speak her language'.[107] Saint-Aubin's lament regarding Christine's allegedly fundamental differences is echoed more spitefully by Geneviève, who predicts Christine's reaction to Robert's extramarital affair on the basis of pre-existing stereotypes: 'Christine has remained a woman of her country. A Parisian woman would understand but not her.'[108]

During the scene of Robert and Geneviève's discussion, it becomes abundantly clear that both Robert and Christine embody origins that were indexically linked with two of the most problematic conceptions of identity in Europe during the rise of the Front populaire and the Exposition Universelle and, now more than ever, on the eve of war. Hence the décor of the la Chesnaye residence, viewed directly before and after our view of Geneviève's apartment, recalls the latter's home on all counts except Geneviève's view of the city. Robert's *petite négresse* and Christine's exoticised black bust, much like Geneviève's ornaments, directly relate to their stratum's exoticisation of France's colonies and, as in the case of Geneviève, the la Chesnayes only appropriate foreign cultures with the twin aims of bolstering their conception of their own class identity among *les Français de souche* and supplanting contemporary images of France's fragmented national identity. However, this décor does not suffice for the la Chesnayes, who must simultaneously disregard radical contemporary attitudes towards Jewish and Germanic identity.

Quite unlike the photography of *La Chienne* and *Boudu*, the camera constantly refrains from staging interior and exterior spaces in depth throughout the remainder of the scenes set in the la Chesnaye residence, and there are no windows or doors that could topographically situate their home. Mirrors and curtains obscure the la Chesnayes' topographical relationship with the public space of Paris in long shots of Christine's room, in shots of her sitting at her dressing table, and in shots taken from the dressing table as Christine prepares to leave. When Christine rises to don her coat, we finally see a door in the background, which Octave uses in a later scene to access the main vestibule. Christine exits through yet another door only to reveal an opulent, ceiling-length mirror that reflects the opposite side of the vestibule, expanding the apparent depth of her space without connecting it to the physical space beyond the residence. Christine's arrival to the opposite room provides us with our introduction to Robert's quarters. This room is devoid of windows but, like Christine's room, contains numerous mirrors and even his bedroom doors contain panes of mirrored glass that denotes the fragile opulence of the la Chesneyes' anachronistic domestic realm.

This delusive effacement of the residence's topographical relationship with the broader space of Paris persists the following morning before Robert has even dressed to visit Geneviève. As Octave walks into Christine's room, followed by Robert, the camera remains outside their doorway, revealing only a mirror located in Christine's room in the background. Although light shines through her window, our view of the area beyond is obscured by blinds. Ornate mirrors only reflect Octave and Christine as he convinces her to invite Jurieux to La Colinière. Similarly, during Octave's subsequent conversation with Robert, natural light shines through two large windows, but both are veiled with partly transparent curtains and neither of them allows us to view the world beyond. Far more prominent in the room is the large, multifaceted mirror that hangs on the wall behind the characters, reflecting the room and the people who pass through.

The interior architecture of Christine and Robert's residence clearly expresses their efforts to create an impossibly closed space that conceals the social upheavals made manifest by the view from Geneviève's apartment. The interior design of their home strengthens their own confidence in their ability to impress and, as a result, crystallises (in the Deleuzian sense) their place in French society whilst paradoxically signifying their failure to coherently integrate into it. The sense of social alienation in the la Chesnayes' residence is augmented by the narrative's refusal to divulge the precise location of their residence (unlike, for example, Geneviève's apartment or, to take an example from another film analysed in this chapter, Lestingois's residence) or to even situate it in relation to other buildings (in *La Chienne*, the precise location of Legrand's apartment is never revealed but it is viewed in relation to neighbouring apartments through the view from his apartment windows). Instead, our introduction to Christine's boudoir takes place via the radio transmission from the airport: as Jurieux voices his discontentment, the camera cuts from the geographically precise airport at le Bourget and rises from behind a radio kept in Christine's geographically imprecise room. No effort is made to clarify even the general location of Christine's apartment. All that is certain is that the la Chesnayes are based in an area within receiving distance of the radio transmission and that their home is close enough to Geneviève's apartment to permit Robert to casually visit her at ten or eleven o'clock in the morning (the two times that he proposes). Interestingly, Christine was originally included in the scene at le Bourget airport and Renoir hesitated as to who should turn off the radio following Jurieux's outburst – Lisette or Christine – before finally settling on the latter.[109]

Christine's possible affair with Jurieux and the latter's vociferous public defamation of Christine provoke scandal within the la Chesnayes' circle and remind the la Chesnayes of the volatility of their domestic space and projected social image. Observing that 'there is imagined to be the security of a (false [. . .]) stability and an apparently reassuring boundedness' in places representing home, Massey is careful to note that the identity of a place derives not only from an internalised history but also 'precisely from the specificity of its interactions with "the outside"'.[110] In Paris, Robert and Christine mobilise a conception of space modelled on physical (and, with it, social) inclusion and exclusion. Therein lies the temptation of the deceptive emancipation permitted by the rural landscapes and the cultural heritage embedded in La Colinière. As the remainder of this analysis demonstrates, the space-time encapsulated by La Colinière is inextricably connected with the urban space of Paris, and the château's distance from mainstream society only further underscores the futility of any endeavour to bolster their receding social space.

The country and the city: retreat to La Colinière

In accordance with the demands of the la Chesnayes, much of La Colinière is decorated in the same taste as Christine and Robert's Paris residence. Set designer Eugène Lourié recollected that he 'tried to keep a certain similarity between the decoration of the Paris house and the castle'.[111] Indeed, the château's interiors are adorned by large paintings, statuettes, mirrors, and ornately crafted bed-posts that also feature in the la Chesnayes' home. Deleuze's description of La Colinière as a setting that embodies the past is worth analysing in relation to the la Chesnayes' attempt to efface the intrusion of the ongoing present and reassert their dominance, and to the problematic conceptions of national identity explored by the film. The theatricality that holds the past in tension with the ongoing present is expressed through two key aspects of the manor's physical layout, each of which caters to Christine and Robert's efforts to cement their status among the *haute bourgeoisie*. The first is the château's expansive hunting grounds, which complement its embodied history of past hunts. The second is the proscenium arch, which provides a centrepiece of the celebrations and a podium from which to mock the contemporary social issues impinging on the la Chesnayes' (im)mobility in Paris.

The château sports ornately designed walls, stuffed pheasants, stag antlers, and a range of firearms, all of which evoke a sense of dominance over the landscape that fuels Robert's own adherence to a policy of no rabbits and no fences on his property. Whereas the la Chesnayes' apartment operates through attempted physical (and, with this, social) insulation, La Colinière offers a physically liberating and deceptively isolated space. Thus, the shooting party serves the double function of situating the la Chesnayes within the French cultural heritage visible in material form on the previously described walls of La Colinière and bolstering their impression of their social mastery over the physical space of La Colinière. It is now what O'Shaughnessy describes as a site of 'ritualised destruction', in which the la Chesnayes, along with their peers, can continue to convince themselves of their domination over the space occupied by La Colinière.[112]

Examining Robert's trajectory through Massey, it becomes abundantly clear that the assets indicate Robert's need for a physically, socially, and temporally insulated locus:

> When black-robed patriarchs organize ceremonies to celebrate a true national identity they are laying claim to the freezing of that identity at a particular moment and in a particular form – a moment and a form where they had a power which they can thereby justify themselves in retaking.[113]

For Massey, the use of material objects to resort to 'some particular moment/location in time-space when the definition of the area and the social relations dominant within it were to the advantage of that particular claimant group' implies that 'the identity of any place, including that place called home, is in one sense for ever open to contestation' and, insofar as the corpus is concerned, no less transient than the original intentions that underwrote the organisation of the Exposition Universelle.[114]

Like the two puppets who try to introduce Legrand's story in *La Chienne* before being beaten into submission by Guignol, Robert and Christine are convinced that they can reduce the contemporary historical narrative with which they are inextricably connected to a controlled mould that corresponds with their own vision. The camera does not merely frame La Colinière; it juxtaposes La Colinière with the Paris metropole circa 1939, reminding us that the characters live in 'a space of loose ends and missing links' theorised by Massey, which, no matter how apparently secure, 'is neither a container for always-already constituted identities nor a completed closure of holism'.[115]

Robert's agenda is threatened by the very revue that he organises for his guests. Rather than function as a cohesive device for the la Chesnayes and their peers, the theatre reminds Christine of her home country's current political gridlock and serves to propagate further stereotypes pertaining to Robert's identity. The Tyrolean costumes worn by the singers of the first song performed, 'En rev'nant de la revue', are not only a reminder to the contemporary audience that Hitler has taken control of Austria (as observed by O'Shaughnessy[116]), but are also a reminder to Christine of her problematic identity as a dual citizen of France and Austria, and of her inability to return to her family home despite her high social ranking. Robert's social standing is also challenged. As the revue continues, the guests perform 'Nous avons levé le pied', a darkly humorous satire of Jewish exiles. Whilst the performers and spectators indulge in the Jewish stereotypes propagated during this rendition, Robert conceals himself behind the stage-curtain and waits for the song to end, unable to join in the buoyant anti-Semitic spectacle (Figure 1.4). Each of these moments signals the limits of the la Chesnayes' social agency, contesting core aims of their retreat to La Colinière and reminding the spectator of the dynamic space-time that the guests endeavour to expel beyond the ornately decorated walls of the château.

Because Robert cannot similarly mock his Jewish extraction without disparaging his own roots, he must compensate by flaunting his newest acquisition, the Limonaire. Viewing Robert's expressions upon the successful unveiling of the Limonaire twenty-seven years after the film's release, Renoir declared: 'What a shot! I think that it's the best shot that I ever filmed in my life. Ah! It's fantastic. The mix of humility and pride, of success and doubt . . .'[117] This pride is contingent on La Colinière and its many assets, a fact which becomes evident when Geneviève demands that he elope with her without considering the

Figure 1.4 Guests perform 'Nous avons levé le pied' whilst Robert (behind curtain) looks on

import of the château and its assets towards his identity. In response, Robert insists upon staying:

> GENEVIÈVE: Let's leave together Robert!
> ROBERT: Where to? I am at home here. I cannot just abandon it!
> GENEVIÈVE: Oh you're so irritating with your sense of property! As if a house were that important!
> ROBERT: I have to talk to Christine first.[118]

Robert's unspoken response is, of course, that his residence is just that important to him: the house's cultural identity provides Robert with his last physical and social bulwark against the disintegration of his stratum, the public denigration of his ethnicity, and the democratisation of French culture in the capital. At a time when contemporary socio-political furore has put the la Chesnayes' potential strategies (to borrow de Certeau's term) out of the question, La Colinière and the la Chesnayes' insulated Parisian residence provide a social space to allow Christine and Robert to circumvent the public sphere. Following Schumacher's rampage, Corneille remarks that, although no guests were injured, 'the birds in the armoury suffered a little and I found a bullet in a door. Of course, the glassware is another story.'[119] Corneille's humorous observation is only too fitting: human life, as Jurieux's death shall prove, carries little currency in this society unless it contributes to the endurance of the *haute bourgeoisie*. By extension, it becomes clear that when Deleuze notes that it is Schumacher 'who breaks the circuit, who shatters the cracked crystal and whose gunshots make the contents disperse', he is observing that physical damage to La Colinière undermines the la Chesnayes' social status and, as a result, the ongoing presence of the embodied past.[120]

Although *La Règle du jeu*, in Deleuze's view, is exemplary of many of the core formal and thematic characteristics that he associates with Renoir's *mise en scène* of temporality, it is worth noting that the film envisions the effects of time from a far more negative perspective than either of the previous films analysed, primarily as a result of the narrative's portrayal of a socially and morally bankrupt France. In fact, the images of a decadent stratum verging on extinction coincide more closely with the four primary qualities that Deleuze associates with Visconti's depiction of time. As in the case of the aristocratic societies featuring in Visconti's *La caduta degli dei* (1969) and *Ludwig* (1973), Renoir's *haute bourgeoisie* is constructing a 'synthetic crystal' whose contents – including its members and opulent status symbols – are 'inseparable from a process of decomposition which eats away at them from within'.[121]

The implications of the noticeably fatalistic *élan vers l'avenir* in *La Règle du jeu* are emphasised by the limited mobility of Renoir's characters within Paris and its outskirts. La Colinière and the la Chesnayes' Paris residence, although topographically distant from one another, constitute mutually implicated nodes on a dynamic and extensive network that also includes the heart of the French capital. Although these two domestic settings provide the *haute bourgeoisie* with a provisional escape from the traumatic realities of urban Paris, the elusiveness of any *point de fuite* within either of them only underscores the importance and the futility of the *haute bourgeoisie*'s agenda. The stratum's rejection of what Massey calls the 'shared historical process that differentiates the world as it connects it' does nothing to generate new possibilities within the world they inhabit, for they rely not on the creation of new possibilities, but on the evocation of a past that has long since dissolved and which, like any tactical action, 'cannot [. . .] take charge of a global project or overcome the adversary in a distinct, visible and delineable space'.[122] As Deleuze remarks on a broader level, 'the repetition of the past is materially possible, but spiritually impossible, in the name of Time'.[123]

The Parisian apartments and La Colinière are only deceptively isolated from the imminent war which will hasten the decay of this privileged stratum, as in the case of Visconti's work, in which 'History is rumbling at the door'.[124] As Renoir himself recalls in his autobiography, *Ma vie et mes films*, 'It is a war film, yet not one reference is made to the war.'[125] Just as history fatally precludes salvation within Visconti's work,[126] the la Chesnayes and their peers are content to pretend that no solution to their impending demise is even necessary, and no *point de fuite* is established: whereas the nomadic tramp in *Boudu sauvé des eaux* is open to what Massey understands as space's 'dynamic simultaneity, constantly disconnected by new arrivals, constantly waiting to be determined', the future is a harbinger of doom for the *haute bourgeoisie* and its anachronistic space.[127]

By the end of the film, Jurieux has been accidentally assassinated by Schumacher, and Robert reminds his peers that they will all be returning home the following day. One may wonder how Robert and Christine in particular will contend with the cauldron of competing ideologies seething in Paris. What is clear is that Jurieux's murder restores Robert's faith in himself. Renoir himself provided some valuable comments on the social import of this single death:

> The people only live through sacrifices so one of them must be killed to appease the gods. Here, this society will live for another few months, until the war and even later, and this society will continue to exist because Jurieux was killed. Jurieux is the person who was sacrificed on the gods' altar so that this kind of life might continue.[128]

Robert's unparalleled ability to mediate perceptions of the murder within his society's pervasive web of expectancies and, in doing so, to create 'a new definition of the word "accident"' further serves to bolster his confidence in his dextrous control over domestic space in Paris.[129] In particular, it articulates his talent for conditioning the social impact of legally impermissible events on his peers, securing him in his ability to exploit the etiquette of his class and preserve its superficial integrity amidst public scorn for his identity. Because his peers accept this explanation without dispute (albeit with some scepticism in the case of Saint-Aubin) and, in the case of the general, even accept it as a sign of Robert's affiliation with the *haute bourgeoisie* ('That la Chesnaye has plenty of class', remarks the general, 'and that's becoming a rare thing these days, my dear Saint-Aubin. Believe me, that's becoming a rare thing'[130]), Robert's speech is not only one of apparent grief and remorse, but also one of relief. The la Chesnayes can return to their exclusionary domestic space in Paris, delusively confident in their ability to fix their status despite the turbulent political crosswinds that buffet the city.

Conclusion: Renoir's *ville-concept*

Sue Harris rightly states that Renoir's Paris embodies an 'ambiguous and fluctuating significance' and constitutes 'a rich site of meaning, even when the city itself seems incidental to the narrative action'.[131] By reading Deleuze's philosophical reflection on Renoir's work through Massey, it becomes clear that three aspects – social space, the ideological perspective informing each narrative, and Renoir's shooting style – interact expressively to expose open space-time to the spectator. Furthermore, these elements enter into dialectic with the spatio-temporal tension invoked by the juxtaposition of the *surcroît de théâtralité* and urban space.

It is important to emphasise the importance of ideologically informed perspective, particularly an awareness of tensions among social classes, to our interpretation of Renoir's techniques. Without considering class tensions, Renoir's use of montage in *Boudu* and wide shots in *La Chienne* would elude this analysis. Coinciding with the emergence of what O'Shaughnessy terms 'chronological depth' in Renoir's work of the late 1930s, *La Règle du jeu* most notably demands a knowledge of both class relations and contemporary French history in order to fully appreciate how its radically different *élan vers l'avenir* – an unflinchingly negative projection of the future – compares with *La Chienne* and *Boudu*.

Although it would be an exaggeration to claim that each individual shot within each of the films discussed invokes open space-time, it is clear that certain shots frame the *ligne de fuite*, during which the past is discarded (the 'mis-meeting' in *La Chienne*), or foreground the lingering presence of the past amidst social upheaval (the shot of the Place du Trocadéro beyond the apartment window in *La Règle du jeu*). Furthermore, it is apparent that these images condition the spectator's perception of other deceptively simple shots (the wide shots during Legrand's first journey to Lulu's residence) and techniques rarely associated with Renoir (such as montage, as employed in *Boudu*) to create an image of open space-time through the cumulative effect of narrative sequences.

By distinguishing between the stultifying *surcroît de théâtralité* and fluctuating urban dynamics, this study does not seek to dismiss conceptualisations of the city as *teatro mundi*: James Donald rightly observes that 'the city provides an imagery for the way we represent ourselves as actors in the theatre of the world, and for what it feels like to present ourselves in that way'.[132] Similarly, both Sennett and Donald encourage the wearing of 'masks' as a method of concealing emotional states in the public sphere.[133] However, Deleuze's reduction of Renoir's urban spaces to theatres, much like these metaphorical theorisations read out of context, prevents us from engaging with the production of urban space. In Renoir's films, the roles alternately donned and discarded emerge from spatial processes that both contribute to and emerge from the city's own unending process of self re-creation.

The lack of any rigid coordinates in space is emphasised by the subjectivisation of the relationship between characters and landmarks in each narrative. Renoir's disorientating reconfiguration of Paris suggests that as social strata disintegrate, landmarks corresponding with our traditional, preconceived image of the city no longer offer reliable guidance. In each of these films, Renoir weaves a variety of elements together to portray urban spaces that are decidedly tentative and incomplete. Furthermore, the possibility for change in all three of the films discussed is presented as a characteristic of everyday life in the city's physical structure and a diverse social tissue. *La Chienne* and *Boudu*, as Harris notes, portray Paris as 'a place in which ordinary people work, live, interact, and a place in which social difference and class tensions break through to the surface'.[134] Similarly, *La Règle du jeu* recounts but one of many excursions to a familiar retreat. The process of self-actualisation is an integral, ongoing process in the urban hermeneutic experience in Renoir's Paris, in which deceptively minor incidents constitute crucial social fulcrums within the context of the fictional characters' lives. Inherently predisposed to temporal flux, Renoir's urban streets, landmarks, dwellers, and interiors can never constitute more than a Certelian 'city-concept' ('ville-concept'), an indeterminate, dangerously splintered site (and sight) within which Renoir's characters are unable to subjugate the inherent openness of space-time, and where the present consequently remains open to the ineffaceable uncertainties of the future.

CHAPTER 2

From Desert to Dreamscape: Viewing Renoir's Rural Landscapes as Spatial Arenas

> Renoir's camera is another kind of explorer, one who hasn't gone ahead of us into the territory and can't presume to know exactly what to show us.[1]
>
> – Gilberto Perez, *The Material Ghost*

> This land, these fields play a role.[2]
>
> – Jean Renoir on *The Southerner* (1945)

Introduction: Opening the Natural Landscape to Space-time

As noted in the introduction to Chapter 1, this book does not aim to dismiss the similar constitution of urban and rural space by assigning separate chapters to each. Since Raymond Williams's disintegration of the preconceived dichotomy between the country as 'a natural way of life' and the city as 'an achieved centre', E. Melanie DuPuis, Brian Short, and David Bell have also related illusory images of the rural idyll to a broad range of social factors including industrialisation, urbanisation, and bourgeois values.[3]

Despite the similar theoretical and social grounding of rural and urban space, each merits separate analysis because of Renoir's repeated appropriation of each over the course of his career, representing a key exception to Susan Hayward's observation that 'French films have focused on the city (in particular Paris) with landscape appearing as a mere dot on the French cinematic horizon.'[4] Natural landscapes provided Renoir with some of his core settings in the silent period, across the 1930s and also during his exile in Hollywood: *La Fille de l'eau* (1925) was filmed in Marlotte, his mother's homeplace; *Le Bled* (1929) was filmed in the Algerian desert; *Toni* (1935) is based on a farm in Martigues; *Partie de campagne* (1936) was filmed almost entirely outdoors at Champs-sur-Marne; *La Règle du jeu* (1939) was largely shot at la Sologne; *The Southerner* (1945) unfolds on a Texan plantation; *The River* (1951) was shot on location in India; and *Le Déjeuner sur l'herbe* (1959) was mostly filmed at Les Collettes, where Pierre-Auguste spent his final years. Even works that would be difficult to class as rural 'landscape' films reveal Renoir's penchant for natural settings: *Boudu sauvé des eaux* (1932) was partly filmed in the Bois de Boulogne and the outskirts of Paris; *Swamp Water* (1941) is set in Georgia's swamps; and much of the drama in *Woman on the Beach* (1947) is set on an unspecified American beach.

Gilberto Perez writes that the natural landscape, as filmed across a variety of genres,

> is not engaged as an actual place, a stretch of the world we inhabit. Whether relegated to a background, or brought forward as a spectacle, it is made to play a part in a fiction and made subservient to that fiction.[5]

Interestingly, Perez singles out Renoir's *Partie de campagne* as an exception that 'does not assign [the landscape] a role and a meaning defined by the fiction. Rather it has the fiction define itself and its characters against the character of a landscape that was there first.'[6] With Perez's comments and Renoir's crystalline city in mind, the present chapter aims to determine the import of the rural landscape towards Renoir's *mise en scène* of the *ouverture d'avenir* in *Le Bled*, *The Southerner*, and *The River*. Two obstacles that did not feature in Chapter 1 are immediately apparent: firstly, whereas Paris incorporates a dense myriad of social trajectories conditioned by urban architecture, the rural landscape in these films often appears sparsely populated and, therefore, may initially seem socially inert; secondly, the motif of the theatre, which formed a crucial counterpoint to urban dynamics in Chapter 1, is surprisingly unimportant (and often entirely insignificant) to *The Southerner* and *The River*.

Interestingly, however, three aspects of Deleuze's writing suggest an affinity between Renoir's natural landscapes and the passage of time. Firstly, the majority of the films that feature in Deleuze's discussion of the inevitable emergence of a new present from the crystal are set in the countryside: *Partie de campagne*, *The River*, and *Le Déjeuner sur l'herbe* all feature within a single extended paragraph, and resurface later within Deleuze's discussion of Renoir's crystal. Furthermore, *Boudu sauvé des eaux* also features within the aforementioned paragraph, but Deleuze tellingly focuses on the tramp's relationship with the Seine rather than on the film's urban setting. Secondly, Deleuze describes the affective force of Renoir's landscapes by drawing on Guy de Maupassant's and D. H. Lawrence's literary representations of the rural: for Deleuze, *The River* is 'strangely close to Lawrence' and Renoir's use of windows in *Partie de campagne* is 'close to Maupassant', the author of the source novella.[7] Thirdly, the river, a frequent motif of Renoir's rural landscapes, is the only plastic aspect of Renoir's *mise en scène* that Deleuze distinguishes from Renoir's settings, which are otherwise reduced by Deleuze to theatres. In particular, Deleuze remarks that rivers provide Boudu and Harriet (protagonist of *The River*) with an escape from the cracked crystal, implying that water represents a smooth space that allows characters to exit beyond the *point de fuite*.

Deleuze's own application of these observations is impeded by his conflation of the literal and the metaphysical, and his general reliance on formal aspects of *mise en scène* elides any in-depth discussion of the import of the natural setting towards Renoir's portrayal of temporality. Even Deleuze's commentary on Renoir's rivers is developed into a metaphor rather than a tool for systematic analysis: after discussing the rivers that feature in *Boudu* and *The River*, Deleuze likens Nini's climactic dance at the end of *French Cancan* (1954) to 'a means through which theatre opens into life, pours out into life, carrying Nini along in a turbulent current'.[8] The examples cited above nonetheless point to specific aspects of Renoir's *mise en scène* that demand consideration within our examination of open space-time. In particular, Deleuze implies that new futures may emerge within rural landscapes in the form of new social relations, possibly at the behest of the elements. However, before engaging with Renoir's films, it is important to establish some basic theoretical and textual groundwork regarding physical and social elements of the cinematographic landscape.

Graeme Harper and Jonathan Rayner's introduction to *Cinema and Landscape* foregrounds the social and physical aspects of space as well as the role of the camera as an 'enabling device' that frames a richly textured site which is replete with relations ready to be enacted by the spectator's mind.[9] This three-fold model incorporating the camera, the landscape, and the spectator is valuable in two key respects. Firstly, it emphasises the social and physical aspects of any landscape, be it urban or rural, indirectly underscoring Howard Newby's assertion that the characteristics of rural space are shared by urban space, and lending credence to Raymond William's assertion that 'country' and 'city' constitute words that 'seem to stand in for the experience of human communities' rather than representing fundamentally different spaces.[10] The respective observations of Williams, Newby, and Harper and Rayner serve as a crucial reminder that rural space is, potentially, no less striated than urban space, and that alterations to the physical landscape recast what Massey calls 'relations-between, relations which are necessarily embedded in material practices which have to be carried out'.[11] Thus, the landscape is open to factors that allow the filmmaker to frame it as a major agent in the ongoing production of space-time, rather than merely as a backdrop for the framing of human interrelations. Discussing the history of capitalist development, David Harvey astutely reminds us that the physical landscape embodies dynamic properties: 'geographical differentiations [. . .] frequently appear to be what they are not: mere historical residuals rather than actively reconstituted features within the capitalist mode of production'.[12] How Renoir frames the impact of the physical rural landscape on the dynamisation of social relations is a core concern of this chapter.

Secondly, drawing on Bergson's likening of the body and its surroundings to an image constantly absorbed by an independent memory within the general process of becoming, Harper and Rayner write that 'cinematic landscapes, whilst obviously part of a continuum, and equally composed of frames, can also be considered conduits to memories, and a form of time, that transcends the cinema itself'.[13] Each of these aspects of the natural landscape – the striated landscape and the recollected dreamscape – are of varying importance to the films discussed within this chapter. Much like Harper and Rayner's analysis, the diversity of the three films discussed within this chapter points to the lack of any precise unifying point of departure for the analysis of rural space-time, and the futility of defining a specialised set of terms on which to exclusively analyse rural settings. In fact, the landscapes discussed in this chapter pose an additional challenge, for all three were filmed in entirely different countries and ideological contexts: *Le Bled*, Renoir's final silent film, was financed by the French and Algerian governments, and was filmed on location in Algeria; *The Southerner* was filmed in Hollywood with the backing of independent producer David Loew as the Second World War drew to a close; *The River*, financed once again by an independent producer, narrates a young girl's experience of growing up as part of a privileged colonial family in British India, and was released four years after the 1947 Partition. Furthermore, whereas *Le Bled* and *The Southerner* constitute incisive portraits of fluctuating spatial politics and more generally serve as thoughtful responses to the contemporary social, political, and economic circumstances in which they were produced, *The River* relegates spatial politics in favour of portraying space itself as a realm of memory. Because of the radically different national settings and discursive positions of each of the three films discussed, the only immediately apparent similarity between them is, incidentally, the occasional staging of the rural milieu in depth, so it is unsurprising that Deleuze focuses primarily on this aspect of Renoir's works (except in his discussion of *The Golden Coach*[14]). Nonetheless, by integrating Massey's theorisation of space-time into Deleuze's examination of Renoir's narrative style, the remainder of this chapter proposes a reading of all three of these diverse landscapes 'in terms of a dimension of the future'.[15]

Le Bled (1929)

'This world divided in two': colonialism and class in l'Algérie française

By 1929, France's Exposition Coloniale Internationale (1931) was on the horizon, and the nation was planning centennial celebrations of the 1830 'pacification' of Algeria, which had been declared an integral part of France in 1848. The anniversary provided the French with the opportunity to commemorate what *Les Éditions du Centenaire de l'Algérie* described as 'the memory of soldiers who, 100 years ago, liberated Algeria of its barbaresque yoke, then guided it to its rightful destiny by introducing "French peace"'.[16] One of the many cultural contributions to the celebrations was *Le Bled*, Renoir's final silent film. The French and Algerian governments provided funding for the film, which was intended to display the country's exotic attractions and lure tourists to the centennial celebrations of the French conquest.[17] The plot of *Le Bled* (a colloquial military term defined by Philip Dine as 'the bush'[18]) focuses on Pierre Hoffer's (Enrique Rivero) attempt to extract exorbitant amounts of his uncle's (Christian Hoffer, played by Alexandre Arquillère) money to pay off personal debts and, in parallel, Claudie Duvernet's (Jackie Monnier) arrival in Algeria for the hearing of her late uncle's will. Pierre and Claudie's trajectories converge in Sidi Ferruch, where they fall in love. When Claudie's ill-wishing cousins, Manuel (Manuel Raaby) and Diane (Diana Hart), attempt to steal Claudie's inheritance, Pierre saves her from Manuel's clutches and the film ends with the couple's engagement party in Sidi Ferruch. Frantz Fanon lambasted the French colonial powers represented by Claudie and Pierre, most notably in *Les Damnés de la terre*, in which he discussed the French occupation of Algeria as 'not simply domination but the decision, literally, to occupy nothing but a territory'.[19] By no surprise, the film's glorification of *l'Algérie française* has largely precluded *Le Bled* from serious analysis, largely because Renoir's involvement in pro-colonial projects sits uncomfortably with his engagement with the French Left (discussed in detail in Chapter 3).[20] However, Renoir himself was contemptuous towards the French colonial powers: his son, Alain, recalled that Renoir 'was sickened by the way in which the French regarded and treated the Algerians'.[21]

The tensions between Renoir's own vision and that of the French colonising powers are expressed through the Algerian landscape, which has guaranteed France wealth and international prestige. The prologue not only 'indulges documentary interest, with glimpses of picturesque native customs and settlers' daily routines', as Raymond Durgnat observes, but also emphasises the social stratification of the landscape: an intertitle states that Algeria is 'a land of a prodigious industrial and commercial activity', and subsequent documentary-like images of miners and a train emphasise the economic efficiency of the country under French rule.[22] Furthermore, it is difficult to overlook the ideological implications of the railway, whose taming of 'the bush, the mosquitos, the indigenous populations, and diseases' is equated by Fanon with 'the ignorance of the political and economic existence of the indigenous population'.[23]

Reflecting the film's purported ideological aims, Arab Algerians occupy a consistently minor role in the film's narrative thrust. Almost invariably assimilated into shots as extras, they confirm the links established by the camera between the landscape and the colonial class structures that striate it. As the Duvernets drive along to their late uncle's land, Algerian men congregate on nearby hills (Figure 2.1), recalling the composition of Pierre-Auguste's *La Mosquée* (1881, also known as *La Fête arabe*).[24] On other occasions, as when Algerian children rush to clean Pierre's shoes and when older Algerian men carry Pierre's suitcases as he walks with Christian, the Algerians and their country are clearly at the disposal of the dominant white French colonisers. This depersonalisation of the

Figure 2.1 The Duvernets' view of Sidi Ferruch recalls Pierre-Auguste Renoir's *La Mosquée* (1881)

Algerian populace exemplifies Fanon's assertion that, under the French, the Algerians merely formed 'the landscape, the *natural* backdrop for the French presence'.[25] Even Pierre's former military comrade, Zoubir (Aîssa Berardi) and the latter's large sheep farm and luxurious villa located in the south of Sidi Ferruch are merely exploited by Pierre to appease his own interest in the Algerian lifestyle and as part of his plan to meet Claudie at the hunt. The narrative thus emphasises Fanon's vision of 'this world divided in two, [. . .] inhabited by different species'.[26]

Crucial to the portrayal of the possibility for change on the hierarchised natural landscape is the introduction of the newest generation of French immigrants to the molar line engendered by the French colonial powers. Pierre is a womanising Parisian who has squandered his inheritance and is primarily determined to extract money from his uncle in order to settle his own outstanding debts. Claudie has travelled to Algeria to hear her late uncle's will, from which she inherits her uncle's villa and a vast agricultural plot in Algeria. Claudie's cousins, Diane and Manuel, are debt-laden and bitter following the revelation their uncle has cleared their current debts but has bequeathed them no other assets. Although Manuel and Diane's attempted kidnapping of Claudie may encourage us to view Claudie and Pierre as the 'good' colonisers, the privileged lifestyle sported by all four locates them collectively within a stratum which, although derived from the older generation of colonisers, embodies a new set of superficial values and a lazy sense of entitlement, which open the future of the French colonial legacy to question. Claudie is only going to Algeria, as Christian suspects, to obtain her inheritance which she probably intends to sell to the highest bidder, as she initially demonstrates no intention of staying there. Furthermore, Claudie's distinctly bourgeois stuffed mink scarf, worn as she arrives at the port, indicates her taste for dead animals long before the climactic hunt. Even her penniless cousins, dismayed following the brutal disclosure of the will, are dressed lavishly whilst they consume cocktail after cocktail in dismay.

Pierre's similarly superficial preoccupations are also exemplified through his clothes. Upon arriving at his uncle's farmland, Pierre takes no fewer than three suitcases and a large valise off the coach that drops him there. Further satirising Pierre's materialism, the departing coach returns momentarily to drop off yet another suitcase belonging to him. Another key incident in this regard occurs at his uncle's farmhouse when Pierre emerges in front of his uncle and the latter's peers wearing a tuxedo. Although suitable on such occasions in his homeland, his attire is highly unsuitable in his new surroundings and provides what Richard Abel terms a 'comedy of costumes'.[27] Décor complements this incident, serving as a commentary on both Pierre's perception of himself and his uncle's perception of him: when Pierre exits his bedroom, the flat blank background lends him the importance which a tuxedo would acquire in metropolitan society and conveys his inflated opinion of his own appearance. When he enters the dining area, however, Pierre's dark tuxedo is pitted against the pale white walls of the dining area on a raised platform that elevates him above the farmers as though he were standing on a proscenium arch, reducing Pierre to a spectacle before the camera cuts to a travelling shot of the farmers' shocked expressions. After Christian laughs mockingly, the camera cuts to a view of the platform and tilts upwards to reveal Pierre's own embarrassed and confused expression as he belatedly realises that this symbol of bourgeois etiquette is not universally appreciated for its superficial merits.

This satire continues during a tour of Christian's land. Jokingly warned not to don a tuxedo by Christian, Pierre's alternative is little better: Pierre breathes on his shoes in an attempt to shine them and, as he sits down to tie them, we see to his right, in the background of the image, a vast array of ties, one of which he selects before descending the stairs to his uncle outside. This excessive range of ties (a possible reason for Pierre's numerous cumbersome suitcases) and his uncle's reaction to Pierre's fedora, double-breasted jacket, and knickerbockers ('Well then! Today, he is dressed as a zouave'[28]) once more indicate Pierre's preoccupation with appearances that acquire new comedic resonance within the Algerian landscape, and are valued only by his fellow compatriots who are no longer with him. Although these sequences do not directly invoke open space-time, this prior knowledge of the preoccupations of the newest generation of French metropolitan immigrants is central to Renoir's dynamisation of the landscape, and the framing of the *point de fuite* later in the narrative.

Sidi Ferruch revisited: staging the point de fuite *in depth*

Central to the narrative's *mise en scène* of open space-time is the threat that Pierre's ambitions pose to the landscape's embodied history of colonial intervention. The narrative further emphasises the history of colonialist intervention and international relations personified by the Algerian farmer. As Christian tours his land with Pierre, he correctly assumes that Pierre has no idea what 100,000 francs represent to workers who endure labour and hardship, and proceeds to inform his nephew that 'One hundred years ago, our forefathers found nothing but marshland here.'[29] The subsequent conversation leaves no doubt that the deeply staged background represents both Christian's and France's legacy as well as Pierre's responsibility towards it: 'And before transforming them into fertile fields, thousands of colonisers died with their boots on . . . whilst our grandparents were there, they should have made better roads. We have been waiting for you for just that, my lad.'[30]

The landscape in the background enters into dialectic with the individual figures of Christian and Pierre Hoffer to signal the instability of the French colonial regime. The tension between molar lines and molecular flux (to employ Deleuze and Guattari's distinction), which are respectively embodied by Christian and Pierre, dynamises the landscape that dominates the background. Their differing political perspectives are underscored by elements of gesture and costume design: the stocky uncle leaves his jacket unfastened, does not wear a tie, and wears a common rural-style cap. He also walks in a far less refined manner than his nephew, hunching his back and tying his arms behind his back. Pierre, on the other hand, walks with a cigarette pursed between his lips and his hands presentably sitting in each pocket of his fastened jacket which even has a handkerchief perched in the upper-left-hand pocket. Through his allegiance to the image of the nation as an essential agricultural and industrial catalyst amidst an otherwise stagnant, infertile landscape, Christian embodies Fanon's conception of 'the coloniser [who] makes history' and whose life represents an epic odyssey: 'He embodies the very beginning: "It is we who have made this land." He guarantees its continuity: "If we leave, all will be lost and this land will return to the Dark Ages."'[31]

Conversely, Pierre expresses no ambition to contribute to France's colonial prowess, and is interested only in the financial aid that his uncle has to offer. Although Pierre subsequently agrees to work on his uncle's land for six months in exchange for 100,000 francs, he only does so after witnessing Claudie riding by on her horse. Furthermore, he accepts Christian's offer with a view to securing the money required to pay his debts rather than to contribute to the colonised landscape which he, like Claudie, may one day inherit from his uncle. Clearly, even the rousing vision of imperialist expansion that informs Christian's determination has failed to convince Pierre of his duty to France's *mission civilisatrice*. The *mise en scène* of the Hoffers' tour of the farmland therefore challenges any easy acceptance of the narrative's prologue, which portrays Algeria as an enduring composite of domestic resources and colonial rule. In fact, no other shot within the narrative so succinctly encapsulates the competing ideologies embodied by the two generations of colonisers amidst the striated space of Algeria, which stubbornly resists permanent colonisation.

The staging of this shot in the field (Figure 2.2) demonstrates Renoir's conceptualisation of the French colonial powers as structures that

Figure 2.2 Christian (left) teaches Pierre (right) about the history and future of Sidi Ferruch

Massey's treatise on space reduces to '(temporary, provisional) stabilisations', suggesting that the land's future is contested by Pierre who, like Claudie and her cousins, was born into the economic privilege earned by farmers such as Christian.[32] The presence of anonymous labourers working the fields in the background of the image almost one century after the conquest further emphasises the undeniable fact that, without future leagues of immigrants to maintain French power abroad, France risks losing the legacy evoked by Christian's hallucinatory vision of the 1830 arrival of Général de Bourmont's troops. The potential disintegration of colonial power over the Algerian landscape suggests that the apparently rigid class structures that stratify the landscape are only provisional constructs. Christian further emphasises the volatility of these social relations when he reveals his decision to bequeath his property to Pierre, and even informs his nephew of this security, somewhat undercutting the patriotic initiative that Christian himself aims to inspire, and challenging the future of the French presence in Sidi Ferruch.

Ironically, a frustrated Bazin marvelled at *Le Bled*, viewing it as 'a perpetual technical aberration: although its *mise en scène* is frequently conceived in depth, Renoir persists in using large-aperture lenses that grant a soft photo without any clarity in backgrounds'.[33] Bazin's analysis risks misleading us towards an erroneous belief that *Le Bled* is dominated by shallow cinematography. On the contrary, many shots within the film testify to an effort to stage multiple events in depth. Deleuze distinguishes between 'a depth *in* the field' (in which the foreground, midground and background of the image remain autonomous in their ensemble) and 'a depth *of* field' (in which elements across different planes interpolate one another), the latter best exemplified as Christian Hoffer grants Pierre a tour of his land.[34]

At this point, it is worth distinguishing between the *point de fuite* that Deleuze locates in Renoir's work, and the *ligne de fuite* theorised by Deleuze and Guattari in *Mille Plateaux*. Although no visible change within Franco-Algerian relations occurs during Pierre and Christian's tour of the farmland (at least, not of the kind that emerges when Legrand happens upon Lulu and Dédé near St Jean de Montmartre in *La Chienne*, and participates in a collective *ligne de fuite*), this staging makes the *point de fuite* evident: more specifically, Renoir's *mise en scène* portrays the introduction of the molecular flux embodied by Pierre to the French colonial system, and the resulting tension which leaves spatial politics open to the truly new. Because the landscape, like any physical space, resists overcoding, the control effected by the French ruling powers relies primarily on future generations of immigrants who, in this case, are portrayed as avaricious consumers placing France's legacy at risk.

We must similarly remind ourselves that Claudie has only come from France to obtain her inheritance and that, prior to her visitation of her newly acquired land, she demonstrates no active intention to permanently reside in the country. Furthermore, when Claudie finally decides to retain her land, it is partly because of the appeal held by the country's very cultural attractions (such as the trained falcons) which the film itself likely displays in an effort to encourage viewers to emigrate to Algeria. This implies that the newest generation of *pied-noirs* has lost touch with the drive to modernise which secured Algeria in 1830 and that they stay there simply because they wish to absorb the exotic delights marketed throughout the film, particularly during the prologue, and which are unavailable in their own country.

'What we have done is shameful . . .': foreshadowing the French retreat from the Empire

If Claudie's right to her uncle's heritage is, in Abdelkader Benali's analysis, 'the primary symbol of the achievement of the process of appropriating Algerian territory', Claudie's inheritance also signals the inherent fallibility of colonial space, particularly at generational junctures where national values undergo change.[35] Claudie's participation in and reaction to the hunting scene later in the narrative interrogate the savagery of France's colonial activities but simultaneously suggest that the newest generation of colonisers are unwilling to renounce the exotic appeal of the colonial activities available in a country that they do not fully appreciate or understand. Claudie enthusiastically seizes a gun from the Algerian chauffeur and determinedly stalks the gazelle behind her dogs, rapidly firing at it until it can be mauled by the party's savage hounds. 'What we have done is shameful', Claudie subsequently laments, 'this hunt is too barbaric'.[36]

Her reaction to the dead gazelle is, rather than an expression of colonial guilt, a crashing encounter with the reality of this slice of upper-class leisure that has provided the mink scarf that she wears upon her arrival at the port in the film's opening scenes: there is a sharp irony in her content retention of her uncle's assets which, as suggested by the cannons accompanying the French army in Christian Hoffer's vision, were violently stolen from the country's indigenous population during the French nation's drive to exploit the country. Thus, Claudie's emotional outburst aligns with the film's strategic critique of the new generation of bourgeois immigrants, who thrive on the products of colonialism, but derive noticeably less pleasure from the colonising process.

Interestingly, Pierre and Claudie's shared indifference towards Christian's rousing call for continuity and mechanised progress is further expressed when they both take shelter from the rain beneath a hut. A close shot of both characters fades to a sunlit land in an image which clearly evokes an Algeria unspoilt by colonisation. None of the symbols of modernity that triumphantly till the land in Christian's vision are to be seen in their antithetical vision of an Algeria that remains untarnished by civilisation and its discontents. Their evocation of the solace to be found in unravaged land marks Christian's vision of de Bourmont's conquest as a rather dystopian triumph of progress and modernity. Pierre and Claudie's dream marks them as manifestly unconcerned for Algeria's future. Yet Claudie's decision to take the reins at her uncle's villa in Sidi Ferruch, where the French invaders established their beachhead in 1830, affirms that she, like Pierre, represents a new generation of landowners who shall now inherit French Algeria's legacy. Claudie's problematic place within Algeria's wider social context is even more firmly established when she finally declares 'I could spend my entire life here', and later, when her lady-in-waiting burns the 'for sale' ('propriété à vendre') sign erected by Manuel and Diane on Claudie's newly inherited property.[37] Each of these moments reminds us of the financial benefits represented by Algeria for Claudie and other women of her generation: Rebecca J. Pulju notes that women's rights were 'severely restricted' in France where, until 1965, husbands acquired automatic legal control of family property.[38]

Conversely, as David Henry Slavin notes, Algeria provided French women with 'an arena where women could act autonomously in economic and social realms'.[39] Thanks to the economic policies of France's colony, Claudie's inheritance provides her with a significant degree of financial independence which would be legally impossible to attain in her home country.

The ideological tension between Christian's patriotic, enterprising imperative on the one hand and, on the other, Pierre's selfish dismissal of his uncle's glorification of colonialism, and Claudie's decision to remain in Algeria because of its cultural and economic attractions, is only partly resolved by the film's ending: at a party celebrating his engagement to Claudie, Pierre is finally wearing farm-suitable attire, which provides a counterpoint to the tuxedo and 'dandy' appearance that he sports earlier during his tour of Christian's land, signifying his assimilation within the Algerian farming community and, by extension, the legacy of the French colonial army. However, the fact remains that Pierre has remained solely in order to marry Claudie who, as noted earlier, wishes to stay because she is confident in what Algeria has to offer her rather than in what she has to offer to Algeria. Benali argues that Claudie's deprecated character will be revalorised by her decision to stay in Algeria.[40] O'Shaughnessy similarly argues that the impending marriage re-establishes 'the broken link between generations of men', and 'announces the broader restoration of order that will come when France turns its back on hedonistic materialism and re-embraces its colonial destiny'.[41] However, these points of view are ultimately irreconcilable with the political tensions articulated through Renoir's landscape: the couple officially fulfils the *mission civilisatrice*, but whether or not they are sufficiently responsible to retain the colonised land remains open to question, and the inability of the film to subsume this reflexive critique beyond the world of *Le Bled* remains problematic. Their projected future together introduces a *point de fuite* to Christian Hoffer's enterprise, further enriching the narrative's framing of the *élan vers l'avenir*.

Given that Algeria would eventually achieve independence in 1962, it is doubly interesting that Renoir offers no convenient resolution to these ideological tensions that infuse the world viewed. Instead, by spatialising colonial rule through molar and molecular elements, Renoir exposes flaws, contradictions, and tensions – in short, the *points de fuite* – within the French colonial process, and the inherent dangers incorporated by endeavours to crystallise space. By visualising the tension between the history of French colonialism and the fluctuating space-time engendered by the socialised landscape, the rural landscapes of *l'Algérie française* become a visual repository of both past histories and potential future narratives of disenfranchised space.

The Southerner (1945)

Socialising the landscape: class and capitalism after the New Deal

As in *Le Bled*, the physical and social composition of the rural landscape permits characters to exploit *points de fuite* in hegemonic class structures and, as a result, produce new power relations. The plot of the film revolves around the everyday efforts of Sam Tucker (Zachary Scott), his wife Nona (Betty Field), and his children to eke out a marginal living on an unspecified farmland in the American South. Encouraged by his dying uncle, Sam Tucker abandons his position as a rural labourer in an effort to raise his family on his own crops, despite the threats posed by the weather, illness, and his malicious neighbours.

Much like *Le Bled*, Renoir's subject-matter is conditioned by the political context underlying the film's production: although *The Southerner* conspicuously avoids engaging directly with the Second World War, which provides the core focus of Renoir's *This Land is Mine* (1943) and *Salute to France* (1944, co-directed with Garson Kanin and also released in a French-language version), the film intimately engages with the socio-economic impact of the New Deal on American sharecroppers. Anthony J. Badger notes that the New Deal's impact on the American agrarian sector was inconsistent at best: prosperous farmers capable of contending with others on the free market 'were given permanent protection by the government at the expense of the national interest', whereas sharecroppers, in Badger's analysis, remained 'economically and politically powerless', even though their income already 'scarcely attained bare subsistence levels'.[42] Thus, although the New Deal enabled surplus farm labour 'to stay on the land at a time when there was nowhere else to go', its ambitions to eliminate rural poverty were 'largely still-born'.[43] Unsurprisingly, the unprecedented technological advances achieved during the four decades that followed the ratification of the New Deal were accompanied by 'the virtual disappearance of the family farm' and a 'massive flight' from the rural landscape,[44] the latter continuing through the 1940s, when *The Southerner* was in production.[45]

The film's opening shots specify both the rural Texan setting and capitalist economic system which provide twin axes of the film's *mise en scène*. The establishing shot of the plantation frames a cotton plant, and tilts upwards to reveal the labourers working in the fields. After a tracking shot of the plantation, the camera cuts to a shot of Sam's uncle, Pete (Paul Burns), as he collapses in the heat of the sun. Numerous workers are visible in the distant background within this shot, and their ongoing activity implies that Pete's death represents a momentary aberration within the capitalist mode of production that striates the landscape. Before Pete dies, he beseeches Sam to grow his own crops. We learn after his funeral that the workers are operating on minimal wages, and that Pete himself has died a poor man, leaving nothing to even pay for his tombstone.

Although Sam's current *rôle mort* condemns him to the same impoverished circumstances as his uncle Pete, the American rural landscape is presented as a fluid space that permits a high degree of social mobility for those who desire to risk their minimal welfare. This potential for socio-economic change is most clearly evoked when Sam visits the office owned by his boss, Ruston (Paul Harvey), following Pete's funeral. The grounds beyond Ruston's office are staged in depth, clearly establishing both Ruston's economic power and the potential for others such as Sam to attain Ruston's degree of success. Beyond the window located behind the two men, we see a water tower bearing Ruston's name in large letters and a group of men seated beneath it (presumably Ruston's employees), emphasising Ruston's ownership of the complex (Figure 2.3). Despite Ruston's economic power and social standing, his casual appearance (compared with the tuxedos worn by Manuel and Pierre in *Le Bled*) and the lack of vain status symbols in his office (which clutter upper-class quarters in Renoir's Front populaire output) suggest that he is a self-made man who has acquired his fortune through his own labour and continued interest in other enterprising

Figure 2.3 Sam (left) discusses his goals with Ruston (right)

ventures rather than through the timely inheritance of his forefathers' legacy. The similarity between Sam's and Ruston's respective appearances suggests an accord that does not exist between the two generations of *Le Bled*, and that Sam may repeat Ruston's success through his engagement with the land that Ruston agrees to allow Sam to rent during this scene.

The staging of Ruston and Sam in front of Ruston's grounds visually recalls the *mise en scène* of Christian and Pierre Hoffer on the Algerian landscape, lending form to the social relationships governing the stratification of Ruston's land. Complementing the ideologically informed staging of fluid rural power relations in depth, the framing of Ruston's office subsequently registers Sam's exit through a *point de fuite*: the two men occupy different social rankings within American society, as suggested by the shadow of the window frame, which is projected between them after they walk away from the window and discuss their arrangement in front of the calendar. However, this vertical line is transgressed by their parting handshake which binds their accord and consolidates Sam's lease (Figure 2.4), denoting Sam's transition to a new position in American society and setting a spatio-temporal blueprint for the rural landscapes that appear in the remainder of the narrative.

Staging rural relations in depth

In a televised introduction granted in 1961, Renoir himself suggested that deep space was intended to visually consolidate the relationship between Sam and the farm:

Figure 2.4 Sam secures his lease in Ruston's office

> By and large, I proceeded with largely closed lenses that granted a great depth of space [*profondeur de champ*] so that I would never lose sight of the fields behind my characters. Because, in reality, this land that my hero was absolutely intent on cultivating and on which he counts to become *independent*, this land, these fields play a role. It is also a character in the film, so it is essential that we see it. It is the reason for which I employed these lenses which lend depth and permit one to remain in contact with the background, whilst one is nonetheless interested, I hope, by what the character in the foreground has to say.[46]

Deep space emphasises the import of the rural landscape towards Sam's desired position in society, illustrating the dynamic relationship between the land and American society. Crucially, Sam does not endeavour to create a new future in the same way as Boudu recklessly escapes bourgeois social imprisonment, or the *haute bourgeoisie* strives to retain the embodied past. Nor does he attempt to prevent the creation of *points de fuite* in the same manner as Christian Hoffer of *Le Bled*. Although Sam hopes to someday fix his position within the American market, the deeply composed shots of Sam and Nona taming the overgrown landscape (see Figure 2.5, for example) demonstrate that Sam is currently endeavouring to establish a *ligne de fuite* through the *point de fuite* represented by the American capitalist landscape and the countryside's ever-developing socio-economic relations, reminding us of the inconsistency of the New Deal's economic benefits.

The range of elements incorporated by the shot in Figure 2.5, including Sam and Nona, the fields, and the sky, is essential to our understanding of the spatialising forces operating within the world viewed. As Paul Little

Figure 2.5 Sam (left) and Nona (right) tame the land

astutely writes, 'There needs to be a creative relation to the nonhuman as another participant in this making of places (places are not just human constructs).'[47] For although Sam's ambition and labour have afforded him a new position in society's 'cartography of power', the juxtaposition of Sam and his unsheltered fields holds Sam's current social status and his potential social ascension in tension, emphasising the dual possibilities to which his enterprise is subject: Sam's current social status exists within 'the shifting geographies of power-relations', and his projected *ligne de fuite* is clearly subject not only to Sam's labour, but also to the elemental forces ranged against the landscape.[48]

Deleuze observes that 'the turbulence of the river swollen by the storm and stung by the rain' cracks the crystal in Renoir's *Partie de campagne*, suggesting that shifting weather conditions may actualise a genuinely new set of characteristics within Renoir's worlds.[49] The potentially destructive forces operating beyond the metaphorical *point de fuite* are evoked when a prolonged drought parches Sam's seeds, and when the climactic storm later washes Sam's long-anticipated crop of cotton away. Renoir's *mise en scène* forges 'the relationship between individual or group disposition and landscape', which is recognised by Harper and Rayner as a crucial product of the photography of any landscape in cinema.[50] In doing so, the narrative dynamises Sam's fields, elevating them from a mere backdrop to an active social catalyst and emphasising that Sam's mobility is the product of both social interrelations and the natural landscape that moulds them. Although elemental forces ultimately recrystallise around Sam's *ligne de fuite* by the end of the film, and the molar reasserts dominance over the molecular, Sam's efforts are not presented as futile endeavours: the narrative nonetheless presents a social space in which his ambitions may be realised in more favourable weather conditions.

The rural idyll in dissolution

Interestingly, although Renoir frames the land belonging to Henry Devers (J. Carroll Naish), Sam's decidedly uncooperative neighbour, with characteristic attention to deep space, the portrayal of space-time on the former's land is evocative of a radically bleaker future. Renoir stages Devers's ranch in depth, allowing the spectator to view Devers within his shed in the foreground, and his home and animal pen in the background (Figure 2.6). Unlike the staging of Sam's land, however, a dense barrier of trees circumscribes our view of the space beyond his house and the space beyond his barn, confining our view of Devers's property to his house, barn, and animal pen throughout the film. Reflecting E. Melanie

Figure 2.6 Sam (left) attempts to win Devers's (right) favour

DuPuis's assertion that 'social elites create the rural idyll either through excluding others from rural communities or by making them invisible', this physical insulation testifies to Devers's attempt to establish an impossibly 'closed' space in which his social dominance has permanently overcoded a geometrically defined section of the landscape, and hints at an illusory control that extends even beyond the confines of his property.[51]

This attitude is later articulated on numerous occasions, as when Devers unjustly insists that 'Lead Pencil', a catfish caught by Sam, cannot belong to Sam, owing to Devers's own repeated (and failed) attempts to ensnare the same fish. Devers's ruthlessly autocratic regime contributes to his steadfast refusal to aid Sam in the latter's struggle to farm his land: Devers refuses to grant milk and typhoid-free water for the ailing Jot on two separate occasions. Even when Sam offers his services in exchange, Devers demonstrates little sympathy, insisting that 'I don't need no extra help. [. . .] Too bad about your boy. I know what that is, a sick kid, pretty sorrowful.' Devers remarks that his own crops once fell victim to hail, his animals were struck by blackleg, his wife died, and his son was claimed by pellagra. Devers's identification with Sam, rather than provoking compassion, encourages him to establish a social bulwark against prospective competition. After denying Sam the milk he needs, Devers declares:

> But I told you before, it's wrong for a man to get too big for his britches. Whenya got no money ya work for them what's got it, that there's the rule. Why don't ya go back to Ruston, get your six bits a day, some milk for your child, maybe some doctorin' even?

This distorted outlook is merely a scapegoat for Devers's avaricious externalisation of unwanted intrusions on what he perceives as his own space. Although Devers himself once undertook such a feat, he wishes to prevent others beyond his enclosure from establishing social hegemony through the rural landscape. What Sam sees as 'some old-fashioned idea I had about neighbourliness', Devers disparages as 'always comin' around asking the neighbours for help'.

If a job without prospects is 'the rule', then Devers has also broken it, but stubbornly believes that he can implement class barriers through his steadfast refusal to grant assistance to others, and through his illegitimate domination of others' property within capitalist society. Devers's personal interpretation of the American social ladder is based not on the value which people like Ruston place on experience, but on the price that Devers himself arbitrarily places on success within each phase of sharecropping in light of his own personal woes and distorted perception of social space. As in the case of Sam's property, the deep staging of Devers's property creates an image of open space-time. Crucially, however, the dialectic between on-screen and off-screen elements reveals an *élan vers l'avenir* whose social implications differ radically from those conveyed by the framing of Sam's farm: the trees, juxtaposed with the open space of Sam's farm, draw our attention to what they conceal and suggest that Devers's opposition to change is counterproductive and ultimately futile.

Although the shots of Sam's land are evocative of the cracked crystal, in which a genuinely new future can be implemented beyond predetermining elements, the framing of Devers's land recalls the decidedly isolated *haute bourgeoisie* of *La Règle du jeu*, whose enclosure at La Colinière, as noted in Chapter 1, evokes the crystal in dissolution. Like Visconti's characters who, in Deleuze's analysis, are rendered defenceless against the external histories impinging on their worlds, and are deprived of any *point de fuite*, Devers has blinded himself to the socio-economic implications of new spatialising forces beyond his ranch.[52] Although he is now wealthy and successful, he also appears to lack the initiative to purchase new plots. Following a fight with Sam, Devers declares that 'Before you come, I was alone in this place. [. . .] I was figurin' on buyin' your farm. It was cheaper then.' No price is mentioned and it is quite possible that Devers was simply unwilling to invest any sum. The decline of Devers's world is further suggested by his battered family unit, which parallels the corporeal decay featuring in Visconti's works: unlike the stabilising family unit that contributes to Tucker's determination, Devers is deprived of his wife and son, and fate has spared only Devers's daughter Becky, and nephew

Finlay, leaving the legacy of his farm open to change. As in *Le Bled*, the likely future of Devers's farm is not envisioned in the positive terms suggested by Deleuze's conceptualisation of Renoir's *ouverture d'avenir*: decidedly blind to the production of new agrarian powers in adjacent fields, his physical enclosure only underscores his receding power.

The country and the city

Corresponding with the narrative's broader emphasis on the socialisation of the rural landscape, *mise en scène* and dialogue evoke the circulation of capital between the countryside and urban space. The film refers to two examples of urban space, specifically a city and a town, each of which remains anonymous. Our awareness of the city, which hosts the infamous factory where Sam's cousin works, is granted exclusively through verbal references, whilst the city itself is relegated to off-screen space. Although Sam denounces the city's factories as unnatural environments, his friend, Tim, remarks at the end of the film that rural and urban space simultaneously operate as producer and consumer within a symbiotic capitalist relationship: 'Your plough, she sure didn't grow on no tree. And your gun that you feed your bunch with in the winter, you didn't plant no seeds to get that. [. . .] Believe me friend, it takes all kinds to make up this whole world.' Secondly, there is the town which Sam and Nona visit when their son falls sick. The presence of Harmie's general store and the doctor's surgery mark it as a harbour of resources. The importance of the surgery within the context of Sam's social mobility cannot be overestimated: without the doctor's advice, Jot's death would be far more likely, even inevitable – both Devers's son and many of Sam's grandmother's siblings were claimed by the ailment in the past – and could rupture the nuclear family unit, leading to the personal, professional, and social disruption that is embodied by Devers and expressed through the crystalline state exhibited by shots of his property. Thus, Leo Braudy's assertion that 'nothing good can come from the town' represented in *The Southerner* is inappropriately drastic.[53] Clearly, the representations of urban space within the narrative do not merely operate through the reductive Manichaean rural/urban contrasts detected by O'Shaughnessy, but through their respective places in the larger American society: without the town, Sam cannot exploit what Massey calls 'the constantly-being-produced new geometries of power' through his work in his fields.[54]

It is worth noting that the import of the mutual implication of the country and the city is inaccessible unless we consider the ideological structures exposed by Renoir's *mise en scène* and interpret them 'in terms of a dimension of the future'.[55] Armand-Jean Cauliez understandably maintains that *profondeur de champ* in *The Southerner* is uncharacteristic of Renoir's work because scenes '*constrain* more or less scattered elements into a montage which is at once concise and harmonious'.[56] However, by integrating temporality into our analysis of space, it becomes clear that the camera, recalling Renoir's framing of the Algerian landscape, entrenches questions regarding ownership of the rural Texas within society's various intercontingencies and reveals the resulting *points de fuite*, one of which may allow Sam to actualise his American dream.

The River (1951)

Eliding colonial civilisation and its discontents

The River centres on the young Harriet's (Patricia Walters) life on the banks of the Ganges river with her parents, brother, and five sisters. Over the course of the film, she falls in love with Captain John (Thomas Breen), a wounded war veteran who has come to visit his cousin, Mr John (Arthur Shields). Captain John is also pursued by Mr John's Eurasian daughter, Melanie (Radha), and by Valerie (Adrienne Corri), the daughter of the owner of the local jute factory managed by Harriet's father (Esmond Knight). A dismayed Harriet unsuccessfully attempts suicide after Valerie's conquest of Captain John and the accidental death of Harriet's younger brother. By the end of the film, Captain John has left and the three girls – Harriet, Melanie, and Valerie – witness the arrival of Harriet's newborn sister to the world.

The River is at once like and unlike both *Le Bled* and *The Southerner*: like *Le Bled*, the film portrays social relations within a colonial setting, in this case Calcutta in British India; like *The Southerner*, the film presents an intimate portrait of family life. However, whereas the *élan vers l'avenir* in each of the two previous films analysed within this chapter is conveyed through responses to the contemporary social, political, and economic circumstances in which they were produced, *The River* relegates spatial politics in favour of portraying space itself as a realm of human memory imbued in temporality.

Although Renoir maintained the essential plot of Rumer Godden's source novella, he decided to introduce the character of the mature Harriet, witnessed only through voiceover as she invokes the memories viewed and heard by the spectator on-screen. It is perhaps because of this effacement of political concerns in favour of examining recollections and the very act of recollection – a central preoccupation of both Bergson's and

Deleuze's writing – that *The River* should happen to be the only one of the three films explored by this chapter to appear in Deleuze's discussion. Although the exploitation of the landscape's natural resources is central to the family's social status in *The River* (as in *Le Bled* and *The Southerner*), the continuity of the jute factory managed by Harriet's father is ensured by the benevolence of the elements. As the mature Harriet recalls, the river that runs through the jute mill

> came from the eternal snows of the Himalayas. [. . .] It flowed slowly between banks of mud and white sand, rice fields, and jute fields. The jute grew in flat marshes, nourished by monsoon floods. Country boats of all shapes and sizes brought the jute to the factories. Some of them came [. . .] through the winding arteries of the Delta.

She later surmises that 'jute was the reason we lived in India' and that 'our whole life depended on it', but recounts no traumatic disturbance to 'the never-ending procession of men carrying [jute] piled on their heads' in the film's prologue or during Captain John's guided visit. In fact, a long shot that captures the lines of workers carrying jute in the midground and background of the subsequent documentary-like shots of the workers implies a rigorously striated space within which a new future is neither desirable nor envisaged. Rather than provide a metaphor for the dislocation of the colonisers (as in *Le Bled*), the landscape provides a site of collaboration for the British colonising forces who sell processed jute as string, and the colonised Indian bodies, who receive sea-shells in exchange for raw jute.

Unlike either of the previous films, the potential for the creation of a new future does not lie in change related to social class or demand an understanding of the socio-economic framework within which the British colonising powers operate. Contrary to the portrayal of *l'Algérie française* in *Le Bled*, *The River* does not frame colonialism as a provisional regime subject to revision. Nor is the British family, on whom *The River* centres, put on trial, a move that evoked contempt from contemporary critics and an impassioned defence of the film from Bazin.[57] The spatio-temporal continuity of colonial power is particularly striking since the Partition of the British Indian Empire had already been ratified four years prior to the release of the film. In fact, this depiction of British colonialism unapologetically elides the reality encountered by Renoir and his crew during production: Renoir's regular set designer, Eugène Lourié, wrote that in India, 'the sky was red from flaming Muslim houses'.[58] Even Renoir himself, who marvelled that India was 'still living in an aristocratic style which has about completely disappeared in our mechanized civilization', likened modern Calcutta to 'the Bronx of India', with its 'ugly factory chimneys reminiscent of Liverpool or Pittsburgh'.[59]

Clearly, Renoir's framing of open space-time can only be understood if, building on Massey's assertion that 'memories [. . .] are also spatial', we consider the importance of the act of recollecting to the visual and aural design of the interactions between the landscape and the various characters evoked by the mature protagonist's psyche.[60]

Landscape as dreamscape: staging memory in depth

Given the centrality of Deleuze to any study of the relationship between film and memory, and the importance of *The River* to this chapter, it is important to assess Deleuze's examination of the film, which features in *Cinéma 2*. As in the case of Deleuze's other textual observations, he offers a tantalising albeit underdeveloped suggestion regarding the creation of a new future: Deleuze writes that Harriet and her siblings, 'sheltered in a sort of crystal or Hindu kiosk, try roles out, some of which take a tragic turn, as a result of which the little brother dies tragically'.[61] Deleuze does recognise the centrality of Harriet's personal story to the narrative of *The River* and mentions that Harriet 'will be saved because she will be able to renounce the role offered by her first love', thus outgrowing the *rôle mort* embodied by her childhood state.[62] However, Deleuze likens the children's home to a theatre of roles without examining how the screen holds these childhood roles in tension with the potential creation of a genuinely new future. Most importantly, he neglects the centrality of memory to Renoir's *mise en scène* of the *ouverture d'avenir*, even failing to distinguish between the young and the mature Harriet and to examine the relationship of the *images-souvenir* with the coexisting present-day vantage point occupied by the older Harriet's commentary issues. Deleuze's negligence in this instance is particularly surprising since Deleuze himself appropriates three central Bergsonian models pertaining to memory and becoming over the course of his analysis of the *image-temps*, and their influence is prevalent in Deleuze's discussion of the flashback structures employed by Marcel Carné (*Le Jour se lève*, 1939) and Joseph L. Mankiewicz (*All About Eve*, 1950).[63]

Whereas Godden's novel is largely recounted by an omniscient narrator and features occasional instances of free indirect speech articulating the young Harriet's fleeting thoughts,[64] the film alters the narrative's discursive position by elevating the newly conceived mature Harriet to the narrator of the entire story. The decision to provide the mature Harriet's voiceover was made relatively late in the production and did not feature in the first script, provisionally entitled 'Eastward in Eden'. However, Renoir wrote during cutting that he had repeatedly envisaged a commentary which would be justified by the fact that Harriet is a writer.[65] This decision coincided with a broader shift in the film's style which, prior to filming, was planned by Renoir as being 'as close to reality as possible' but which, following his collaboration with Godden, changed radically.[66] As Renoir wrote, 'this script [. . .] is now a kind of poetic drama, very far away from the film adaptation of the novel we were considering in the beginning'.[67] The saturated Technicolor hues recall Bachelard's assertion that 'space that has been seized upon by the imagination [. . .] has been lived in, not in its positivity, but with all the partiality of the imagination'.[68] The film's accompanying commentary transforms Renoir's conception of the film into a retrospective visualisation of life in India in which time, space, and change are articulated entirely through Harriet's subjective dreamscape.

Deleuze specifically elaborates on the relationship between memory and crystalline images in his discussion of Max Ophüls's *Lola Montès* (1955). Deleuze suggests that bifurcation invoked by flashback structures can enter into dialectic with a crystalline state, resulting in the representation of 'the dividing in two of time, which makes all the presents pass and makes them tend towards the circus as if towards their future, but also preserves all the pasts'.[69] Unlike Ophüls's 'perfect' crystal, however, Renoir's crystal allots the potential creation of a new future beyond predetermining elements, and *The River* challenges us to determine how *profondeur de champ* interacts with other visual and aural elements to articulate the *ouverture d'avenir* within both the memories of the younger Harriet and the world of the older Harriet.

Interestingly, Deleuze elsewhere proposes that the function of *profondeur de champ* in Orson Welles's *Citizen Kane* (1941) is 'to explore an entire region of the past, a continuum, every time'.[70] Drawing on Bergson, Deleuze asserts that *profondeur de champ* creates 'a certain type of *image-temps* that can be defined by memory, virtual regions of the past [. . .] a function of remembering, of temporalisation: not exactly a recollection but "an invitation to recollect"'.[71] In *Kane*, Welles's composition of shadows, ceilings, and oblique lines in depth forms 'sheets of the past'[72] that constitute realms of virtual memory. These visual elements, although defined by '*optical* aspects or elements borrowed from interacting planes', are irreducible to the dimensions of space, creating 'a set of non-localisable connections, always from one plane to another'.[73]

However, such a perspective on Welles's deep focus compositions seems irreconcilable with the *élan vers l'avenir* articulated by Renoir's staging of multiple events in depth. The contradictions between Deleuze's analyses of Renoir's and Welles's respective uses of *profondeur de champ* are underscored by Deleuze's assertion that the only precursors to Welles's particular appropriation of *profondeur de champ* were Erich von Stroheim's body of work and Renoir's *La Règle du jeu*, and by Deleuze's assertion that Renoir and Welles both pioneered a kind of *profondeur de champ* that rendered the cinema 'more demanding, more constraining, in some sense *theorematic*'.[74] Apart from integrating space into our analysis of the temporal implications of *profondeur de champ* in *The River*, it is essential that viewers address the potential of flashbacks to act as a *mise en abîme* of *une profondeur de champ mémoriale*, in which the spatiality of memory is addressed, in Deleuze's words, 'in terms of a dimension of the future'.[75]

'In a memory-Being, in a memory-world': image-souvenir *as* élan vers l'avenir

Contrary to Deleuze's examination of *The River*, the younger Harriet does not merely renounce her infatuation with Captain John. Her 'changing of roles' is instigated by the embrace shared by Captain John and Valerie, and the traumatic nature of this incident challenges us to consider Harriet's reason for dwelling on the incident and to examine the mutually affective relationship between the composition of the extended flashback and the mature Harriet as she beholds her younger self. Prakash Younger surmises that the film's narrative style 'constantly makes us aware of the subjectivity of the older Harriet's "objective" perspective' and also of the limited viewpoint 'hidden within her "objectified" younger self'.[76] This establishes a juncture between the past (the younger Harriet and the Indian landscape which are visible on-screen) and the ongoing present (established aurally through the mature Harriet's commentary), which challenges us to examine the very role of the flashback structure in the film for the mature Harriet. The particular challenge posed by *The River* is to determine how the image of the past conveys the *ouverture d'avenir* (either in the form of a *point de fuite* or a *ligne de fuite*) in both the world inhabited by the younger, imagined Harriet and the ongoing present moment experienced by the mature Harriet.

The rupture between the younger Harriet and Captain John occurs late in the narrative following a discussion between Captain John and Melanie at the latter's home, which is separated from Harriet's home by a wall. An outdoor shot grants us a view of Melanie exiting the house, Harriet perched behind a tree located in front of the house, and Valerie hiding behind a wall in the foreground of the image (Figure 2.7). Both Harriet

Figure 2.7 Melanie (left), Harriet (centre), and Valerie (right) pursue Captain John

and Valerie are carrying flowers for Captain John following his personally humiliating fall and pursue the captain as he searches for Melanie. They progressively disappear within the obscure darkness that lies beyond the lush green trees that dominate the background, whilst the mature Harriet verbally recollects that 'I was caught in an unexpected intrigue, but my adolescent pride would not let me turn back.'

Younger notes that this shot is both objective in its wide scope and subjective in its inclusion of the younger Harriet.[77] Central to the spatial and temporal scope of this shot is the mature Harriet's voiceover which, recalling Deleuze's analysis of *Kane*, enters into dialectic with the deep space of the garden to represent 'the virtual sheets of the past that we explore to find the sought-after memory'.[78] Simultaneously, in accordance with the role Deleuze associates with Renoir's use of *profondeur de champ*, change in the younger Harriet's world is about to be instigated through the departure of the girls 'in the background, in depth, through the third dimension, through the crack':[79] the adolescent protagonist's progressive distantiation from the wall surrounding her home in the foreground reminds us that the mature Harriet is evoking her experience of breaking with her childhood state. The adult Harriet hints at the crucial juncture that this precise moment represents as she remarks that 'suddenly we were running away from childhood, rushing toward love'. Somewhat gravely, she proceeds to state that 'the enchantment began and ended in the grove'. Upon this final line, Valerie too disappears into the trees in the background.

This shot of Harriet and Valerie running towards the trees in the background challenges us to think further about how the *ouverture d'avenir* that Deleuze associates with the cracked crystal enters into dialectic with 'the coexistence of every sheet of the past'.[80] More specifically, the organic emergence of Harriet's commentary relates the characters' spatio-temporal trajectories to Deleuze's Bergsonian assertion that 'memory is not within us, it is us who move in a memory-Being, in a memory-world', and therefore provokes us to consider temporal trajectories operating in the worlds occupied by both the mature Harriet and the young, imagined Harriet.[81] The extended take of the girls' disappearance through the background reflects Harriet's introspective act of digging further into the recesses of her memory and signals the possibility for change in both the past (the story recounted) and present (the adult Harriet who narrates the story).

As the mature Harriet reminds herself of the pivotal role this moment played in her life and that of the other girls, she is forced to confront herself with exactly how the event affected and continues to affect her. In the shots that follow, Harriet and Melanie look on, both morally depleted after Valerie and Captain John's embrace. Harriet's voice in the following lines suddenly sounds wounded: 'The kiss on her lips, terrifying and fascinating, burned into my heart and hurt. It was my first kiss, but received by another.' The audible grief in Harriet's tone indicates the mutually affective link between each version of herself which is absent from conventional voiceovers. As Mary Ann Doane usefully clarifies, voice-off '*belongs* to a character who is confined to a space of the diegesis, if not the visible space of the screen' whereas in interior monologues, although voice and body are represented simultaneously, 'the voice, far from being an extension of that body, manifests its inner lining'.[82]

Interestingly, although the older Harriet 'displays "the inner life" of the character' in accordance with Doane's definition of interior monologues, the younger Harriet challenges this definition because she embodies a composite of both the young girl of times long since past and the mature Harriet's own subjective recollections of her younger self.[83] The image of the young Harriet becomes the embodiment of what Deleuze terms 'the point of indiscernibility' within the crystal of time, in which the actual and virtual, respectively manifest as present and coexisting past, become unassignable.[84] The adult Harriet's interior monologue is not solely a voice signifying 'the privileged mark of interiority, turning the body "inside out"'.[85] Her speech reveals that, like Lola Montès, she is mentally implicated in her younger self's spatio-temporal trajectory.

Deleuze himself remarks on a category of the *hors-champ* (or 'out-of-field'), which

> is connected to the Whole that is expressed in sets, to the change that is expressed in movement, to the duration that is expressed in space, to the living concept that is expressed in the image, to the spirit that is expressed in matter.[86]

This field can be evoked 'through very particular speech acts, which are reflexive and no longer interactive (the voice that evokes, comments, and knows, endowed with an omnipotence or a strong power over the sequence of images)'.[87] Because this category extends to the mature Harriet's voice, it is only by listening closely to her commentary that the spectator can understand how the recollected event challenges the mature Harriet to break with childhood in the present day. In light of the cathartic effect of the mature Harriet's recollections portrayed by the narrative, this sequence demonstrates that each of Deleuze's temporally defined views of *profondeur de champ* – as *image-souvenir* and *élan vers l'avenir* – may be subsumed within the visual and aural aspects of Renoir's *mise en scène*.

Apart from challenging the spectator to apprehend the dual temporalities operating within *The River*, this sequence also evokes the question of the function of Harriet's deliberate recollection, and how it corresponds with the future that she desires. Defining the flashback as 'a privileged moment in unfolding that juxtaposes different moments of temporal reference', Maureen Turim notes that 'some flashbacks directly involve a quest for the answer to an enigma posed in the beginning of a narrative through a return to the past'.[88] Harriet's recollections in *The River* largely adhere to Turim's definition: through the expressive relationship between voiceover and other visual aspects of *mise en scène*, a juncture is wrought between the ongoing present and the present that has long since passed. However, the narrative initially refrains from offering an enigma to be restored. Of more importance is Turim's remark that 'the past is an object of desire, due to its personal, intense, and even liberating attitudes'.[89]

Over the course of the film, it becomes progressively apparent that the impact of the mature Harriet's oscillation between various emotions in the ongoing present is itself a crucial role of her extended recollection. Deleuze writes that the act of thinking, by drawing on the past 'as it is condensed in the inside, in relation to oneself', invokes a dialectic between the present and our accumulated past that is potentially conducive to evolution:[90]

> [One can] think the past against the present and resist the latter, not in order to effect a return but 'in favour, I hope, of a time to come' (Nietzsche), that is to say, by making the past active and present to the outside so that something new will finally emerge, so that thinking may always reach thought.[91]

It is only when the mature Harriet reflects on the moment in the grove that her goal in recollecting becomes entirely clear. The mature Harriet's reflection on her younger self's failed pursuit of Captain John brings her older self through the sheets of the past, producing a new, sympathetic understanding of her childhood years that liberates the mature Harriet from the stultifying influence of the past. Her younger self's experience of love and guilt, reinterpreted years later, has become a *rôle mort* and the mature Harriet has escaped the metaphorical crystal. In short, repetition results in difference.

'The river runs, the round world spins': escaping the crystal au fil de l'eau

One final aspect of Deleuze's interpretation of *The River* must be located within the context of open space-time. As noted in the Introduction, the only space that Deleuze distinguishes from the theatrical roles that proliferate throughout Renoir's output is the river. Discussing the guarantee that 'something forms within the crystal which will manage to escape through the crack and dispersing freely', Deleuze remarks:[92]

> This was already the case of Boudu, who finds the water's stream [*le fil de l'eau*] by leaving the intimate and enclosed theatre of the bookseller's where he has tried numerous roles. It will be the case of Harriet in the grandiose film, *The River*, where the children, sheltered in a sort of crystal or Hindu kiosk try roles [. . .] which will provide the young girl with her learning process until she finds in it the powerful will to live which coalesces with the river and unites with it outside.[93]

The disparity between Deleuze's interpretation of water and the two films already discussed in this chapter further flags the dangers of overreading Deleuze's discussion of rivers: in *Le Bled*, the only source of water is the desert oasis at which local camels drink and in which Manuel's car becomes trapped. In *The Southerner*, a river runs alongside Sam's land, providing sustenance through fish but, on the other hand, it harbours typhoid that renders its water undrinkable and it floods Sam's land. In *The River*, unlike these examples, the Ganges provides an important source of creative inspiration for Harriet as well as a source of recourse when she attempts suicide. Furthermore, this river plays an important role in the mature Harriet's transcendence of the past and incorporates its own temporal implications within Renoir's *image-souvenir*.

In his discussion of Boudu's escape from Lestingois's milieu, Deleuze evokes a rhizomatic quality of water which irresistibly transports characters towards a genuinely new social setting. Interestingly, Deleuze and

Guattari elaborate on the following verse from 'Ol' Man River' to describe the rhizomatic circulation of knowledge:

> He don't plant tatos
> Don't plant cotton
> Them that plants them is soon forgotten
> But old man river he just keeps rollin [sic] along.[94]

Deleuze's assertion that Harriet's will to live coalesces with the river risks distracting us from the relationship between the mature Harriet and her imagined image of the river.[95] It is not just the young Harriet who unites with the object of her poetry in her attempted suicide, but also her older self, whose narrative opens and closes with shots of the flowing Ganges.

The river itself signifies the very capacity of the mature Harriet's recollections to instigate escape from the past. Bachelard, one of Deleuze's key influences,[96] counterposes the liquidity of water with the rigid durability of crystals during his reflection on the material imagination of water in *L'Eau et les rêves*: '"Images" whose basis or matter is water do not have the same durability and solidity as those produced by earth, by crystals, metals and precious stones.'[97] Anticipating Deleuze's favoured metaphor of the seed forty-three years before the publication of *Cinéma 2*, Bachelard elaborates on the potential of the imagined image of water to catalyse the imagination's capacity for interpreting objective reality:

> Water swells seeds up and causes springs to gush forth. [. . .] The spring is an irresistible birth, a *continuous* birth. The unconscious that loves such great images is forever marked by them. The unconscious that loves such great images is indelibly marked by them.[98]

The inspiration provided by the Ganges is evidenced by the young Harriet's own poem 'Big River', the river-bank setting of the story she recounts to Captain John and Valerie, and, most notably, by her attempted suicide in the Ganges.

Bachelard's discussion of the relationship between water and death in Shakespeare's *Hamlet* valuably illuminates the import of the mature Harriet's recollected image of water to the casting aside of her *rôle mort*. Drawing on the image of Shakespeare's Ophelia, Bachelard writes that 'water carries [things] far away, water passes like the days. [. . .] Each of the elements has its own type of decomposition, earth into dust, fire into smoke. Water dissolves more completely. It helps us to die completely.'[99] More importantly, drawing on examples of water featuring in reveries and literature, Bachelard proposes that water invokes a process of becoming within the imagination rather than an exclusively literal death: 'A being devoted to water is a being in flux. He/she dies every minute. Something of his/her substance is constantly dissipating.'[100] Within the context of this analysis, Bachelard's statement may be most productively aligned less with the corporeal deaths evoked by Bachelard (including that of Ophelia and of Goethe's Faust) or even with the young Harriet's attempt to end her own life than with Deleuze's conceptualisation of 'the gushing forth of time as doubling, as scission', specifically the mature Harriet's mental transitions, which are signalled by her own grief-stricken voice.[101]

The younger Harriet's later attempt to drown herself is less a reaction to Captain John and Valerie's embrace than a guilt-ridden response to her implication in the death of her brother, who is killed by a cobra bite whilst Harriet is pursuing the captain. The mature Harriet, visualising her younger self's immersion in the Ganges, remarks: 'There were so many unsaid things I'd forgotten to tell Bogey and now I would never tell him.' Harriet's guilt has evidently haunted her since the death of her brother. It is only by revisiting her infatuation with Captain John that she manages to understand that her childhood self does not merit reproach for its limited perspective. Like the water that flows towards the future in Deleuze and Guattari's discussion of the rhizome, the imagined river subsumes the past within the mature Harriet's own orientation towards the future. Within her memory, which is visualised through the *image-souvenir*, 'a single matter has taken over everything. "Everything is dissolved."'[102]

The progression of the mature Harriet's imagined narrative reflects her own renewed understanding and sympathy towards her younger self's childish infatuation with Captain John. There is a humorous irony in the rapid dissolve from Harriet's attempt at drowning to the shot of her, crouched and soaked, sitting inside the docked river-boat. Whereas Lola Montès experiences 'a dizziness, an oscillation', and remains within the crystal following her climactic dive, Harriet has finally transcended the past, which she has hitherto felt obliged to recollect.[103] Turim observes that 'flashbacks in most cases terminate at precisely the point at which they must be sealed off, in which the imperatives of fixing interpretations and reaching judgements in the present must be imposed. Made aware of the past, the spectator is freed to forget it once again.'[104] Compelled to revisit her adolescent years, Harriet herself is now capable of discarding the grief that they brought upon her. This cycle of death and renewal is at the heart of Harriet's poetic summarisation of life as she finally recalls the birth of her youngest sister, and the closing shot of her mind's eye lingers on the Ganges:

The river runs, the round world spins.
Dawn and lamplight. Midnight. Noon.
Sun follows day. Night stars and moon.
The day ends. The end begins.

Conclusion: Dynamising the Natural Landscape

Harper and Rayner rightly remark that any cinematographic landscape is the product of a 'complex combination of found or chosen features – some visual, some aural, some relating to movement, some based in innate understanding'.[105] Although this chapter has deliberately sought to study a wide range of aspects of *mise en scène* beyond *profondeur de champ* (among them off-screen space, characterisation, and interior décor), the fact remains that Renoir's use of deep space is crucial to his portrayal of open space-time across all three landscapes analysed. This continuity within the implications of Renoir's *mise en scène* is particularly interesting given the range of social, political, and cultural contexts underlying the production of each film: the spatio-temporal tropes visible in *Le Bled*, which was directly commissioned as a propagandist project, are visible in *The Southerner* and *The River*, neither of which was subject to the same ideological control exercised by the French (or any other) state. However, the prominence of this unifying technique should not prevent us from respecting the diversity of Renoir's rural landscapes: each challenges any easy attempt to derive an image of open space-time through our established methodological framework in at least one of two particular ways.

First of all, the *surcroît de théâtralité* that provides a formal and thematic keystone of Deleuze's framework and a spatio-temporal counterpoint to Renoir's portrayals of Algeria and Paris is of little concern to Renoir's *mise en scène* in *The Southerner* and *The River*. Rather, Renoir exclusively foregrounds the landscape in its social, physical, and metaphysical aspects, and juxtaposes it with the hopes and histories embodied by individual characters. In doing so, Renoir frames the natural landscape as a temporally imbued locus that contributes to the emergence of new *points de fuite* or *lignes de fuite* in both films in ways that recall *Le Bled*.

The second challenge posed by the natural landscape is that it often appears physically and socially inert, and devoid of the unique architecture that catalyses characters' imbrication in the scission of time. Renoir's natural landscape can only be viewed as an active force if we view these rural spaces from at least one of two perspectives that each inform Renoir's *mise en scène*. On the one hand, we may view Renoir's landscapes as sites of what Harvey terms 'actively reconstituted features', which are subject to both the elemental forces of nature and capitalist activity, and in which, as Jonathan Murdoch reminds us, 'gender relations, forms of ethnic belonging, sexual identities, and so forth will [. . .] be recast'.[106] In *Le Bled* and *The Southerner*, as in the case of the films analysed in Chapter 1, Renoir's open space-time is not only a technological product but also an ideological one, which emphasises the mutually affective relationship between physical and social space. In both of these films, the landscape itself becomes a *point de fuite* through its innate defiance of overcoding and its impartiality towards hegemonic social strata existing within overarching social structures, specifically colonialism and capitalism. The precise import of the landscape towards the production of new positions of economic power is emphasised in both films by the presence of an off-screen *ailleurs*: to Algeria's landscapes, there is France, and to the Texan fields, there is the town. In all of these areas, the characters' social standing would inevitably differ, and each narrative emphasises the socialisation of the landscape as both a factor and product of adjacent spaces: Claudie would have neither the rich inheritance granted by her uncle nor the economic return that it provides for her and for Hoffer's labourers, and the security of work and regular pay in a factory would preclude Sam Tucker's potential rise to Ruston's lofty heights.

This same structure informs *The River*, in which it is unlikely that the colonial family would live with the same privileges that they currently enjoy in India. However, although the landscape in *The River* situates the jute mill run by Harriet's father within a geographically precise context, these specificities are subjugated to the narrative's focus on the spatiality of memory: the visual and aural elements of *The River* transform India's natural landscapes into what Harper and Rayner describe as 'conduits to memories'.[107] Yet within the mature Harriet's *mémoire-monde*, the possibility of exiting through a *point de fuite* remains, invoking dramatic personal consequences in the ongoing present moment that provides her with a vantage point on the entire visualised narrative. As Perez observes of *Partie de campagne*, 'rather than assigning meaning to the landscape, the fiction becomes a foray in quest of meaning'.[108]

Because Renoir portrays the *ouverture d'avenir* in all three films regardless of their production context, geographical setting, and ideological perspective, it is unsurprising that Renoir's natural landscapes appeal to Deleuze, even if he misguidedly analogises them with theatres. Interestingly, the relegation of an ideologically informed narrative style denoting the mature Harriet's passage through the 'sheets of the past' is where Deleuze's film philosophy is most enlightening, and the relevance of both Deleuze's and Massey's spatial thought tends to wane. As in the case of the urban narratives studied in Chapter 1, the camera only occasionally frames the confluence of heterogeneous forces that engender a *point de fuite* or *ligne de fuite*, but such shots condition the manner in which the spectator views each entire film. As a result, all three films exemplify Harper and Rayner's theorisation of cinematographic landscapes whose frame 'allows for, or even encourages, the audience to move over, or scan, the image; and the overall effect of a film is to place the audience in a dynamic and extensive experience'.[109]

CHAPTER 3

Portraying the Future(s) of the Front Populaire

We must address a relational politics for a relational space.[1]

– Doreen Massey, *For Space*

Our great Jean, if he had a heart for the left, had no head for politics.[2]

– Roger Leenhardt

Introduction: Theory and Texts in Context

By analysing the *mise en scène* of space-time in Renoir's Front populaire output, this chapter argues that *Le Crime de Monsieur Lange* (1936), *Les Bas-fonds* (1936), and *La Grande Illusion* (1937) articulate Renoir's lack of confidence in the new future envisioned by his communities. In particular, this analysis demonstrates that the subjugated social groups featuring in each of these films are helpless to comprehensively apprehend or overcome the hegemonic social structures that striate space. Apart from representing some of the most aesthetically audacious work of their director's career, Renoir's films of this period implicitly occupy a central position in Deleuze's conceptualisation of Renoir's crystalline oeuvre. Asserting that Renoir is the director who came closest to conveying 'an acute awareness of the identity of liberty with a future, be it collective or individual', Deleuze proceeds to ground the director's outlook in 'Renoir's political conscience, the manner in which he conceives the French Revolution or the Front populaire'.[3] Deleuze's discussion of the relationship between Renoir's ideological messages and shooting style in his films is surprising within the context of a work that largely elides such discussions and generally depoliticises Renoir's *mise en scène*, and testifies to the undeniable impact of Renoir's *engagement politique* on his social and aesthetic development. At its peak, the Front populaire introduced collective contracts, salary increases averaging 12 per cent, a forty-hour working week, and paid annual holidays. Although Deleuze's optimistic statement necessarily simplifies both Renoir's involvement with the Front populaire and Renoir's *mise en scène*, his comments on Renoir's political affiliation remain valuable nonetheless, as they suggest a direct link between Renoir's contemporary political outlook and the range of futures available to Renoir's characters.

On the one hand, Deleuze's optimism regarding the relationship between Renoir's public commitment to the Front populaire and the *élan vers l'avenir* expressed by Renoir's cracked crystal of time within an analysis that largely depoliticises Renoir's work is entirely understandable. First of all, a cycle of films directed by Renoir between 1936 and 1938 'certifies a leftist humanism even down to our own day' and complements Frontist prisms of analysis.[4] Renoir's left-wing sympathies were already manifest in *Toni* (1935), which treats a group of exploited Italian immigrants based in Martigues. Considering the narrative's clear engagement with the tribulations of the proletariat, issues concerning the rights of women, and the value of international solidarity, Keith Reader suggests that the film is, if only in part, 'a precursor of, and of a piece with the director's work of the Popular Front years'.[5] *Lange* was produced in collaboration with le groupe Octobre, whose members included the film's screenwriter, Jacques Prévert, and premiered at the Aubert Palace in Paris on 24 January 1936.[6] The production and distribution of *Lange* (September 1935–April 1936) coincided with the Front populaire's campaign preparations for the May 1936 legislative elections and, as Brett Bowles notes, the film 'in its time [. . .] appeared as militant and unconcealed support for the left'.[7] Indeed, the critics of *Premier Plan* even asked: 'Will it be necessary to reformulate the credits? *Le Crime de Monsieur Lange* – a film by le groupe Octobre – technical assistant: Jean Renoir.'[8] Renoir later produced the fervently propagandist *La Vie est à nous* (1936), which he later claimed to have envisaged in response to the anti-Semitism he had witnessed in Nazi Germany.[9] Produced shortly after the Radicals, Socialists, and Communists had endorsed the common programme of the Front populaire, the film 'transformed Left filmmaking activity from a hope to a reality'.[10]

Les Bas-fonds, co-adapted by Renoir and Charles Spaak from Maxim Gorki's source text, once more orchestrated the fall of oppressive capitalist structures, this time embodied by an exploitative landlord. According to Spaak, the development of the script was monitored by the Parti communiste, and Renoir 'who, at that point, was flirting a great deal with the communists, received some comments: there was to be no question of taking liberties with Gorki'.[11] Gorki himself declared his satisfaction with the scenario one month before his death.[12] When the film was awarded the first Prix Louis Delluc, it beat *Lange* – now incontestably the better known of the two – by twelve votes to two.[13] As the prize itself had been established by a group of predominantly left-wing journalists and writers unofficially associated with the Front populaire, who sought to provide 'a judgment free from artistic, patriotic, and moral conformism, in opposition to the academic and orthodox Grand Prix du Cinéma', Renoir's victory validated his status as the favourite filmmaker of the Left.[14] Jacques Duclos further underscored the film's association with the Left by subsequently congratulating 'on behalf of the Parti communiste, the great director whose outstanding talent has produced works that will last' and 'the great friend of the people who gave us the beautiful film, *La Vie est à nous*'.[15] *La Grande Illusion*, as Martin O'Shaughnessy remarks, 'is an attempt to make productive sense of the First World War within the French republican and revolutionary traditions while at the same time responding to the challenges of the 1930s', not least the Spanish Civil War (17 July 1936–1 April 1939), the rise of fascism, and the Front populaire's own attempts to eradicate indigenous racism and anti-Semitism.[16]

In the wake of the smash critical and commercial success of *La Grande Illusion*, Renoir directed *La Marseillaise*, which recounts the early events of the French Revolution through the eyes of the French aristocracy and the popular classes. Originally funded through a popular subscription system in association with Ciné-Liberté and the Confédération générale du travail (then France's dominant trade union), the film was regarded from its inception as '*the* film of the Front populaire' and, on 16 March 1937, was launched by Renoir as 'a film by the people and for the people'.[17] However, this programme was eventually aborted when funding fell short and the film ultimately became, in Renoir's words, 'an absolutely normal enterprise', thus ending his public association with the Front populaire.[18] Yet the production of the film, whose Frontist message 'barely seeks to hide behind the historical period it purports to represent', nonetheless suggests that Renoir's apparent commitment even seems to have outlasted the Front itself:[19] Jean-Pierre Jeancolas and Edward Ousselin both argue that *La Marseillaise* already bore a posthumous quality at the time of its release in February 1938, at which point Renoir was still contributing articles to *Ce Soir*.[20]

Secondly, of all the directors associated with French popular cinema of this period, Renoir was the Left's closest public collaborator. Although not an official member of any political party, Renoir publicly supported Secretary General Maurice Thorez at the Eighth Congress of the Parti communiste français in 1936.[21] Renoir served on the administrative council of Ciné-Liberté, a production company that helmed a number of films (including Renoir's own *La Marseillaise*) in association with the Parti communiste français's Maison de la Culture, and was also a member of the editorial board of the company's journal, *Ciné-Liberté*.[22] When *Commune*, the journal of the Association des écrivains et artistes révolutionnaires, published a letter of support for the Soviet Union in November 1936, Renoir was the only filmmaker among the signatories, who included André Gide, Le Corbusier, and Picasso.[23] Renoir was later offered carte blanche by Louis Aragon to write for the Communist newspaper *Ce Soir*, to which he contributed articles from 4 March 1937 to 7 October 1938.[24] During February–March 1935, before commencing pre-production work on *Lange*, Renoir visited Moscow to present *Toni* with Marguerite Houllé (Renoir's lover and editor of fifteen of his films), Claude Renoir (cinematographer for ten of Renoir's films including *La Grande Illusion* and *La Vie est à nous*), and Georges d'Arnoux (actor in a number of films directed by Renoir, most notably as the male protagonist in *Partie de campagne*).[25] Renoir was also giving speeches on Soviet cinema in France, including discussions regarding the image of Lenin in Soviet film, as late as July 1938.[26] It is no surprise that by February 1937, Roger Leenhardt had baptised Renoir 'the genius director of the Left'.[27] A chapter entitled 'Le Front populaire' in Renoir's autobiography depicts a nation enlightened by a blissful glimmer of hope: 'It was a moment when the French truly believed that they were going to love one another. We felt ourselves being carried along by a wave of generosity.'[28]

Because questions regarding Renoir's confidence in the Front populaire necessarily concern the tension between his country's past and the range of potential futures that it faced, it is important to retain Deleuze's remarks as a valuable avenue of enquiry towards our examination of Renoir's Front populaire output. However, it would be misguided to interpret these films as though Renoir believed in what Reader calls 'the imaginary resolution of political contradictions'.[29] Rather, it is worth reminding ourselves that the Front populaire was weakened from the outset by national political and economic instability, owing in part to the prolonged impact of the Great Depression in France and to the financial scandal generated by the suicide of embezzler Serge Stavisky in 1934. In the wake of Léon Blum's notorious refusal to intervene on the Republican side in the Spanish Civil War, the Front populaire collapsed, having held power for only 380 days. A second government, established under Blum in March 1938, lasted barely a month.

Moreover, scholars have established that Renoir's commitment from 1936 to 1938 was neither absolute nor unconditional. The very fact that

Renoir did not obtain membership of any political party during this period hints at his own reservations regarding the true (un)feasibility of Blum's agenda. Elizabeth Grottle Strebel labels Renoir 'a humanist socialist' and Claude Gauteur criticises those who doubt the sincerity of Renoir's brief commitment, somewhat helplessly arguing that 'Saint Renoir does not exist, nor has he ever existed. [. . .] Jean Renoir was a man, with all of the strengths and weaknesses engendered by the human condition.'[30] François Poulle is less forgiving, and although he understands that 'Renoir was a man of many political colours', he criticises Renoir for not declaring his true sympathies in public.[31] Some of Renoir's own associates were more scathing. Pierre Braunberger (producer of Renoir's *Tire-au-flanc* [1928], *La Chienne* [1931], and *Partie de campagne* [1936]) aligned Renoir's Front populaire output with the director's opportunistic search for a target audience:

> On the political chessboard, he was rather on the right. [. . .] He was social without being socialist. [. . .] I strongly encouraged him to accept [the communists' proposition], explaining to him that there he had the opportunity to finally find a real public.[32]

Spaak, co-writer of *Les Bas-fonds* and *La Grande Illusion*, claimed Renoir 'forgot that Marxism and Nazism were not synonyms' and was 'a complete traitor'.[33] All of these interpretations of Renoir's attitude towards the Left, whether sympathetic in nature or not, only leave his motives and the political messages of his Front populaire output open to further speculation.

Furthermore, Renoir's career from 1938 to 1940 provides enough grounds in itself to question his previous public commitment to the Left during the rise of the Front populaire. Renoir followed *La Marseillaise* with the dark naturalism of *La Bête humaine* (1938) and, the following year, delivered the scathing satire of *La Règle du jeu* (1939). Moreover, the very Renoir who had claimed that 'by filming abroad, we betray France and the cinema at the same time'[34] and had condemned Marcel Carné's *Le Quai des brumes* (1938) as a fascist film[35] was, by 1939, planning an adaptation of *La Tosca* in fascist Italy and, in 1940, accepted Mussolini's invitation to offer a master class at the Centro sperimentale di cinematografia, a move for which many of Renoir's former Communist allies never forgave him.[36] Renoir claimed that he was simply following the French government's orders as part of his country's broader aim to dissuade Mussolini from forming an alliance with Hitler.[37] However, Pascal Mérigeau remarks that the contract for *La Tosca* dispatched by Scalera studios is dated 12 July 1939 whilst Renoir's orders from the army are dated 2 September, concluding that

Renoir 'subsequently chose to be quiet, preferring to situate his decision to film [*La*] *Tosca* after the war with Germany had been declared'.[38]

Because Renoir himself wrote relatively little on his public affiliation with the Left following the outbreak of war, O'Shaughnessy's lament that Renoir pre-1936 'is largely unavailable to us except through the films' still remains true over fifteen years later.[39] Assessing Renoir's attitude towards the Front populaire, and the extent to which this outlook is evidenced by Renoir's *mise en scène*, demands that we examine the limited documents detailing Renoir's personal sentiments prior to the May 1936 elections, from which point inadequate documentation and Renoir's public involvement with the Front populaire largely efface any personal misgivings which he may have harboured. One noteworthy instalment in Renoir's Front populaire output has yet to be sufficiently examined. After the release of *Toni* and prior to the production of *Le Crime de Monsieur Lange*, Renoir penned *Ida*, an ultimately unfilmed screenplay. Two drafts of *Ida* survive, each of which was written during the pre-production stages of *Le Crime de Monsieur Lange*: the first was written on 8 August, the second on 26 August 1935. *Ida* recounts the tensions between two factions – the woods people and village people – living in La Cordelière, a fictional town located near Paris. The first draft centres on the ill-fated relationship between the titular protagonist and her suitor, Pierre, who respectively live in the forest and the village, and whose fathers forbid their union. This aspect of *Ida* has been situated by Gauteur within the development of Renoir's ultimately unfilmed *Roméo et Juliette*.[40] The second draft develops the political contours of both fathers through the addition of a critical omniscient narrator who relates the two figures to the screenplay's contemporary context in striking ways that demand further elaboration.

The leader of the woods people, Taillefer, is commonly addressed by the characters and the narrator as 'the King of Prussia' ('le roi de Prusse'), directly relating him to Kaiser Wilhelm II, the last king of Prussia, whose aggressive *Weltpolitik* and personal relations with Archduke Franz Ferdinand laid a foundation for the July crisis. Taillefer thus provides a direct link between the memories of the Franco-Prussian War and the outbreak of the First World War, during which Renoir himself fought in the French cavalry and air force. The narrative further suggests that such volatile political figures are still active, not only within the fictional world of La Cordelière but also in contemporary Europe. The script notes that Taillefer was once unconstitutionally granted jurisdiction by the local mayor and that 'in a few years, his authority was no longer discussed and one could say that he was a sort of Mussolini or Hitler of the forest'.[41] The possibility of historical repetition is also embodied by Vandeuvres, the most prominent member of the village people, who works as a butcher in the village centre. His enterprise is described as 'the most dreadful burstone house imaginable', and contrasts with the 'simple and harmonious mentality' exhibited by the small church located opposite it.[42] Most alarmingly, the narrator proceeds to locate the building within the screenplay's contemporary national context: 'This butcher's is distracting me a good deal but we must speak about it. These are the horrors that have dishonoured the banlieues of Paris as well as the surrounding areas of every big city.'[43] As in the case of Taillefer, the narrator directly equates Vandeuvres with the two rising fascists of the interwar period: 'Germany creates HITLER, Italy creates MUSSOLINI. In France, the same category of arrogant petits bourgeois creates burstone houses and they are almost as dangerous.'[44] The fact that Vandeuvres ranks no higher than the *petite bourgeoisie* serves as a distinct reminder of the right-wing sentiment and authoritarian ambitions that proliferated within French society, even among middle-class ranks, before Renoir began filming *Lange*. In an introduction to the setting, the narrator even comments on the provocative parallels between the fictional narrative and contemporary society:

> This tiny agglomerate of two hundred people will be the centre of the story that I am going to try to transcribe. Naturally I am changing the name of the country and the people. Someone could recognise him/herself and get angry. But my replacement names are not false – they are borrowed from real people and places which could very easily have been the actors and formed the frame of a similar drama.[45]

This chapter does not merely aim to criticise Deleuze's generalisation on the basis of biographical details of Renoir's engagement with the Front populaire, prior readings of Renoir's films, or by revisiting *Ida*. Rather, by drawing on Renoir's simultaneous involvement in both *Ida* – a cautionary tale of seething tensions in French society – and *Lange* – the first French film to solidify Renoir's public commitment to the French Left – this chapter argues that Renoir's *mise en scène* of coeval spatial politics during this period is informed by his own pessimism regarding the rise of the Front populaire, and that the forces ranged against Renoir's characters should not be relegated in favour of examining the hopes and dreams projected by his communities.

From *point de fuite* to *ligne de fuite*: Framing the Future in Rhizomatic Space

Because of the tension between the propulsive force of the characters' endeavours to implement new projects leading to the potential creation of a new future and the external spatio-temporal forces ranged against these projects, it is important to distinguish further between the *point de fuite* conceptualised within Deleuze's description of crystalline states in *Cinéma 2*, and the *ligne de fuite* which he discusses in *Mille Plateaux*. As noted in the Introduction, Deleuze and Guattari assert that although 'one may make a rupture, draw a line of flight [*ligne de fuite*]', the fact remains that 'groups and individuals contain micro-fascisms simply waiting to crystallise', and therefore, 'there is still a danger that one will re-encounter organisations that re-stratify everything'.[46] Deleuze and Guattari's emphasis on the forces existing beyond any *point de fuite* signals the potential futility of implementing a new future by those who exploit a 'line of chance, line of hips, line of flight' ('ligne de chance, ligne de hanche, ligne de fuite').[47] Deleuze and Guattari's allusion to the molecular flux introduced by an insurgent community is particularly pertinent in the case of the three films discussed in this chapter, within which subjugated communities endeavour to consolidate a collective project that offers them a *ligne de fuite* from oppressive circumstances. By virtue of the fact that space is, in Doreen Massey's words, 'so unamenable to a single totalising project', the restructuring of cartographies of power (or molar lines, to use Deleuze and Guattari's term) can only be achieved through 'the construction of (temporary, provisional) stabilisations' that inevitably vie against one another within a 'sphere of dynamic simultaneity'.[48] Therefore, the molar may reassert dominance over the molecular, and society may recrystallise around the *ligne de fuite*, nullifying the escape effected through the *point de fuite*. As the *mise en scène* of open space-time in the three films will demonstrate, the trajectory of a rhizomatic '*ligne de hanche*' is constantly contested by hegemonic molar lines, and is never assured.

Le Crime de Monsieur Lange (1936)

Les Éditions Batala and the courtyard: staging politics in depth

Le Crime de Monsieur Lange recounts the efforts of the eponymous protagonist (René Lefèvre) and his fellow employees at a publication house to establish a socialist cooperative following the apparent death of their exploitative boss, Batala (Jules Berry). Backed by the jovial Meunier *fils* (the son of one of Batala's creditors, played by Henri Guisol) and assisted by the workers of the adjoining *blanchisserie* owned by Valentine (Florelle), the community markets Lange's *Arizona Jim* comics. At the peak of the cooperative's financial success, Batala returns unscathed but is shot by Lange. Aided by Valentine, Lange is escorted across the Belgian border by a group of men who deem the murder a necessary one.

Unsurprisingly, Renoir himself regarded *Lange* as 'an essay of links between backgrounds and foregrounds within the same shot'.[49] During the first third of the narrative, the deep spaces that provide a lynchpin of Deleuze's interpretation of Renoir's *mise en scène* convey the vacillating vitality of the workers' presence in the courtyard and publishing house as they work at Les Éditions Batala. On the morning of work in the opening sequence, deep staging and lateral movement offer what Lyall Bush describes as 'frequent excesses of information that are irrelevant except that they suggest a film world as semiotically rich and as seamlessly detailed and unpredictable as the world in which the audience lives'.[50] As the workers arrive, Lange's eyes follow Édith's (Sylvia Bataille) legs as she quickly ascends the stairs to Batala's office. The camera cuts to a frontal view of Lange and, after we hear a voice call, 'Lange!' off-screen, the camera pans to the left to reveal Valentine. As she jokingly mocks Lange, we realise that she occupied this formerly off-screen space as Lange was ogling Édith's legs. As Valentine walks back to her deeply staged laundry area, Lange looks up towards off-screen space once more before an inspector intrudes on the left-hand side of the image and asks him where Batala may be found.

Throughout this sequence, Renoir's camera depicts the social relations as the 'sphere of dynamic simultaneity' theorised by Massey's treatise on space, 'constantly disconnected by new arrivals, constantly waiting to be determined (and always undetermined) by the construction of new relations'.[51] The physical proximity and social interaction between each of these businesses establish a precondition for the horizontal merger effected through the consolidation of the cooperative: Valentine effects a significant degree of mobility in both the launderette and the workers' quarters of Les Éditions Batala, interlinking the social space of each enterprise by supplying linen to Batala and his employees, and occasionally walking around Batala's publishing house. Although these sequences lend credence to Sesonske's assertion that the characters share an 'essentially topographical relation', he is incorrect to assume that the cooperative enterprise 'simply becomes one through the interpenetration of the areas around the court'.[52] These early moments in the narrative portray the elements required for the creation of politics rather than the future potentially invoked by these politics. The camera's framing of the fleeting passages of workers in the buildings displays the very lack of a cohesive political agenda that could implement a new future.

The workers remain socially gridlocked within the exploitative workplace, where Batala refuses to allow his workers to exercise their own creative liberty. Furthermore, he has accumulated multiple debts that he does not intend to repay, placing not only his own future but that of his unwitting workers at risk. The photography of two spaces – Lange's room, and Batala's office – demonstrates the social imprisonment imposed by Batala's regime within the world of the courtyard. Lange's room, although replete with items that fuel his imagination, insulates him and his ideas from mainstream society, and its only window looks out onto the opposite side of the courtyard. This social gridlock is also visible in Batala's office, located within Les Éditions Batala. When Batala presents Lange's ideas to Baigneur, a representative of one of the publishing house's many creditors, in an effort to prolong his own solvency, deep space registers the tensions between capitalist production and artistic creativity: in the foreground, Lange, Batala, and the debt collector agree to write off Batala's soaring debts through the publication of *Arizona Jim*. The unceasing pace of work in the background conveys the assimilation of the workers within the rapid pace of the capitalist workplace and its sheer drive to produce within the hierarchical structure of Batala's company. Clearly, neither Lange nor any other worker can strive to secure their own reputations as artists or a better quality of living within their stratified workplace.

The obscurity of any *point de fuite* from the gridlocked social space of Les Éditions Batala even remains when the camera frames an aperture leading from the courtyard to mainstream society: an archway breaches the apparent insulation provided by the wall, permitting the constant ebb and flow of people, values, and ideas to and from the courtyard. After Batala finds a letter from a creditor and angrily expels Lange from the office, Lange recounts the incident to two fellow employees whilst the window behind them frames the archway in deep space. On another occasion, Valentine plays with a dog in front of the archway. The camera subsequently pans to the left, revealing that Valentine is being watched by Lange from an upstairs window of the publishing house. The camera pans further left until we are granted a clear view of the door to Batala's office, located in the background, thus contrasting the liberty of the courtyard and its connection with mainstream society with the stultifying capacity of Batala's workplace. Later, as Lange speaks to Valentine in the courtyard, they are both pitted against the archway whilst people walk through it, to and from the courtyard. On all of these occasions, the oppression of the workplace is contrasted with the potential opportunities existing beyond the courtyard. Because the employees of the *blanchisserie* and the publishing house lack any cohesive political agenda, they are incapable of creating a revolutionary social project, and no future can be guaranteed, let alone plotted.

Each of the above cases, be it set in the courtyard, Lange's room, or the publishing house, lends credence to Christopher Faulkner's assertion that 'there may be an argument for saying that Renoir's moving camera and shooting in depth have the effect of leaving the visual field continually open to the play of difference'.[53] Crucially, however, the camera's framing of the social and physical space of Les Éditions Batala underscores the absence of a collective project that could liberate any of the characters from the stultifying inadequacies of their professional lives. Whereas Massey emphasises 'the necessity for the political' in any attempt to harness 'a space of loose ends and missing links', Batala's exploitative brand of capitalism striates the space within the publishing house.[54] Although the circulation of people between the courtyard and the city through the archway presents the courtyard as a socially open milieu that accommodates new configurations, the lack of any rhizomatic *ligne de hanche* that could carry characters through the spatio-temporal *point de fuite* renders such a prospect opaque.

Arizona Jim vs Cagoulard *as doomed* ligne de fuite

The framing of the courtyard and the archway repeatedly signals the cooperative's inability to comprehensively implement its socialist project. Moreover, Renoir's *mise en scène* demonstrates that the cooperative is leaving itself open to assault from external social forces. Before proceeding to this analysis, it is worth noting that scholars other than Deleuze have interpreted Renoir's *mise en scène* as a positive conception of socialist projects. O'Shaughnessy's Deleuzian analysis of the historical moment in *Lange* particularly lauds the removal of the billboard from Charles's (the concierge's son, played by Maurice Baquet) room. The camera first frames the advertising panel placed over the window of Charles's room. After Lange begins to remove the panel, the camera cranes upwards diagonally, revealing groups of workers leaning out of the first-floor windows of Les Éditions Batala, who all watch Lange. Tracking left, the camera reveals another group of workers looking out of a window. The camera cranes downwards, as Meunier *fils* prevents the concierge from interfering with Lange's efforts. More and more workers gather at the window. The camera switches to Charles's room, as we view the panel being removed by the workers, opening the physical space of the bedroom to the exterior courtyard. Discussing the political and temporal implications of this sequence, O'Shaughnessy insightfully writes that 'the frame itself is no longer immutable in either its physical or its symbolic dimensions but, becoming an object of dispute between the workers and their boss, it is opened up to collective intervention'.[55] Although O'Shaughnessy's analysis is convincing, he overestimates the import of this local landmark towards a genuinely new future within the narrative's overall context, primarily because he fails to remark that the significance of this historical moment is limited to the space of the courtyard, and consequently neglects the forces ranged against the budding cooperative during Batala's absence.

Much like Deleuze's easy acceptance of Renoir's apparent confidence in the Front populaire, O'Shaughnessy's optimism regarding the creation of a genuinely new society is understandable. The archway, of little political import earlier in the narrative, acquires a completely new social significance following the apparent death of Batala and the arrival of Meunier *fils*. Following the decision of the employees to consolidate a cooperative, Meunier *fils* shakes hands with one of Batala's ex-employees at the window of the publishing house (Figure 3.1). The window behind them frames the archway located in the background, as well as the space enclosed by the courtyard walls. The camera does not frame merely the archway and an employee, as in many of the previous cases, but the establishment of a new relationship between a capitalist investor, a member of the cooperative, and the off-screen space evoked by the archway, foreshadowing the agreement between Sam Tucker and Ruston in *The Southerner* (1945). The manifest amenability of the smooth space beyond the window to the cooperative's venture renders the potential creation of a new future limpid. In short, the camera frames the possibility of a *ligne de fuite*.

Figure 3.1 Meunier *fils* (left) backs the cooperative

The *élan vers l'avenir* articulated by this scene is challenged later within the narrative. Having consolidated the cooperative and discarded the embodied memories of Batala's regime, the workers are in a position to produce the *Arizona Jim* comics conceived by Lange in the privacy of his bedroom. Reflecting the ongoing circulation of ideas from the space beyond the courtyard to the interior space of the courtyard, within which the comic-covers are shot, a cover announcing 'Coming Soon: Arizona Jim vs Cagoulard' ('Prochainement: Arizona Jim contre Cagoulard') appears on the screen. The corresponding cover, which the cooperative is later shooting, shows Arizona Jim standing victoriously above the titular black-hooded villain (Figure 3.2). This cover immediately signals the limits of the cooperative's impetus. 'Cagoule', the French word for hood from which 'Cagoulard' is derived, was the press name given to the Organisation secrète d'action révolutionnaire in recognition of the hoods its members allegedly wore during secret meetings.[56] Led by decorated bourgeois Great War veteran Eugène Deloncle,[57] la Cagoule emerged from l'Action Française, a reactionary organisation which suffered severe losses during the riots of 6 February 1934.[58] Catalysed by the rise of the Front populaire during 1935, the year in which Lange was filmed, la Cagoule made an attempt on the life of French Prime Minister Blum the following year.[59] The presence of la Cagoule is reminiscent of Renoir's own memories of his *séjour* in Berlin during Hitler's election as chancellor (30 January 1933), where he was shocked that

> this old Berlin was a peaceful city with good bourgeois people who were smoking their pipes and discussing the elections as one would have discussed normal elections

Figure 3.2 Photographing a forthcoming cover image for *Arizona Jim*

> [. . .] and then on the morning after the election, another part of the population – unless it was the same part – rose up destructively.[60]

The image of la Cagoule, exploited by the cooperative for its financial viability within the pages of *Arizona Jim*, is darkly indicative of the very real social threat posed by fascist movements beyond the insulated enthusiasm of the cooperative and testifies to Dudley Andrew and Steven Ungar's vision of contemporary France as 'an internally riven nation'.[61]

Crucially, at the peak of the cooperative's success, a wooden door is shut across the archway for the first time. In fact, none of the workers is even seen outside the courtyard following the consolidation of the cooperative with the notable exceptions of Charles, who exultantly delivers *Arizona Jim* to the kiosks, and Meunier *fils*, before he announces his news of the *Arizona Jim* film. Despite the active collaboration of the cooperative, Renoir's framing of the closed archway obscures the likelihood of any change in mainstream society: the emphatic shallowness of the foreground enters into dialectic with the off-screen space beyond the archway, invoking a tension between the cooperative and the world that it exteriorises. O'Shaughnessy optimistically remarks on 'the positive transformation that the co-operative can bring about in a space from which conflict has been removed'.[62] However, the appropriation of la Cagoule within this insulated setting alarmingly implies that the decidedly myopic cooperative risks immanent subjugation to an unduly trivialised social menace which potentially impedes the growth of the cooperative, constituting what Deleuze and Guattari term 'micro-fascisms just waiting to crystallise'.[63]

The members of the cooperative superficially suspend the past, blinding themselves to potential threats to the space of the courtyard and whitewashing their projection of a new future. They also transform their world within the courtyard into a new Arizona: during Lange's final conversation with Batala, the map of Arizona that was once pinned in Lange's room now features in Batala's former office. Much like the billboard removed from Charles's window, the movement of the poster to Batala's former office suggests that the workers have redefined their past through their present successes, neglecting their original motivations and misinterpreting the requirements of the future. If the film holds the weight of the past and the potential creation of a genuinely new future in tension, it does so by pitting the determination of the cooperative against the public beyond the courtyard. Although *Arizona Jim* has amassed major income for the cooperative, the domestic Fascist movements operating at a local level threaten the existence of the cooperative's hopes and dreams long before the extrusion of Valentine and Lange.

Although Deleuze does not discuss *Lange*, the film justifies his emphasis on the stultifying influence of the 'dead roles or roles of death' available within Renoir's theatres:[64] this scene portrays the courtyard as a theatrical space within which the new roles acquired ensure entrapment rather than the liberty that the community of workers aims to secure. As in La Colinière, the *ligne de hanche* has ceased marching and solidified as a centralised socio-economic structure that remains open to contestation by 'organisations that re-stratify everything'.[65] Such is the cooperative's effort to preserve the spatio-temporal 'closure and stasis' spurned by Massey that their world, although devoid of the opulent surroundings that characterise Visconti's films, constitutes a synthetic realm of the kind recognised by Deleuze in Visconti's work.[66] Despite the apparent promise embodied by the cooperative's collective venture, its prospects remain subject to the incohesion of its own members (note the problematic inclusion of the reluctant concierge) and the force of history from the outset. Indeed, much like the *haute bourgeoisie* of *La Règle du jeu*, their inability to either subjugate the inherent openness of space-time or to synchronise with the broader spatial politics of Paris dooms them to extinction.

Suspending the past, obscuring the future

The futility of implementing a new future on a limited, geographically circumscribed local level is underscored by the eventual return of Batala, who withdraws a gun from his former desk, only further emphasising the superficiality of the cooperative's attempted expunction of the past. The ensuing murder sequence simultaneously marks the definitive fracture not only between Lange and the cooperative but also between Lange and the Parisian public. The staging of the murder sequence begins with an exterior shot of Lange holding Batala's pistol in the latter's former office and culminates in a 270° pan that sweeps laterally across the circumference of the courtyard. Two interpretations of the pan are particularly significant within the context of this study.[67] A sceptical Colin Davis remarks on 'the striking [. . .] absence of the community that is supposedly encompassed by [the pan]'.[68] Central to Davis's interrogation is 'the contrast between the *visual* absence of the community and its *audible* presence' which, for Davis, suggests 'Lange's solitude, his position outside the community, and the foundation of the murder in desire and rivalry rather than political commitment'.[69] O'Shaughnessy specifically argues that Davis 'is wrong [. . .] in suggesting that there is an implicit separation of Lange from the rest of the co-operative'.[70] Interpreting Lange's escape from the 'totalizing circling gaze' of the camera as a 'step into the uncharted space of the authentic political act', O'Shaughnessy purports that 'the sound [of laughter] surely serves to remind us of exactly in the interests of whom or what Lange is acting'.[71] Although Davis's argument is more convincing than that of O'Shaughnessy within the context of this analysis, neither sufficiently addresses the breadth of physical space incorporated by the bravura camera movement, and each fails to interpret the pan in relation to the *mise en scène* of the courtyard in earlier narrative sequences, or to the space that becomes the subject of the camera's fleeting gaze.

Through the formally radical camera movement, space is foregrounded in its capacity as a 'precondition for the temporal', an aspect effaced by Deleuze's depoliticisation of the pan and by Bazin's famous map of the camera's movement, in which, like any map in Massey's analysis, 'space is completely and instantaneously interconnected', and the 'loose ends and ongoing stories' are ignored.[72] The pan is primarily preoccupied not only with the absent cooperative but also with the very vacancy of the physical space between Lange and his co-workers and beyond the courtyard. The detachment of the camera acknowledges the possibility of hitherto invisible trajectories interfering with Lange's solitary course of action within a manifestly open space, but neither the public nor the cooperative is present in Lange's hour of need. Unlike the fluid shots that elsewhere track the fleeting entrances and exits of other characters within the world of the courtyard, the view beyond the archway is now uninhibited by passing bodies. Readers of the *Arizona Jim* comics, through their absence, are portrayed as avid consumers whose purchases ensure the financial growth of the cooperative, but who do not personally contribute to the expansion of the cooperative's network in any notable way. In fact, the financial success reaped by the comics renders the cooperative even more oblivious to the threats potentially admitted by the impartial archway than during the photo shoot of the *Arizona Jim* comic-covers, and their laughter during Lange's off-screen approach to Batala articulates their blindness to both Lange's plight and the limits of their own collaborative project. Whether or not we agree with O'Shaughnessy's assertion that Lange is reminded of the cooperative as he commits murder, the fact remains that neither Lange's comrades nor the Parisian public are present to assist Lange during the cooperative's darkest hour. As Reader's lucid consideration of the contradictions inherent to the cooperative's socio-political identity suggests, the pan 'operates less as the agent of [harmonious] closure than as a "holding together" that incorporates antagonism and splitting itself into rather than seeking to deny or transcend them'.[73]

If the pan is, as Bazin proposes, 'the pure spatial expression of the entire *mise en scène*', it is because it further dismantles the pre-existing perceptions of any reassuringly fixed spatial coordinates projected by the spectator and the cooperative, revealing a malleable space that is, as Massey writes of public spaces, 'riven with antagonism, always contoured through the playing out of unequal social relations'.[74] Given the inherent political fissures within the alleged cooperative which are constantly evoked by the narrative, the pan hardly represents a sudden, radical shattering of the cooperative but the final statement on its inevitable dissolution.

By the end of the film, Lange and Valentine have been forced into exile whilst the fate of the cooperative remains uncertain. The shot of the beach, notes Tom Conley, represents 'an indistinct border between air and land or "molar" and "molecular" states of being'.[75] Although Conley is referring to this distinction as it appears in Deleuze's differentiation between the liquid and solid masses that contrast with one another in the classic French cinema,[76] it would be even more suitably read through Deleuze and Guattari's spatially informed interpretation of these terms: the cooperative's temporary success holds no currency as they venture towards an uncertain future, unsure of their ability to navigate the social structures of the as-of-yet invisible world beyond the border. If, as Faulkner writes, '*Le Crime de Monsieur Lange* is not a mirror held up to life [. . .]; it is a mirror held up to a measure of desire circa 1936', it is also, in hindsight, a starkly realistic moral lesson on the self-destructive blindness that provisionally ensured the survival of the Left's delusive hopes.[77]

Les Bas-fonds (1936)

Many elements of set design featuring in *Lange*, such as the courtyard and multi-storey building, are explored by Renoir's camera to lend renewed social resonance to Gorki's source-text play, *Na Nde/The Lower Depths* (1902). Unlike Gorki's drama, which focuses exclusively on the marginal existence of tenants in the titular shelter, the first third of Renoir's film portrays a heavily indebted baron's (Louis Jouvet) fall from grace and his chance encounter with Pépel (Jean Gabin), a thief who attempts to rob the bankrupt baron's home only to find it holds nothing worth stealing. Over the course of the film, the baron readily sheds his prestige and joins the dosshouse in which Pépel and various other lost causes live. The shelter itself is run by the exploitative Kostylev (Vladimir Sokoloff). Pépel is conducting an affair with Kostylev's wife, Vassilissa (Suzy Prim), but loves her younger sister Natacha (Junie Astor). When Kostylev and Vassilissa try to blackmail a policeman by granting him Natacha, Pépel and the other tenants kill Kostylev. Pépel serves a spell in prison and, at the film's close, walks away into the country with Natacha. Beyond these events, much of the film narrates Pépel's first encounter with the baron, and its marginal tenants' daily suffering at the hands of Kostylev. As we shall see, the *mise en scène* of space-time in *Les Bas-fonds* would only seem to confirm Renoir's reservations regarding the hopes and dreams ignited by the rise of the Front populaire.

Framing the archway as social point de fuite

Les Bas-fonds borrows two key elements of set design from *Lange*, specifically a courtyard and a rigorously hierarchised building overlooking it, which together hold the joint possibilities of social imprisonment and escape in tension. Although *Les Bas-fonds* does not feature within Deleuze's corpus in either *Cinéma* volume, his concept provides a useful method of mapping the relationship of Renoir's characters to the topography of the *bas-fonds* and mainstream society beyond.

The stultifying import of striated space on the creation of a new future is centrally articulated through Kostylev's shelter, which, much like Les Éditions Batala, is located within a courtyard incorporating an archway that leads to mainstream society. Kostylev's *petit bourgeois* protocol impedes any social or economic liberty desired by the lower class. Durgnat relates Kostylev to the archetype of the Russian 'ghetto Jew' who has succeeded through swindling others and dreams of prosperity and solid bourgeois connections that will preserve him from persecution.[78] The interior décor of Kostylev's quarters, tellingly based in the upper floor of the building and adorned with numerous items stolen on his behalf by Pépel, illustrates his upwardly pretensions as a member of the deserving rich. Kostylev's financially prohibitive regime entraps characters within the shelter, and he reminds Pépel, 'You forget that I am the boss here and that you owe me respect.'[79]

Beneath Kostylev's quarters are the titular *bas-fonds*, which are essentially composed of a cellar divided by ramshackle walls and curtains, and are inhabited by a range of vagrants, only some of whose names and pasts are ever revealed. What is most alarming about this film, within the context of Renoir's unofficial affiliation with the Front populaire, is that the abused residents of the shelter, far from collaborating on any social project, have no desire to plot a new future for themselves, either as individuals or as a group. Of all the tenants, three – Anna (Nathalie Alexeeff), an anonymous actor (Robert le Vigan), and Nastia (Jany Holt) – are characterised in depth: Anna, a woman dying of an undisclosed ailment (possibly the loss of the will to live), remains in her bed and finds solace in the possibility of a blissful afterlife; an alcoholic actor dwells on the fabricated glories of his past and dreams of a utopic sanatorium instead of opening his eyes to a reality in which such far-fetched wishes will never materialise. Whereas Gorki's actor quotes Shakespeare in front of the other tenants,[80] Renoir's actor refuses to demonstrate his ability to recite such monologues until he has finally exited the shelter to hang himself. Nastia condenses her quarters with decorative patterns and pollutes her memories with her book, *L'Amour fatale*. All perform their lethargy, pessimism, and individual pasts, testifying to Braudy's assertion that 'the life of the tenement is basically self-involved theatre'.[81] Whereas the community of Lange – however internally fragmented and synthetically insulated – collaborate on the production of *Arizona Jim* comics, these tenants are utterly directionless and demonstrate no interest in collaborating on any collective project. Potential collaboration with the upper classes is not possible. The only member of the upper classes who joins is the baron himself, and he is entirely penniless, with nothing to love, no confidence in the class to which he now subscribes, and nothing to invest in it, financially or morally.

Sesonske criticises Renoir's apparently unambitious framing of characters:

> the scenes in the asile feel essentially static; the flow of the film seems to stop here [. . .] and though the camera does move, it seems both less fluid and less resolute in its movements. As no action occurs in these scenes but merely aimless talk and pointless motion, so the camera too seems to have lost purpose.[82]

This is precisely the point of Renoir's narrative, for these characters embody 'the *danse macabre* of memories' from which any *point de fuite* is decidedly obscured.[83] The camera subjectivises the tenants' experience of their ability to blind themselves to an ongoing present as it unfolds within the world beyond the courtyard and their downright refusal to actualise a new future, liberated of oppressive social circumstances: on the one hand, the potential liberation of the tenants from their current circumstances is made manifest by the mainstream society that is barely visible beyond the archway in the exterior shots of the courtyard, and through the visible existence of other social settings beyond the courtyard. On the other hand, none of the characters demonstrates any intention of transgressing this *ouverture d'avenir* leading beyond the shelter. In fact, the majority of the tenants languish within the confines of the *bas-fonds*, where this very potential for departure remains opaque.

Crucially, whereas the entirety of Gorki's play is set within the dosshouse, Renoir juxtaposes shots unfolding within the lower depths of the shelter with the space of the courtyard and with various other settings such as the aristocratic home formerly occupied by the baron, and the banks of the Marne visited by the baron and Pépel. (Indeed, Sesonske notes that whereas Gorki's source text is set entirely within the shelter, less than a quarter of Renoir's film's 236 shots occur in locales that we actually see in the play.[84]) By balancing the spectator's exposure to the *bas-fonds* with various other *ailleurs*, the narrative grants the spectator a greater view of the various socialised spaces existing beyond the insulated shelter, thus allowing the spectator to critically interrogate the tenants' insulation within their squalid world. This serves as an insightful reminder that the embodied past is not exclusively engendered through upper-class *règles* and that the lowest strata of French society are as susceptible to *rôles morts* as the outmoded uppermost echelons of society whose inevitable extinction, as Deleuze observes, is foreshadowed in *La Grande Illusion* and *La Règle du jeu*.

The courtyard constitutes the film's nerve centre of the ongoing tension between the subsistence of the embodied past and the potential creation of a new future. Prior to the consolidation of the cooperative in *Lange*, the courtyard is framed in way that 'displays the very lack of a cohesive political agenda that could implement a new future', eventually proceeding towards a vision of the workers collaborating on the collective production of *Arizona Jim*.[85] Conversely, the rare scenes in which the tenants enter the space of the courtyard simultaneously emphasise the possibility of circulating in modern society and the lack of any cohesive project that could elucidate and exploit potential prospects beyond the archway. With the exception of the unpremeditated murder of Kostylev, the courtyard never provides the communal meeting point that we see after the consolidation of the cooperative in *Lange*. Rather, it provides a locus for uneventful meetings between the characters who dwell in Kostylev's shelter and in the other buildings surrounding the courtyard: in the beginning of the film, Nastia lingers inside the arch, watching Pépel as he exits to the street; on another occasion, a small number of the tenants including the baron, Nastia, and Louka among others sit in the courtyard outside the shelter, their utter directionlessness hinted by the broken-down, horseless carriage in which Nastia and the baron sit (Figure 3.3). Rather than portraying an *ouverture d'avenir*, these shots depict perpetual idleness. As Sesonske notes, 'none of these characters can conceive of their lives as really different'.[86]

Three different pairs of characters are pitted against the archway to signal its value as a potential *point de fuite*, as well as the necessity of what

Figure 3.3 Nastia (centre) defends her fabricated past against an incredulous baron (left), Louka (right), and former telegraph employee (below)

Massey terms 'stabilising projects', one of which could establish a *ligne de fuite* from the dilapidated *bas-fonds*: Pépel and Natacha, Vassilissa and Pépel, and Natacha and the policeman. Early in the film, as Vassilissa warns Pépel against crossing her, the archway features in the background, behind the door to the balcony. The same motif re-emerges later in the film as the oppressed Natacha is courted by a commissaire to whom Vassilissa and Kostylev have proffered Natacha in order to prevent him from holding them liable for their unsuitable living conditions. Upward mobility is contingent on sexual bargaining in each of these cases.

The deep staging of Pépel and Natacha in relation to the boarding house and the broader space of the courtyard visually recalls each these two moments, yet the distribution of elements within the frame differs noticeably. As Pépel tries to convince Natacha to leave with him, the camera captures them sitting on the stairs that lead to Kostylev and Vassilissa's quarters, facing the shelter entrance that looks directly on to the deeply staged archway (Figure 3.4). During this scene, Pépel tries to convince Natacha that their lives may turn out differently, stating that 'Drunkards are not always drunk, and thieves are not always in prison' and suggesting that she leave with him, thus proposing the only realistic project amongst the tenants.[87] The staging of Pépel and Natacha in relation to the archway suggests that a joint escape by Pépel and Natacha is a possibility. Crucially, Pépel advocates an understanding of how they might change their circumstances rather than merely projecting lofty dreams. Such a perspective is justified by Pépel's room in the *bas-fonds*, which testifies to

Figure 3.4 Natacha (left) and Pépel (right) consider their respective futures

his downright refusal to lie to himself or to patiently listen to the lies of others: Pépel personalises his space through meaningful objects including the statuette of the horses, given to him *gratis* by the baron, which serves as a reminder to him of his own 'occupation' of thief through the very fact that it was originally awarded to the baron for his equestrian feats. As Sesonske observes, Pépel's space-time is 'merely overlapping that of the derelicts who sleep or smoke or just lay open-eyed'.[88]

Interestingly, the three scenes outlined above frame the characters concerned in relation to the archway but relegate the other tenants of the *bas-fonds* to off-screen space. As a result, the visual composition of each implies that the characters endeavouring to escape cannot do so in collaboration with the other indolent tenants who collectively squander their futures in the shelter without interrogating the validity of Kostylev's authority, justifying O'Shaughnessy's description of the tenants as 'social flotsam and jetsam with no shared labour to weld them together' and antagonising any attempt to view the community as a unified whole.[89]

Collectivising Kostylev's murder: provisional solidarity

As already mentioned, a number of scholars align the film with the dominant themes of Renoir's Front populaire output and the idealistic aspects of the coalition's agenda. The extent to which Kostylev's murder is framed as a revolutionary political event is debatable. The shots that follow Kostylev and Vassilissa's vicious physical assault of Natacha after her rejection of the policeman recall the social criticism embedded in the *mise en scène* of Batala's death in *Le Crime de Monsieur Lange* both formally and politically. The staging of the murder sequence in *Lange* begins with an exterior shot of Lange holding a pistol in Batala's former office. From the courtyard, the camera tracks Lange's descent from the office to the courtyard and, as Lange walks towards Batala, the camera pans laterally across the circumference of the courtyard, framing the shooting of Batala in the final moments of a 270° pan. Throughout the camera's sweeping motion, the celebrations and laughter of Lange's absent co-workers remain audible.

Whereas the pan in *Lange* emphasises the disintegration of the provisional relationship between Lange and the other members of the cooperative, the camera in this scene from *Les Bas-fonds* frames a nascent collective project budding amongst the numerous residents and passers-by in the courtyard. The camera begins with a medium shot of the closed window of Kostylev's quarters through which Natacha's screams can be heard. The camera gradually tracks backwards and pans downwards to the courtyard where Louka is now visible, looking up at the window which is now off-screen. The camera pans to the right, and we see a group of four children standing still, looking in the direction of the window. The camera pans further right and pauses to frame a man standing at the door of a house within the courtyard. Two women standing beneath a washing line also watch and a man opens a window above the archway to listen, also looking towards the window. Within the same shot, the resident accordion player and the baron walk through the archway, singing and playing music until they pause, shocked to hear the screams emerging from behind the closed window. Louka runs towards them and tells them that it is Natacha who is screaming. For the first time in the narrative, the camera has framed the entrance of socially disparate characters to a communal space. In this instant, all of the characters are joined in their preoccupation with the event taking place behind the closed window. The shared response to Natacha's screams during the pan marks the awakening of a collective spirit amongst the residents around the courtyard, most of whom we have not even seen before.

Still, the impetus germinating within the courtyard does not permeate the entire complex. When the baron alerts Pépel to the violence ensuing in Kostylev's quarters, Pépel immediately runs out from his quarters to Kostylev's floor. As Pépel ascends the stairs, the accordion player who earlier listened to Natacha's cries in the courtyard now sits on the stairs, still listening, with a blend of curiosity and helplessness. Three other tenants stand at the foot of the stairs, roused but ineffectual, unwilling to come to Natacha's aid.

The cohesion of the tenants is further challenged in three shots that follow Kostylev's descent from his quarters and depict the collective revolt resulting in his murder as a senseless albeit subversive act, devoid of any clear political strategy. When Kostylev exits, the doorway leading to the courtyard frames him exiting towards the bystanders who were earlier dispersed across the courtyard. As they drag Kostylev away, Pépel runs into the courtyard, followed by a number of other tenants. During this shot, our view of the uprising is obscured by the narrowness of the door frame and the mobile bodies exiting through it. The course of action becomes progressively unclear once again in the next shot as the camera pans from a close shot of Kostylev, roaring and at the mercy of the mob, to a close shot of Pépel, who is being restrained from violence by the tenants. In each of these two shots, the camera vainly endeavours to obtain clusters of information regarding the action at hand. In the subsequent shot, it follows the baron as he struggles through the vengeful mob towards an anvil on which Kostylev's head has fallen. The camera pauses at the anvil as the baron walks off-screen and tilts upwards to reveal Pépel gazing down towards the defunct landlord. Throughout, the frame provides an inadequate window on the mass of disorganised, impulsively scurrying bodies with no centralised thrust or collectively coordinated points of articulation. The *mise en scène* of this sequence provides a revealing contrast with the physical and social negotiation of the parameters of the frame during the cooperative's removal of the billboard in *Lange*, where the cooperative acts systematically in perfect unison, cheered on by their peers. Although the courtyard in *Les Bas-fonds* provides a locus for a shared project, the abused tenants are bound only by a shared manifestation of combustible hatred.

Although the mob attempts to collectivise responsibility for Kostylev's death, suggesting the potential birth of a new social project within the shelter, their efforts pass unrewarded. The baron authoritatively declares, 'we are all as much to blame as Pépel'.[90] The shoe-mender admits, 'I also dealt blows', and Louka astutely declares, 'it is the lower depths that killed him, but not Pépel any more than anyone else'.[91] However, the police listen only to Vassilissa's vindictive assertion that Pépel is responsible and arrest him without even noting the comments of the latter's co-tenants, demonstrating the futility of lower-class collective negotiation with social structures responsible for upholding justice.

'The singing ends tonight . . .': pursuing the ligne de fuite

In an ending that does not feature in Gorki's original play, we witness a newly freed Pépel and Natacha walking towards the screen and into their new world, evoking the final scenes of René Clair's *À nous la liberté* (1931) and Chaplin's *Modern Times* (1936).[92] As Natacha and Pépel walk towards the screen, a passage through a *point de fuite* is framed for the first time in the narrative as the camera tracks backwards in an extended take, implying that their every step is one into the unknown.

Conversely, the tenants' potential actualisation of a new future is, disappointingly, no more apparent in the scenes that follow Kostylev's death than in those that precede it, even though Vassilissa has departed and Louka is now absent (and possibly dead). As in our introduction to the *bas-fonds*, the individual characters persist in their standard daily behaviour, loitering aimlessly in the shelter, and no shots frame the insular interiors of the shelter in relation to the space of the courtyard. The accordion player is even singing 'Every day is a carnival' ('C'est toujours le carnaval'). Faulkner rightly lambasts the lack of a revolutionary project at the heart of the film, and the tenants' attitudes following Kostylev's death prevent me from fully conceding to Andrew's opinion that the landlord's death must be taken as a reprise of Lange's assassination of Batala.[93]

It is not until the actor's suicide that the tenants collectively exhibit any semblance of initiative, as the baron announces: 'Come here, it's serious. The actor has hanged himself. The singing ends tonight.'[94] Nastia and the baron's glimpse of this brutal eruption of the all-too-real consequences of living in the shelter forces them to confront their peers with their own distorted perception of space, time, and humanity. The baron's position on the staircase, halfway between the courtyard and the lower depths, suggests a call to integrate into broader society. However, whether or not it is too late for the characters to effect a successful integration into the society from which they have been estranged for so long is a question to which the film offers no answer: rather than framing the tenants in relation to the courtyard or archway, the camera dwells on a close-up of the baron's distraught features and the uncertain future that they still face. In the play, on the other hand, Satine (who does not feature in the film) simply complains that the actor has spoilt their song, and the play ends without the sensitive reaction elicited by Renoir's baron.[95]

Echoing Deleuze's interpretation of Renoir's Front populaire output, the majority of scholars agree that the film aligns with the positively Frontist perspectives expressed by Renoir's other politically engaged films of the period addressed by this chapter: O'Shaughnessy locates the film within its Frontist context through the manner in which it 'refuses fatalism, unmasks a corrupt order, and shows the oppressed move from passivity to revolt'; Andrew notes that although *Les Bas-fonds* 'carries contradictory, perhaps incoherent social ideals, [. . .] it is true to a good many Popular Front themes', and Bowles notes that the film 'sharply delineat[es] class divisions and dramatiz[es] their purge through friendship, mutual respect, and shared interest'.[96] Considering the working-class protagonist, the death of the exploitative Kostylev, and the collective will expressed in the latter's murder, Bowles even remarks that the film 'recycles several key motifs from *Le Crime de Monsieur Lange* in a less morally ambiguous, more optimistic and commercial register'.[97]

Contesting such views, Sesonske more convincingly reads the mixture of hope and despair in the film as a reflection of the last stages of the remains of the euphoric moment that followed the victory of the Front populaire and the grim political reality of 1937 that confronted France. The reading offered by the present analysis clearly concurs with Sesonske's view: the portrayal of the tenants as a group who, with a small number of exceptions, must await catastrophes before considering the necessity of change, only further entrenches the film within the inconvenient truths of its contemporary context. Even the few hopes offered in the film amount to little more than personal desires for independence and social mobility which were soon to be drowned out within a country that could soon devote little attention to the cares of such wishful individuals. Despite the enthusiastic responses of Renoir's left-wing critics to *Les Bas-fonds*, it was becoming increasingly clear during the months following the release of *Le Crime de Monsieur Lange* that the French could no longer insulate themselves within the solitary, idealistic pacifism of the French Left, or confidently bank on optimistic promises regarding Europe's future.

La Grande Illusion (1937)

La Grande Illusion, partly based on Renoir's own experience of the First World War, recounts the capture of Maréchal (Jean Gabin) and Boëldieu (Pierre Fresnay) – working-class mechanic-turned-pilot and aristocratic career officer respectively – by German aviator Captain von Rauffenstein (Erich von Stroheim), also of aristocratic birth. The French soldiers are sent to Hallbach prison camp where they meet other prisoners of various class rankings and ethnic origins, among them the Jewish Rosenthal (Marcel Dalio), and together plot to escape from Hallbach. Many futile attempts later, they are sent to Wintersborn, where von Rauffenstein is now serving as commandant. Boëldieu sacrifices himself to allow Maréchal and Rosenthal to escape. The two escapees remain at the home of Elsa (Dita Parlo), a German war widow, for an extended period of time before eventually leaving, narrowly avoiding German troops as they cross the Swiss border.

Three striated spaces

La Grande Illusion was filmed as the hopes promised by the Front populaire were rapidly waning and serves as a response to contemporary political tensions that laid a foundation for the Second World War. As such, the present analysis does not specifically aim to demonstrate that the film exudes a clairvoyant pessimism regarding the French Left or the future of France in general. Rather, it builds on Stanley Cavell's description of *La Grande Illusion* as 'a film obsessed with the entering and leaving of rooms, with the relations between the inside and the outside of a dwelling, with the impassability of sills and frames'.[98] More specifically, this analysis proposes that Renoir frames the alarming influence of social hierarchies on the radical restriction of entire populations in ways that significantly deviate from his previous deployment of his signature techniques, particularly deep staging and framing devices such as doors and windows, problematising Deleuze's assumption that 'depth makes it clear that the crystal is there so that something can escape from it, in the background, through the background'.[99]

La Grande Illusion is particularly worthy of analysis within the context of open space-time as the film provides Deleuze with two key examples of his proposals regarding Renoir's *mise en scène* of temporality: firstly, Deleuze draws on Wintersborn, the last prison camp featured in the film, to illustrate the presence of buildings that lend the embodied past physical form; secondly, discussing heroic characters in *La Grande Illusion*, Deleuze indicates how affective bodies may embody competing temporal rhythms within and across individual shots. Deleuze specifically compares Boëldieu and von Rauffenstein who, by defiantly adhering to their aristocratic etiquette, are 'already doomed to become memories', with the liberating capacity embodied by Maréchal and Rosenthal, 'the two escapees [who] will be saved by the sacrifice of the other one [Boëldieu]'.[100] The present analysis extends the relevance of Deleuze's ideas to three key settings that express the tensions between freedom and imprisonment in order to demonstrate that the influence of spatial politics on the production of a new future is as much the subject of *La Grande Illusion* as *Les Bas-fonds*.

Hallbach: subordination and solidarity

During a reconnaissance mission, Boëldieu and Maréchal's plane is shot down by von Rauffenstein. The two Frenchmen are briefly granted the privilege of eating with the German soldiers before being summoned to

Hallbach, the first of the three settings in question, where they meet a range of prisoners of various social backgrounds including a music-hall entertainer from Paris (Cartier, played by Julien Carette), a schoolteacher (Jean Dasté), an engineer (Gaston Modot), and Rosenthal (Dalio), a French citizen of Jewish descent whose family has absorbed the fixed assets that Boëldieu's elite class has failed to retain over the course of time. The tension between the stultifying force of German regulations and the future projected by the French would-be escapees is expressed through spatial tensions between the prison setting and the off-screen space beyond. The entrapment implied by the physical architecture of the prison actively draws on the visual absence of natural surroundings. Our only glimpse of the proximity of the natural landscape to Hallbach occurs as a horse-drawn cart is brought through the prison entrance (Figure 3.5). The relatively shallow image of the gate contrasts with what it reveals once opened: a deep shot of a field that stretches far to the distant background, interrupted only by a border of trees. The deep staging of four civilians looking past the gate in the foreground and two labourers collecting crops in the background emphasises the visual depth of the image, a device previously employed during the farmland tour in *Le Bled* (1929).

As in *Boudu sauvé des eaux* (1932), montage is not merely assimilated within a classical narrative style but, rather, is employed to mark an emphatic social barrier between two points in space. Most interestingly, the editing of this shot in *La Grande Illusion* precludes the prospect of even viewing the field from the building occupied by the imprisoned

Figure 3.5 Staging the natural surroundings beyond the prison in depth

soldiers. A cut from civilians standing at a gateway to the German soldiers training within the camp and a subsequent cut from these German soldiers to the quarters occupied by the French prisoners only further emphasise each army's physical distance from the fields beyond the gate. In fact, the natural landscape remains an imagined image for the prisoners during their entire stay at Hallbach. Outdoor shots within the camp repeatedly emphasise the domineering buildings that circumscribe the soldiers' views of the surroundings: when Arthur dictates the rules of the camp to the newly arrived soldiers; as the French soldiers dump the earth removed whilst digging their tunnel; and later, within Maréchal and Rosenthal's prison cell, when Arthur reiterates that non-military outfits cannot be worn. On the two occasions where the elusive landscape is evoked by individual characters during the prisoners' stay at the camp, it is relegated to off-screen space: in the first case, the engineer informs Maréchal that the prisoners are building a tunnel, and that 'we aim to end up in a garden, behind the buildings that you can see over there. It's right in the open country.'[101] The framing of their conversation – beginning with close-ups of each man and proceeding to a close shot of the two men – only further emphasises their distance from the off-screen garden. The second example occurs as the prisoners send a cellmate on a false expedition to a latrine to investigate suspicious sounds outside their quarters. Once outside, he is informed by Arthur that the German soldiers caught a would-be escapee in the very outdoor area to which the prisoners' tunnel is due ultimately to lead. Arthur gestures towards an off-screen space that lies beyond the camera, stating, 'we caught him in the gardens behind the buildings and opened fire on him'.[102] As in the case of the world beyond the photo shoot during *Lange* and the society existing beyond Kostylev's *bas-fonds*, the space lying outside the prison remains an imagined concept for the imprisoned parties. Whereas a physical aperture is available to those characters who choose to use it in each of these prior productions, none is present to the characters of *La Grande Illusion*. In fact, following the death of the soldier recounted by Arthur, it becomes clear that their escape tunnel is beset by menaces that potentially preclude the soldiers' place within their imagined future.

What is most interesting about *La Grande Illusion* within the context of this chapter is that the very techniques Renoir previously exploited to explore the tension between the embodied past and the potential creation of a new future in *Le Crime de Monsieur Lange* and *Les Bas-fonds* are used here to emphasise the prisoners' lack of agency and the futility of attempting to actualise or even envision a new future. More specifically, whereas Renoir's deeply staged compositions in *Lange* and *Les Bas-fonds* signal the potential integration of individuals and groups into new social configurations, deep staging is deployed in *La Grande Illusion* to convey the possibility for constant surveillance. The very scenes at Hallbach where the characters converse with one another frequently exploit deep staging to play on the tension between the prisoners' suspension of concern for their present situation and the constant surveillance effected by the prison guards. Before the prisoners first sit down together to indulge in the parcel of food that has been posted to Rosenthal, the stationary camera frames the characters seated around the table. As they speak, a guard discreetly walks through the door located in the background, glances around the room towards the foreground and, satisfied with the proceedings, leaves and shuts the door. This understated action unfolds over the course of approximately eight seconds and risks passing unnoticed by the spectator or even by the prisoners themselves. The impossibility of creating a new future is further emphasised in the subsequent shot, also staged in depth, taken from the opposite side of the prisoners' table. As the soldiers eat, talking about their choice of food, the window behind them frames the German guards on patrol in the yard. The looming threat of surveillance is later evoked in more comical terms when another guard, having already conducted a headcount of the soldiers in the cell, returns for an inspection as Cartier laments the hole in his trousers.

Deleuze's analysis understandably emphasises the agency of the prisoners and the potential future that they embody: the foreground of this deeply staged image creates new configurations established amongst characters of various ethnicities, classes, interests, and occupations within the cell and the theatre, demonstrating the extent to which the openness of space-time and the potential for social change are rooted within human interrelations. In the cell, the prisoners arrive at new understandings of each other, collapsing vertical barriers and threatening horizontal divisions through humour. One key example is Cartier, whose humour appeals to both French and German of all classes, as when he playfully mocks Boëldieu by donning the latter's monocle at the French prisoners' dinner table and, later, when he sings for the German army and multinational group of prisoners.

However, there is an ongoing tension between the foreground and background within the shots of the prisoners dining in their prison cell and singing in the theatre, and the background of these images occasionally contradicts the optimism of the foreground. Despite the shared goal that imprisonment instils in the various characters, these moments serve as clear reminders that German surveillance, if discreet and sometimes invisible, is ubiquitous both within and beyond the walls of the quarters,

Figure 3.6 Cartier entertains the prisoners of war at Hallbach

and almost entirely nullifies the prisoners' efforts to establish a *ligne de fuite* from the camp and its oppressive regulations.

The framing of this system of surveillance is reprised in the theatre. Whilst the camera faces Cartier and the other entertainers, we, as viewers of the film, engage with the spectacle as a distraction, much like the prisoners and German officers who form the mass of spectators. However, during the interlude between Cartier's numbers, the camera grants us a longitudinal view of the deep space of the theatre. Lurking distinctly in the background are two guards who remind us of the diegetic wartime context within which the escapist musical numbers are being performed (Figure 3.6). The reverse shot of the spectators reminds us of the social reality that exists beyond the world of the stage, and which awaits the prisoners when the deceptively liberating musical distraction has ended, implying that the proscenium arch is far more useful when dismantled and used to structure the French prisoners' escape tunnel. Moreover, whereas the tenants of the *bas-fonds* were metres away from the potential liberty offered by the archway, the creation of a genuinely new future remains an even more elusive prospect, to be decided on the distant battlefield.

The jailer jailed: Wilhelm II and imperial authority

The limits of the French soldiers' solidarity are accentuated by the narrative's multiple references to the hierarchical structure that entraps the German army's prison guards within a war that they have no personal reason to fight. Drawing on shots of the German soldiers following orders as they drill and a later shot of the stationary camera gazing through a wire fence that encloses the young soldiers being trained in an adjacent section of the camp, Nicholas Macdonald rightly surmises, 'Who exactly is prisoner and who jailer?'[103] Echoing the previously analysed shots, the narrative repeatedly reminds us of this mutual implication through the staging of the French and German soldiers in depth.

Military hierarchies within the German army are noticeable on a number of occasions. After the soldiers empty bags of earth outside, two German soldiers open the main gate to the camp to allow a horse-drawn cart to enter. The camera cuts to an elderly German woman who remarks, 'the poor boys' and, subsequently, to a close shot of some of the young German soldiers being drilled. The camera cuts once more to the interior of the French prisoners' room where a German soldier is conducting a headcount. It cuts yet again to Boëldieu and the view that the window grants him of the soldiers training outside. Boëldieu succinctly describes their mutual imprisonment: 'On one side, children play soldier. On the other, soldiers play like children.'[104] The camera cuts to a wide shot that incorporates each of the two physical spaces introduced in this narrative sequence, staging the outdoor drill and the prisoners' indoor exchanges in depth. As the camera pans from the engineer to Maréchal to Boëldieu to Rosenthal, the German soldiers beyond the window remain in view. The spectator clearly perceives the soldiers marching, squatting, and performing other drills at the behest of their officers across the breadth of the yard. The camera subsequently views the French soldiers through the window as they look out towards the yard that is now relegated to off-screen space, behind the camera. The haunting, rigorously disciplined sound of their march is not just a hint towards both the German First World War jailers and the contemporary rise of Nazism (as suggested by O'Shaughnessy[105]) but also a signifier of the unquestioning, rigorous uniformity enforced by any imperial will, be it incarnated by Wilhelm II or Hitler.

Rather than offer a reductive prisoner/imprisoner binary, the spaces juxtaposed by the through montage and the staging of characters either side of the window frame interact expressively to illustrate the oppressive structure of power that dominates both the prisoners and the German soldiers who remain its devoted instruments. The German soldiers in this scene are similarly entrapped as they answer to the officers who train them for war, and their officers in turn answer to the royal authority that forces these men to battle. Thus, the possibility for mutual understandings amongst the prisoners to effect change within the broader social context are hampered not by the visible German characters, but by the imperial authority that imprisons German soldiers within the national war machine and forces them to imprison others who could exploit the 'relations, fractures, discontinuities, practices of engagement' which, in Massey's analysis, open space to negotiation.[106]

Furthermore, the relationship between the spectator and the manifest striation of space in each of the three sequences analysed above invokes a triangular relay of looks between the French soldiers, the German sentries, and the camera's own gaze. This interplay metonymically underscores the conceptualisation of striated space that features within the film on both a thematic and formal level, and recalls Michel Foucault's theorisation of the relationship between surveillance and structures of power in a budding panoptical seventeenth-century society where 'the gaze is alert everywhere'.[107] Foucault asserts that the panoptical *dispositif* engendered through the architectural design of Jeremy Bentham's original model 'arranges spatial unities that make it possible to see constantly and to recognise immediately', making the objects of the gaze permanently aware that they are located within an intensively monitored social field.[108] Renoir's use of deep space and editing correspond with such an instrumentalisation of power within the camp and, most interestingly, with its apparent invisibility.

The validity of imperial authority is directly challenged in the German military station following Germany's first seizure of Douaument. In an extended mobile take, the camera travels left, incorporating the many soldiers who chant in unison. After panning by a map on the wall that hints at rigorous striation of German land on both a local and national level, the camera lingers momentarily on the German guitar player, piano player, and a singing soldier before tilting upwards to reveal the portraits of two figureheads of royal authority, namely Kaiser Wilhelm II and his wife, Augusta Victoria of Schleswig-Holstein.

The presence of the Kaiser interrogates the reasons underlying warfare and the folly of extracting the pyrrhic victories that defined the battles of the First World War, especially since he embodied three qualities that, according to Michael Howard, 'characterized the contemporary German ruling elite: archaic militarism, vaulting ambition, and neurotic insecurity'.[109] Wilhelm II dismissed Chancellor Otto von Bismarck's *Realpolitik* in favour of the politically aggressive policy of *Weltpolitik*, which fuelled Germany's aggressive international diplomacy and military expansion. Furthermore, the Kaiser's flagrant detachment from diplomacy as well as his close personal and ideological relations with Archduke Franz Ferdinand laid a foundation for the July crisis, during which the Kaiser and the German chancellor, Theobald von Bethmann Hollweg, issued their formal assurances to Vienna that Germany would support

Austria in the event of a showdown with Serbia.[110] Wilhelm's operations foreshadowed Hitler's similarly intolerant determination which, as *Ida* suggests, was becoming increasingly clear to neighbouring nations by the 1930s. Juxtaposed with this outmoded relic of recklessly ambitious world policy is the soldiers' collective chant of 'Die Wacht am Rhein', a song that promises an everlasting abundance of German blood to protect the greater glory of Germany, and whose chorus (sung by the German soldiers during the final pan in this narrative sequence) lauds patriotism without asking the price or the results of such unquestioning adherence to imperial authority:

> And even if my heart breaks in death,
> You'll never ever become foreign territory.
> As rich in water is your flood,
> Is Germany in heroes' blood.
>
> Dear fatherland, no fear be thine,
> Dear fatherland, no fear be thine,
> Firm and True stands the Watch, the Watch at the Rhine.
> Firm and True stands the Watch, the Watch at the Rhine.[111]

The soldiers' fervently patriotic celebrations sharply contrast with the image of the Kaiser whose unthinking drive for expansion contributed in no small part to the declarations of war in 1914. The *mise en scène* of our introduction to the portraits reminds us of the soldiers' own national obligation to attack the French and, as O'Shaughnessy remarks, shows 'how this apparently popular attachment to nation [. . .] works to sustain a hierarchical social order and the militarism that goes with it'.[112]

The Kaiser's influence is palpable throughout the film: when Boëldieu and von Rauffenstein speak together for the first time at the German airbase, a picture of Wilhelm that is adorned by the German flag is visible between their heads in the background. Wilhelm's portrait features again as the German soldiers at Hallbach laugh about the British habit of eating plum pudding and later appears once more at Wintersborn as von Rauffenstein sits down and calls out the French soldiers' escape records. In all of these cases, the German soldiers' shared attempt to liberate their circumstances through humour and friendship belies the imperial wartime impetus projected by Wilhelm II's image, but much like the French prisoners at Hallbach, they are helpless to subvert the military order established by the German monarch. Only a few shots later, Maréchal celebrates Douaumont's recapture by the French. However, because the soldiers on either side unquestioningly fulfil their national duty and joyfully celebrate each provisional victory amidst the constant tug of war that defined the four years of battle, the extent to which their future is likely to differ from the decline of the pre-war aristocracy remains open to question.

Wintersborn: the Kaiser's prison

The two central axes of Renoir's *mise en scène* of imprisonment in Hallbach – the ubiquity of German guards and the tension between the prison and outlying natural landscapes – continue to structure the dialectic of confinement and escape that features in Wintersborn, the second of the film's three central narrative settings. The stultifying impact of the extensive network of German soldiers at Hallbach is signalled by the escape records of Boëldieu, Maréchal, and Demolder (Sylvain Itkine), which not only indicate that they share twelve escape attempts between them but also reveal that two of the would-be escapees have gone to extreme lengths to escape: Maréchal has attempted escape on five occasions disguised as a heating engineer and, on other occasions, as a German soldier and even as a woman. Boëldieu has attempted escape on four occasions through a heating duct, in a trash bin, through sewers, and once in a laundry basket. As in Hallbach, Maréchal and Rosenthal embody the *élan vers l'avenir*, sometimes literally donning new roles within an otherwise petrified environment that actively prohibits their escape. In fact, Rosenthal and Maréchal's shared disregard for the imaginary resolutions desired by the tenants of *Les Bas-fonds* becomes abundantly clear during their brief exchange with a Senegalese officer. We first witness him in conversation with the other soldiers when he shows Maréchal and Rosenthal his artwork entitled 'La Justice Poursuivant le Crime' ('Justice Pursuing Crime'). If Maréchal and Rosenthal appear indifferent to the artwork, it is because they instinctively dismiss idealised conceptions of a world where morals structure all outcomes in society, and the guarantee that justice pursues crime rather than the reverse. Further underscoring Maréchal and Rosenthal's impetus, the unnamed officer creates yet another image whilst Maréchal speaks to Boëldieu regarding the escape plan.

At Wintersborn, the forces that striate the natural landscape are emphasised as von Rauffenstein guides Maréchal, Boëldieu, and Demolder to a vantage point where two machine gunners are stationed. A deep shot of the German countryside below tempts the prisoners with a view of the land. As the four men exit behind the camera, the focus shifts to the vast landscape overlooked by the machine gunners (Figure 3.7). Although the shot of the landscape is breathtaking in scope, the presence of the marksmen reminds us that this landscape does not embody unconditional

Figure 3.7 German sentries man a tower at Wintersborn

freedom and is, in fact, rigorously striated. Like the contested landscapes analysed in Chapter 2, the land is intrinsically political and subject to dominant powers, in this case the German army which was earlier visible during the transport of the prisoners to Wintersborn, manning each stop based in the countryside. The forces of the army transform the rural landscape into a stultifying locus, petrified and petrifying, a genuine force of death where physical escape necessarily implies vulnerability and the possibility of detection and demise.

As in Hallbach, the physical structure of Wintersborn defies escape, and prison guards ensure constant surveillance. The impenetrability of the walls and networks of surveillance are primarily emphasised during two moments, namely the French prisoners' introduction to Wintersborn and, later, the death of Boëldieu. After Boëldieu, Maréchal, and Demolder arrive at Wintersborn, von Rauffenstein warns them that any hopes of escape are out of the question. After Demolder remarks on the thirteenth-century walls, the camera tilts upwards to view the domineering fortress, beginning with its coat of arms and panning to the left, emphasising the staggering dimensions and impenetrability of the prison walls. Set designer Eugène Lourié recalled that the crew voted unanimously to use the actual fortress built by Kaiser Wilhelm on Haut-Koenigsbourg for exterior shots of 'the inaccessible castle in the mountains', but that he constructed his own sets in order 'to visually express the severity and grimness of the inaccessible stone fortress. I wanted to make evident von Rauffenstein's words, "*Nobody* escapes from here. *Nobody*."'[113] That the medieval castle which now imprisons von Rauffenstein was besieged, burned, and looted during the Thirty Years War only to be rebuilt during the 1900s by none other than Wilhelm II further emphasises, on an extra-textual level, the role of the German monarchy in imprisoning its military.

As von Rauffenstein guides the French prisoners around the fortress, the ubiquity of the German surveillance is marked discreetly but distinctly through deep staging and off-screen space. The camera frames the French prisoners visiting different areas of the castle, evoking the German soldiers' presence in adjoining spaces as-of-yet unseen by the prisoners themselves: as Maréchal describes his escape attempts to Rauffenstein at Wintersborn, a silhouetted guard is visible in the door behind him; later, as von Rauffenstein remarks that his men 'are not young but enjoy playing soldier', a soldier is distinctly visible in the passageway behind them, through which they have yet to walk as part of their tour.

As in Hallbach, windows emphasise the French and German soldiers' shared state of imprisonment rather than the possibility of escaping Wintersborn. The windows located behind Boëldieu and Rauffenstein as they discuss the impending death of the old order grant the spectator a view of the castle walls that imprison Rauffenstein as much as Boëldieu and the other captive soldiers. The staging of this sequence is echoed in turn once again following Boëldieu's death as von Rauffenstein proceeds towards the window in his quarters where the two officers had previously conversed: a wide shot framing the three large windows reveals domineering walls and a patrol guard whose presence reminds us of the German order that blocks all escape from the enclosed physical space of the prison. That the backing visible through the window in each of these instances is, in fact, a photographic blow-up of the castle walls at Haut-Koenigsbourg and a cardboard cut-out of a soldier animated by Lourié only further emphasises the crew's own endeavour to illustrate the physical and social aspects of the imprisonment imposed by Wintersborn on both the French and German armies.[114]

Elsa's home: deceptive security

Von Rauffenstein dutifully remains assigned to Wintersborn whilst Rosenthal and Maréchal, embodying the *élan vers l'avenir* through their defiant impetus, continue in their attempt to liberate themselves from German rule. However, the *mise en scène* of the natural landscape implies that their attempt to plot a *ligne de fuite* remains subject to 'groups and individuals [that] contain micro-fascisms simply waiting to crystallise'.[115] By this point in the narrative, the German soldiers' map at Hallbach following the German victory at Douaument and the framing of exterior space at both Hallbach and Wintersborn have already testified to the rigorously striated space of the German countryside. Clearly, the rural landscape is just as conducive to entrapment as the sky and each of the prisons through its physical openness and limited protection against surveillance. Maréchal and Rosenthal's joint escape from Wintersborn, although instrumental in approaching the *point de fuite* in oppressive German regulations, does not constitute a liberating *ligne de fuite*: in German territory, the French soldiers are enemies of the country and subject to the suspicion of its people, and they are even forced to hide from a civilian walking casually with her horse. Furthermore, this knowledge almost convinces the escapees to abandon the hope and solidarity that had ensured their joint escape, and without which their prospect of escape from Germany is much less likely.

Elsa's home, the third of the film's three narrative settings, provides a haven for Maréchal and Rosenthal because it integrates the escapees into a supportive domestic unit and also conceals them against suspicion and potential capture. On the one hand, Elsa's decision to hide them from the German soldiers who march to Wölfisheim marks the home as a protective space that eludes the network of German surveillance. In fact, the camera establishes a series of interconnections between interior domestic space and exterior natural landscapes through the formerly restrictive device of the window, and the escapees navigate interior and exterior spaces in ways that are illustrated nowhere else in the narrative: for the first time, the characters integrate with family life and refrain from discussing their projected escape to France; during their stay at Elsa's home, Maréchal leaves her stable and stretches himself in front of a wide, breathtaking shot of the German landscape; and for the first time in the narrative, windows frame the natural landscape beyond the house. In the scene following the Christmas celebrations, Rosenthal opens a window and walks into kitchen where Maréchal and Elsa are also looking out a window. In the next scene, Rosenthal and Maréchal are outside, leaning against a wooden cart as both men conclude that they must announce their impending departure to Elsa. Rosenthal subsequently tells Elsa that they will be leaving that night and, afterwards, opens a window to reveal Maréchal leaning against Elsa's cart. However, it is easy to overestimate both the security provided by the home and the liberty offered by the landscape in these scenes: as evidenced by the passage of the soldiers to Wölfisheim, the fact remains that the natural landscape is surveyed by German soldiers. Thus, although Deleuze likens Renoir's windows to 'frozen water'[116] through which the spectator envisions the scission of time, his otherwise insightful observation only further underscores the extent to which the most Renoirian of framing motifs, insofar as it features in Elsa's home and at Hallbach, represents a complete subversion of Renoir's prior deployment of windows.

The stultifying force of the landscape continues to be held in tension with the future embodied by the escapees: Maréchal and Rosenthal's impetus eventually propels them through a *point de fuite* constituted by the Swiss border, which officially liberates them from German military rule, as declared by the German soldiers who order a ceasefire after the escapees have crossed the border. Before closing this analysis, however, it is important to note that the goal to 'put an end to this damn war' (voiced by Maréchal shortly before he and Rosenthal cross the Swiss border in the film's final scene) will motivate their return to the aerial battles that threaten to relay the escapees' spatio-temporal trajectory to the German prison system once again or to their grave.[117] Deleuze rightly emphasises Maréchal and Rosenthal's temporal orientation towards the future, for they alone represent the insurgent spontaneity introduced by space to hegemonic social configurations. However, by the end of the film, Renoir's *mise en scène* has consistently challenged any easy attempt to look beyond their squandered potential. The camera does not merely sympathise with the two barely discernible figurines marching through snow towards a nameless grave. It pities their valour and laments their inevitable loss.

Conclusion: 'We are dancing on a volcano'

By reading the three films concerned through *Ida* and Deleuze, and interpreting their socialised spaces through Massey, we are in a position to consider the import of buildings and characters towards the portrayal of space-time in Renoir's Front populaire output from a perspective that lends overdue scope to the true extent of Renoir's misgivings regarding the French Left. Characters in all three films endeavour to escape the embodied past at one point or another, but are emphatically myopic and fail to appropriately engage with the various spatialising forces that problematise any implementation of a *ligne de fuite* from the embodied past. Interestingly, all three films feature a central edifice (*La Grande Illusion* features three) that has been striated by various cartographies of power that condition the characters' spatio-temporal trajectories, and problematises any implementation (or, in the case of *Les Bas-fonds*, even the envisioning) of a *ligne de fuite* from the embodied past. Their necessarily short-sighted view of physical space and the social forces that striate it are constantly signalled by Renoir's signature style, notably deep space, lateral camera movement, and calculated use of off-screen space, all of which were developed by Renoir during what arguably represents the most technologically innovative period of his aesthetic and political development.

Although Renoir frequently portrays social projects that can only be achieved in collaboration with another member or number of members of their community, we should not automatically conclude that the characters who do not subscribe to antiquated etiquette or stultifying capitalist regimes are guaranteed to be rewarded for attempting to liberate themselves. *Lange* and *Les Bas-fonds* feature communities that crucially fail to engage with a comprehensive conceptualisation of space (itself an impossibility), inadvertently leaving their spaces open to restratification. As for *La Grande Illusion*, although the impetus of Maréchal and Rosenthal is held in tension with the constraints of German rule, the only true escape from the force of striated space is effected at the end of the film. Space-time is open, but even then, the aftermath of the story is as uncertain as that of *Lange* and *Les Bas-fonds* by virtue of the heroes' projected circular trajectory (notwithstanding their plans for an unlikely reunion at Maxim's in Paris).

Insofar as the specific temporal dimension of these films is concerned, Deleuze's decision to liken each film to a cracked crystal from which time escapes and 'is given a future' is an oversimplification:[118] each film testifies to the constant imposition of social forces upon the *ligne de fuite* embodied by individuals and groups that appropriate a given set of circumstances to enter a process of becoming. Deleuze and Guattari's discussion of crystallisable 'micro-fascisms' provides a useful means of revising Deleuze's categorisation of Renoir's crystal of time and illustrating why Renoir's Front populaire output appears more politically oriented towards the radical pessimism of *Ida* than the hopes and dreams expressed by the Front itself. Each film testifies to the constant recrystallisation of flawed crystals around the *ligne de fuite* that escapes the crystal in which the societies are established (or 'born' to use Deleuze's term[119]), from which individuals and groups must constantly endeavour to extricate themselves.

Before closing this analysis, it is important to observe precisely how it interrogates Martin O'Shaughnessy's relatively recent study of this period in Renoir's career, for his analysis is also concerned with the passage of time, specifically what O'Shaughnessy terms 'the *mise en scène* of history', and is informed by aspects of Deleuze's film philosophy that are central to this book. On the one hand, O'Shaughnessy is not undividedly optimistic regarding the portrayal of social progress within Renoir's Front populaire output: O'Shaughnessy lucidly argues that Renoir's *mise en scène* of history during his Front populaire period involves a sense of 'uncertainty, driven by the co-presence of competing possibilities', and acknowledges that progress in *Lange* can only be achieved through problematic acts of violence.[120] However, by failing to critically interrogate Renoir's own attitude towards the collective enterprises that feature in his work of this period, O'Shaughnessy generally overestimates the social agency of the characters in each film who endeavour to supplant the economic and political molar lines that impede their spatio-temporal trajectories. For example, even though only Pépel and Natacha escape the *bas-fonds*, O'Shaughnessy asserts that the *mise en scène* of *Les Bas-fonds*, 'in contrast to an immobilizing social realism which would tie characters to social roles and locations, [. . .] loosens their bonds to open up the possibility of transformation'.[121] More broadly, although O'Shaughnessy insightfully acknowledges what Massey refers to as 'a notion of becoming', his analysis remains relatively closed to 'the articulation of forms of power within spatial configurations', which Massey surmises as a unifying argument of her treatise on space.[122] Because the projects plotted by Renoir's communities are necessarily subject to social forces articulated beyond their own physically enclosed spaces, the range and potential impact of the futures envisaged by Renoir's communities is alarmingly limited. Clearly, the very 'closing down of possibilities' detected by O'Shaughnessy in *La Bête humaine* and the final scenes of *La Règle du jeu*, should be read as a historical and social process in itself, whose spatial politics are *mises en scène* from the very beginning of Renoir's involvement with the French Left.[123] Indeed, the phrase 'We are dancing on a volcano', a word of caution that was voiced during the reign of Charles X and which later inspired Renoir's portrayal of the *haute bourgeoisie* in *La Règle du jeu*,[124] could well be applied to the diagnostic value of any of the three films discussed.

The numerous interpretations to which they have been subjected over time, including the reflexively critical attitude elucidated by this chapter, arguably result from Renoir's own conception of history. Recollecting the 6 February 1934 crisis, a fatal riot organised by far-right leagues which catalysed the rise of the Front populaire, Renoir commented on his own perspective on the process of interpreting history. The parallels between his memories and the multiple perspectives continuously unearthed within the three films analysed are so salient that they are worth citing in full:

> On 6 February 1934, the day that these riots unfolded in Place de la Concorde, I was eating lunch in a little restaurant that was perhaps about fifty metres from the area where it all happened. And quite a lot happened. Well, it was when I was going home that I met a friend who informed me about what had happened during my lunch! We always believe that an event is immediately and universally perceived. This isn't true. The event remains buried or isolated for a very long time. It only emerges little by little. It only acquires meaning after the fact.[125]

By opening our analysis of Renoir's Front populaire output to Renoir's multifaceted political outlook, Deleuze and Guattari's spatial thought, and Massey's theorisation of space as 'a sphere of coexistence of a multiplicity of trajectories' that simultaneously differentiates and connects the world, we can consider the full range of futures evoked by Renoir's crystalline images.[126] Only then may we fully appreciate Renoir's ability to integrate temporality within its perspective of the mutually affective relationship between social and physical space, and the diversity of the ideological stances embedded in Renoir's narrative style.

CHAPTER 4

Renoir's *crises anti-réalistes*: Framing *le temps gelé*

Everything was false: false realism, false credit and even false harlots [. . .].[1]
– Gustave Flaubert, 29 April 1871

What makes you exist is not the force of your desire [. . .], but the play of the world and seduction; it is the passion of playing and being played, it is the passion of illusion and appearances [. . .].[2]
– Jean Baudrillard, *Les Stratégies fatales*

Introduction: Seeing Time in the *image plane*

Prefiguring Deleuze's own emphasis on the theatricality that infuses Renoir's settings, Leo Braudy states:

> Renoir's world of theater and his world of nature do not exist in mutually exclusive categories, and in fact more of the unique quality of film can be illuminated if one examines their interaction than if one keeps them totally separate.[3]

Previous chapters have sought to avoid reducing Renoir's worlds to theatres, arguing that a full appreciation of Renoir's *mise en scène* demands that we examine the counterpoint through which the *surcroît de théâtralité* and geographical setting (in its physical and social aspects) interact expressively. However, Braudy's and Deleuze's comments are pertinent in the case of *Diary of a Chambermaid* (1946), *The Golden Coach* (1952), and *Eléna et les hommes* (1956): although all three are costume dramas – a genre described by Susan Hayward 'in its broadest sense as [films] set in an historical period that features characters dressed in costumes pertaining to that era'[4] – any general sense of geographical place and chronological point in time is secondary to the theatricality foregrounded by various combinations of costume design, set design, camerawork, music, and performance. It is worth noting that the emphatic theatricality that distinguishes each of the three films from Renoir's previous output and the costume-drama genre was not always a deliberate choice on Renoir's part. Years after its release, Renoir stated that '*Diary of a Chambermaid* corresponds with one of my anti-realist crises [*crises anti-réalistes*].'[5] Renoir further elaborated:

> There are moments when I ask myself if the sole truth is not the inner truth [*la vérité intérieure*] and if the truth of make-up, of costumes, of appearances, of furniture, the exterior truth [*la vérité extérieure*], if we really should not neglect it in order to advance a bit more towards this interior truth. *Diary of a Chambermaid* corresponds with this preoccupation.[6]

This aesthetic watershed disappointed even Renoir's most faithfully appreciative critic, André Bazin:

> What mental aberration, lack of self-judgement, or dangerous taste for paradox led Renoir to film, in America, the subject that was closest to his heart, and which could least be treated outside France? [. . .] We feel the sunlamps on Burgess Meredith's rose-bushes, the entire film is bathed in that aquarium light that is typical of Hollywood studios, and everything – including the actors – looks like Japanese flowers in a fishbowl.[7]

Perhaps as a result of the unflattering reviews, Renoir avoided emphatically artificial *mise en scène* in his following features, *Woman on the Beach* (1947) and *The River* (1951). However, he subsequently returned to the style of *Diary*, filming *The Golden Coach* in its entirety at Italy's Cinecittà studios with a prologue and epilogue set in front of a proscenium arch when his plan to film 'some atmospheric shots in a Latin American country' fell through.[8] Although this film also divided critics,[9] Renoir exploited a similarly saturated colour palette for *French Cancan* (1954), a crowd-pleasing fictionalisation of the opening of the Moulin Rouge, and once more for *Eléna et les hommes*, arguably his most socially incisive study of theatre and artifice.

Despite Deleuze's inadequate conceptualisation of space in *Cinéma 2*, he formulates two key observations that are conducive to a comprehensive understanding of how Renoir's revised aesthetic portrays the relationship between space and time. Remarking that *The Golden Coach* is characterised by a reduced tendency towards staging shots in depth, Deleuze states that the scission of time that is visible in Renoir's deeply composed images is also embedded 'in flat images [*l'image plane*], as in *The Golden Coach*', although 'it was less visible'.[10] Deleuze's characteristically reductive view of Renoir's technical style misleadingly implies that the entirety of *The Golden Coach* is comprised of visually shallow images (deep space is, in fact, a crucial element of this film's *mise en scène*), but he usefully implies that the *image plane*, which nonetheless features frequently in Renoir's post-war work, conveys the tension between the past and the ongoing creation of the present moment. Secondly, Deleuze lends theatres a temporal texture, asserting that by drawing on the virtual possibilities available, characters may find a role that allows them to pursue a *ligne de fuite* and enter 'a new reality that did not pre-exist', liberated of 'frozen, fixed, ready-made, too conformative roles'.[11]

Deleuze valuably encourages the spectator to elucidate a temporal tension between the stultifying force of the past and the ongoing present, regardless of the visual depth incorporated within the image. However, Deleuze's definition of theatre requires further elaboration. Given the variety of theatrical motifs emerging from various molar lines (to use Deleuze and Guattari's term) – colonialism, capitalist hierarchies, and pre-war aristocratic class barriers to name but a few – it would be reductive to ground an analysis of these three emphatically theatrical works within the same methodology that Deleuze employs for films as diverse as *Boudu sauvé des eaux* and *The River*. Just as those two films have been analysed elsewhere in this book within the contexts of urban and rural space respectively, one must avoid conflating the generalities of Deleuze's approach to theatricality and the stylistic specificities of Renoir's *crises anti-réalistes*. To this end, we must distinguish between two particular aspects of theatre that feature in different Renoir films, as dichotomised by Thomas Elsaesser's analysis of films directed by Renoir during the 1930s and the 1950s. On the one hand, Elsaesser states that Renoir's theatre features as a 'formalized game' with an agreed set of rules and conventions that bind performer and audience.[12] On the other hand, Elsaesser argues that theatre incorporates spectacle, a 'riot of color and movement' embodied by 'a firework of energy, ecstasy, and the *élan vital*'.[13] Although spectacle implies a public space, it requires no diegetic audience because 'it is affirming the sense of being fiercely alive'.[14]

Elsaesser's analysis usefully echoes that of Deleuze by suggesting that characters can escape a role through a liberating force that is simultaneously of and at odds with the theatre (escaping theatre through theatricality), thus holding the petrifying force of theatrical roles and the potential creation of a genuinely new future, free of theatrical influences, in tension. However, Elsaesser unjustly emphasises the liberating power of spectacle at the expense of its potential ideological function. In doing so, he unduly elevates spectacle's spontaneity and life-asserting force from a possible attribute of spectacle to an inherent characteristic. For spectacle can be deployed to entertain or to homogenise space and establish hegemonic strata with equal facility.

Theorising spectacle as 'a social relationship between people that is mediated by images',[15] Guy Debord's *La Société du spectacle/The Society of the Spectacle* (1967) associates the increased value of superficial appearance in the modern world with a progressive lack of authenticity in society which has degraded human knowledge and the capacity for critical thought.[16] Debord particularly emphasises the appeal of spectacle and its relationship with social subordination:

> The spectacle manifests itself as something enormously positive, indisputable and inaccessible. It says nothing more than 'whatever appears is good; whatever is good appears'. The attitude that it demands in principle is passive acceptance which, in fact, it has already obtained by its manner of appearing without reply, by its monopolisation of appearances.[17]

The spectacle and its ideology both become the focal point of the subjugated stratum's vision and consciousness but it 'escapes reconsideration and correction', thus precluding revolutionary action.[18] Society is, in Deleuze and Guattari's sense of the term, crystallised.

Most interestingly, in a chapter entitled 'Spectacular Time' ('Le Temps spectaculaire'), Debord emphasises the impact of the appeal of spectacle and its corollary, fixed social relations, on the prohibition of a new future. Asserting that 'reasoning about history is, necessarily, *reasoning about power*', Debord argues that spectacle prevents people from synchronising with the progression of real time by creating '[a] *false consciousness of time*' through 'the paralysis of history and memory'.[19] Debord specifically refers to 'cold societies' as those which 'have slowed down their historical activity to the limit', establishing hegemony through 'a definitive structuring [that] has excluded change' and the construction of 'pseudo-history [. . .] at every level of consumption of life', preserving what Debord defines as 'frozen time [*le temps gelé*]'.[20]

Given that vivid spectacle provides the substance of these films rather than merely operating as a trivial embellishment, it is important to examine the socio-political deployment of spectacle and the temporal stasis that this implies. It is particularly essential that we shift our perspective towards the ways in which Renoir frames the dialectic between politics and spectacle to foreground temporality in his portrayal of social space. In all three films, incumbent power structures established by upper-class institutions, ranging from families to colonial bodies to the French military, exploit spectacle as part of their theatrical regimes in order to enforce a specific set of ideological values within a given space and to nullify space's ability to provide what Massey terms 'a precondition for the temporal'.[21] In doing so, these bodies reassure members of their own class of their own socio-political hegemony and assimilate lower social strata within their theatrical regimes with a view to externalising their values. This chapter aims to demonstrate the ways in which the visual style in each of these *crises anti-réalistes* presents a contrast between the ideological stratification effected through spectacle on the one hand and, on the other hand, those who endeavour to escape its influence, resulting in a tension between theatricality and 'decanted reality' (to employ Deleuze's distinction) that provokes the spectator to interpret spectacle both temporally and spatially.

Diary of a Chambermaid (1946)

Diary of a Chambermaid, based on Octave Mirbeau's *Journal d'une femme de chambre* (1900), traces the experience of a newly hired chambermaid (Célestine, played by Paulette Goddard) who, weary of executing orders, aims to become her own mistress.[22] During her stay at the Lanlaire residence, Célestine encounters the domineering, socially detached Mme Lanlaire (Judith Anderson), who keeps her ineffectual husband (Reginald Owen) penniless whilst doting on Georges, her disgusted, gravely ill son (Hurd Hatfield). She also meets the neighbouring Captain Mauger (Burgess Meredith), who laughs at the Lanlaires' self-assumed importance, and Joseph (Francis Lederer), a fellow servant who, after ten years of service in the Lanlaire manor, is plotting to steal the family's vast collection of silverware and begin a new chapter in his own life as the entrepreneur of a café in Cherbourg. Célestine ultimately opts to leave with Georges instead of Joseph, who wrests Célestine from Georges's hands before meeting his own violent end at the hands of a mob of Bastille Day revellers.

Whereas the previous three chapters have demonstrated that deep staging is a crucial technical component and ideological device in Renoir's films of the 1930s, the few events staged in depth in *Diary of a Chambermaid* generally depict trivial actions that coexist without competing for the enforcement or disintegration of a given social configuration: as Célestine and Joseph speak in the foreground, we witness two men, presumably rail workers, performing work in the background; later, as Célestine walks around Georges's room for the first time with Joseph, M. Lanlaire is visible in an adjoining room, pulling curtains off shelves; on another occasion, early in the narrative, Célestine removes an item of clothing from the washing line in the foreground, revealing M. Lanlaire as he tends to his roses in the background; finally, in a moment which will be discussed later in this section, Mme Lanlaire brings Célestine through the background to a deeply staged boudoir as she offers her maid a new role within the household. Beyond these moments, Renoir largely eschews his characteristic staging of events in depth. Furthermore, Renoir's technique displays far less camera movement than his films of the 1930s. As William Gilcher's formalist study of Renoir's American work observes, the camera is noticeably more mobile during the first half of *Diary*, but is 'largely motivated by character movement' and its actions are 'rigidly executed'.[23]

Renoir himself readily acknowledged that the completed film bore little resemblance to his initial vision. Renoir first considered filming the novel during his silent period 'in an extremely romantic fashion' resembling his lavish adaptation of Émile Zola's *Nana* (1926), but claimed that the producers vetoed the subject matter.[24] Renoir's correspondence with producer Frank Rollmer indicates that later, in the wake of the lukewarm reception of *La Marseillaise* (1938), he was once more considering an adaptation of *Diary of a Chambermaid* before he ultimately opted for Zola's *La Bête humaine* (1938).[25] Describing the finished film's aesthetic style, Renoir himself wrote that *Diary* 'was entirely modified since I directed it at the beginning of that period when I saw scenes in a more concentrated manner, more theatrical, with less cross-cutting'.[26] Deleuze's observations regarding the temporal texture of theatrically defined worlds in Renoir's *image plane* and the interplay between costume design, décor, and characterisation are therefore key to our interpretation of narrative space-time in *Diary*.

'I'm trying to get you to stay with me': freezing domestic space

The physical and social space of the Lanlaire residence initially appears isolated from the impact of time and outlying spaces, recalling Deleuze's description of physical locations in Renoir's work (including Hallbach and La Colinière) where the possibility for the creation of a genuinely new future is nullified.[27] The windows and doors that elsewhere connect domestic interiors with public spaces (see *La Chienne* [1931], *La Grande Illusion* [1937], or *The Southerner* [1945]) only lead to and from the servants' quarters, between each floor of the residence, and out to the garden, which is enclosed by a high wall. The Lanlaires' apparently immutable grandeur is emphasised by the wide shots of their high ceilings, lengthy corridors, ornately framed portraits, statues, and rose gardens that distinguish their residence from the modest abode and untended garden of the neighbouring antagonist, Captain Mauger.

As in the case of Hallbach and La Colinière, the temporal stasis described by Deleuze is enforced through the striation of space. Within the home, Mme Lanlaire's rigorous adherence to right-wing politics renders her husband and son ineffectual. Mirbeau's M. Lanlaire is even more powerless in Renoir's film than in the novel: although Mirbeau's M. Lanlaire succeeds at least in killing three thrushes at one point in the novel,[28] Renoir's powerless patriarch openly remarks that he always has terrible hunts because he never even carries gun cartridges. Although M. Lanlaire temporarily rebels during Mme Lanlaire's anti-Bastille Day celebrations, his spirit is rapidly quenched by his wife's disciplinarian authority. Mme Lanlaire's attempts to crystallise time reach their zenith in her relationship with her son. When Georges returns home early in the film, Mme Lanlaire determinedly declares, 'I'll see that he never leaves me again, never.' Her attempt to perpetually embody this ideal maternal authority is blatantly indicated by the large portrait of her that hangs in his room. Committed to the canvas at a precise moment in the past, it is left hanging beneath a sheet in Georges's room until his return. Later, when Georges rebels against his mother's plot to retain him within the mansion, Mme Lanlaire stifles his impetus to leave: 'You won't be sorry, I'll take care of you. [. . .] I'll watch over you as I've always done since you were a fragile little boy. Haven't I always protected you, sheltered you?' Mme Lanlaire clearly maintains a relationship with her son based on her memories of him as a boy rather than on the fully grown man that he has become, and the outcome falls in Mme Lanlaire's favour despite Georges's objections.

Clearly, like the la Chesnayes who resort to La Colinière, Mme Lanlaire endeavours to isolate her residence from the provincial town within which it is situated, echoing Massey's discussion of attempts by anachronistic social groups to resort to moments and locations in space-time when the area and the social relations that structured it were to the advantage of the group in question.[29] Unsurprisingly, Mme Lanlaire herself displays even less mobility within the physical space of the manor than any of the other characters: whereas M. Lanlaire ventures into the garden on occasion and, when enraged, even pursues Mauger beyond the cleft in the wall that separates their gardens, Mme Lanlaire remains solely within the architectural parameters of her house, never even entering the garden for the entirety of the film. The importance of reading their residence temporally is indicated by the fact that the family's social circle has drastically diminished. Mme Lanlaire remarks that 'We are not as young as we once were. Our friends don't want to visit us as they once did.' Although the action unwinds almost forty years before *La Règle du jeu*, in which the la Chesnayes socialise (albeit in closed circles) with members of high society, Mme Lanlaire's attempt to striate domestic space has already deprived the family of contacts beyond the walls of their residence. In fact, Renoir's narrative generally emphasises the isolation of the Lanlaire residence to a far greater extent than Mirbeau's novel, in which Mme Lanlaire never utters this phrase. However, Mme Lanlaire's rules do not extend beyond the sterile world of their manor. In fact, tensions between costume design and characterisation imply that Mme Lanlaire's regime fails to even maintain control within her home, and evoke its inevitable disintegration.

Vérité intérieure *as* élan vital*: Célestine, Joseph, and upward mobility*

The tension between '[the] frozen, fixed, ready-made, too conformative roles' imposed by Mme Lanlaire and the *élan vital* oriented towards a realm of reality that is liberated of theatricality is chiefly expressed by Célestine and Joseph, most notably through the contrast between their private desires and the professional façades that they both project.[30] Deleuze's discussion of the origins of the crystalline states provides an enlightening framework within which to analyse how a fictional character's private motives may enter into dialectic with superficial aspects of his or her presentation to confront the spectator with competing versions of what we may accept as the characters' true feelings. Drawing on the collaborations between Tod Browning and Lon Chaney (*The Unholy Three*, 1925; *The Unknown*, 1927), Deleuze remarks that the actor, like the crystal, has both an opaque and a limpid face. Prefiguring his emphasis on the relationship between theatricality and the crystal later in the chapter, particularly in his analysis of Renoir's work, Deleuze states that 'the crystal is a stage'[31] within which the actor

> makes the virtual image of the role actual, so that the role becomes visible and luminous. [. . .] But the more the virtual image of the role becomes actual and limpid, the more the actual image of the actor moves into the shadows, and becomes opaque.[32]

Although Deleuze's discussion of '[the] double face of the actor' is intended as a clarification of the figures through which time passes,[33] specifically the limpid and the opaque, it also provides a valuable metafilmic avenue of enquiry towards the relationship between role playing and temporality, each of which is emphasised by Deleuze in his exploration of Renoir's worlds within *Cinéma 2*. Building on his preoccupation with realistic performance, Renoir similarly conceptualised the relationship between *la vérité intérieure* and *la vérité extérieure*, respectively pertaining to the inner characteristics and outward appearance of characters, each of which contributed to what Renoir recognised as a core aim of acting: 'to place the public in contact with a human being'.[34]

Renoir stated that by situating Célestine's narrative within the *fin-de-siècle* context of the source novel, he was in a position to base the *vérité extérieure* in costumes that he had seen in films set in the same era, and he could completely preoccupy himself with descriptions of the inner characteristics of characters.[35] He aligned this approach with that of the formulaic costumes and characters association with the *commedia dell'arte*, which 'could concentrate solely on what is the essential, that is to say on the character, the situations, and the way of treating situations' and, in doing so, respond to one central question: 'In reality, is the human being not hindered by appearances rather than helped?'[36]

Rather than limiting Deleuze's or Renoir's examination to the relationship between the spectator and the on-screen oscillation between the actor and his or her character, we can examine the impact of the ongoing dialectic between an individual fictional character's public displays and private sentiments on that character's relationship within its social environment. In doing so, we may understand how Renoir's emphasis on theatricality and performance, within a setting entrenched in ideologically imbued spectacle, lends the framed theatrical space an emphatically temporal dimension.

Renoir further states in his autobiography that 'the *vérité intérieure* is often hidden behind a purely artificial environment'.[37] In the case of *Diary*, this environment extends not only to the manifest superficiality of the Lanlaire residence, but also to the roles imposed within it: the Lanlaire residence is artificial to the extent that the costumes assigned by Mme Lanlaire bear no true resemblance to the motives of the characters who wear them. Because we are aware of the animosity harboured by Célestine and Joseph towards Mme Lanlaire, the costumes designating socially assigned roles (the *vérité extérieure*) underscore each character's ulterior motives (*vérité intérieure*), invoking a tension between the overtly theatrical social space of the Lanlaires' home and the personal realities embodied by each character, which Mme Lanlaire aims to suppress. The inconsistency between the servants' personal agendas and assigned roles transforms Célestine's and Joseph's respective costumes from symbols of subservient status into Brechtian distancing devices, and demonstrates that Mme Lanlaire's spectacular domestic theatre serves less to seal space than to provide her with a reductive structure of visibility that threatens the continuity of her regime.

The fallacy of judging characters based on the *vérité extérieure* is signalled from the outset. When Célestine first arrives, she assumes that M. Lanlaire is a servant because he sits down in the kitchen and wears unkempt clothes. Similarly, Joseph assumes that the unkempt Mauger can offer nothing to Célestine and is later surprised to learn that he has offered Célestine 25,000 francs for her hand in marriage. Ironically, Célestine herself assumes that Joseph will never rise to any position higher than a valet and is shocked to learn that he is in a position to offer her a steady income at his bar in Cherbourg.

The reductive influence of Joseph's costume is saliently evidenced by Mme Lanlaire's attitudes towards him. On the surface, Joseph carefully corresponds with Mme Lanlaire's demands and shares a rapport with Mme Lanlaire that is unique among all of the servants. Entrusted with a complete set of keys, Joseph is the only one amongst the servants who is permitted to enter the downstairs vault that contains the Lanlaires' fortune. Like Mme Lanlaire, he stands against the Republic, declaring to Célestine that it was 'created for weaklings'. Yet beneath his costume, Joseph aims to break free of his socially assigned role and to integrate with the world of business and upward mobility which has developed through the birth of the very Republic that evokes his disgust. In Mme Lanlaire's company, his *vérité intérieure* is emphatically opaque to his mistress, subjugated to his carefully composed *vérité extérieure*, invoking a tension between the established decorum of the Lanlaire residence and its potential dissolution.

Even when Mme Lanlaire discovers Joseph's plot to elope with Célestine and the silver, she condescendingly insists, 'you're a valet Joseph, you'll always be a valet', failing to realise that Joseph may access alternative options in society in order to shed his pre-assigned role of valet. As Braudy rightly notes, '[the Lanlaires'] world is theatrical and closed because they consciously erected its limits around them through added ignorance and prejudice'.[38] Joseph is a lower-class, non-national resident (as indicated by his accent), but his acquisition of assets pertaining to both the world of business and that of French heritage secures his place as a French citizen. Furthermore, the prized silverware is located under the stairs used by the aristocrats to reach their bedroom, suggesting that Joseph is capable of robbing the house of its very foundations. As Joseph states to Mme Lanlaire on Bastille Day, 'I must have it as you had it for my peace of mind. It represents, as it has to you, my new position in life, my new security.' Like Rosenthal of *La Grande Illusion* (1937), whose French terrain and naturalised father guarantee him the same citizenship as the aristocratic Boëldieu, Joseph's entrepreneurship will guarantee him a steady income. In a world where social status is achieved through a steady source of capital rather than noble blood and family heirlooms, these fixed assets will represent medals of honour rather than an isolated source of wealth and embodied national identity. As Renoir himself stated:

> In its roots and, I think, equally in its direction, the film is a type of vain race on the part of people representing an already-dead society; it is a race of ghosts. These people [the Lanlaires] represent a bourgeoisie which no longer exists, because the bourgeoisie which has replaced them is a bourgeoisie of businesses, an active bourgeoisie, a bourgeoisie which makes money.[39]

From the moment Célestine arrives at the residence, the narrative repeatedly signals Mme Lanlaire's attempt to similarly cast Célestine within her specific role as chambermaid. When Célestine and Louise first arrive, Mme Lanlaire deems Célestine's name 'too complicated' and regards Célestine's insistence on retaining her own name as 'very interesting'. Mme Lanlaire inspects Célestine's body, remarking, 'I like your figure' but stating that she will modify Célestine's clothes. Célestine provides a distinctive contrast with Louise, who fulfils her role as expected: Louise is far more obedient than Célestine, and her name is accepted as 'very proper' by Mme Lanlaire. When Mme Lanlaire finally receives word that Georges is returning home, she determinedly executes the next stage of her social objectification of Célestine in an elaborately designed bedroom: 'I told you I wasn't satisfied with your clothes. Now we'll do something about it. [. . .] I'm going to try an experiment. Undress please.' Mme Lanlaire proceeds to withdraw dresses specially ordered from Paris from the wardrobe. She shows Célestine an old catalogue of hair designs and immediately sprays her with her own choice of perfume, supporting Braudy's observation that 'Célestine's journey into the provincial world of the Lanlaires is temporal as well as spatial'.[40] In a moment dominated by Renoir's characteristically self-conscious theatrical set design, Mme Lanlaire beckons Célestine towards a section of the bedroom in the background which is framed by curtains in a manner resembling a proscenium arch (Figure 4.1). Read through Deleuze, Mme Lanlaire's transformation of Célestine reveals the problems with the choices of roles available within the residence. For although Deleuze suggests that characters must experiment with roles within the crystal, the roles available to Célestine are predefined by Mme Lanlaire, who wishes to retain the chambermaid as her subservient instrument. That the dress is a 'very proper' fit, as Mme Lanlaire remarks, only further emphasises that Célestine's new role is literally tailor-made in Mme Lanlaire's imprisoning anachronistic vision.

Yet Mme Lanlaire's careful composition of domestic space, right down to her theatre of roles, cannot absolutely nullify Célestine's *vérité intérieure*, and Célestine's disruption of social configurations within the residence remains a possibility: although Célestine initially submits to Mme Lanlaire's demands for a new costume out of obligation to her mistress, she inadvertently develops a loving relationship with Georges that

Figure 4.1 Mme Lanlaire (right) creates a new outfit for Célestine (left)

belies her assigned role and threatens the social status of the family unit. Eventually, Célestine does unleash her temper on an unperturbed Mme Lanlaire, when the latter lends Célestine her wraparound and beckons her to bring broth to Georges:

> What do you think I am? A dog, or a cat or an animal or something? That you can send for me one minute and throw me out the next? [. . .] I don't want to dress like you, or look like you, or be like you. I can't stand it here any more! I'm through! I'm through!

Joseph's observation that 'you and I are alike', spoken to Célestine, is no surprise: like the spectator, he recognises the disparity between each of their theatrically defined roles and their own private intentions.

An unperturbed Mme Lanlaire smiles and refuses to acknowledge the gravity of the threat posed by Célestine to the carefully guarded domestic space. Mme Lanlaire's confidence is partly justified. Célestine's position in society is fixed not only in her affiliation with the working class but also within patriarchal society. Mme Lanlaire therefore knows that Célestine's current occupation confines her to a choice between conformity and resignation, and presumes that Georges would never liberate himself from his own role as a bourgeois member of society by marrying below his station. On the final count, Mme Lanlaire is proven wrong: Célestine retains her *élan vital*, which internally supplants her assigned *rôle mort*, inadvertently inspiring Georges to do the same, and they both ultimately elope, leaving the manor behind.

However, it is important to remark that Célestine's position in society problematises the creation of any genuinely new position in society. As a woman entrenched in subservient positions within hierarchical society, Célestine's potential *lignes de fuite* are clearly conditioned by her gender. Her upward social mobility is contingent on the acquisition of money which, realistically, may be obtained only through unfeasible years of service or, alternatively, though marriage to a man of means. Even simple acts of displacement mark male mobility as a prerequisite for female agency, as when Célestine frantically arrives at the train station at the beginning of the film and, later, when she resigns from her post and implores Joseph to 'hitch up the carriage and take me to the station. [. . .] Joseph, get me out of here, please!' Célestine realises this, and the importance of shedding her subservient role, better than anybody:

> Life is life. From now on I'm going to fight and I'm going to fight hard and I don't care who's going to get hurt just so it's not me. And I tell you what, I'm not going to be a chambermaid any longer. No I'm not. I'm going to be a mistress and have a house of my own. [. . .] And I'm going to grab the first man I meet to get where I'm going. Yes I am, the very first man. I don't care whether he's handsome or ugly or young or old. Just so he's got money. That's the main thing, money. [. . .] No more love for Célestine.

The departure of the train that transports Célestine and Georges away from the village may suggest a *ligne de fuite* from the theatre of Mme Lanlaire's socially oppressive residence on initial viewings. However, Célestine's diary implies that she remains entrapped within the crystal due to patriarchal dominance: whereas she defiantly writes 'no more love for Célestine' during her first night at the Lanlaire residence, the film ends with her writing marriage vows into the same diary. As Katherine Golsan writes, 'the narrative concludes in female subservience' and 'her final destination is within the confines of [the] predictable patriarchal feminine'.[41] Célestine's fate is sealed, her spatio-temporal trajectory guided by the rails, and her attempted escape contingent on her submission to her new male partner in life. Although liberated of her subservient occupation, her new role (in the broader, Deleuzian sense of the term) limits her social agency. Destined towards an uncertain future, she remains subject to the potential presence of stultifying spatial forces theorised by Deleuze and Guattari as 'micro-fascisms simply waiting to crystallise'.[42]

Class as spectacle in dissolution

Mme Lanlaire's domestic dictatorship is first and foremost a private *mise en scène* of striated space that cannot be implemented without a stage, and her attention is lent to costume and other aspects of appearance to the exclusion of individual personalities. Given the temporal stasis that Mme Lanlaire endeavours to impose on the manor, and Deleuze's own emphasis on the petrifying force embodied by theatre in Renoir's work, the gradual physical and social erosion of the Lanlaires' lavishly decorated residence should be read in both spatial and temporal terms. Although Braudy remarks that 'Renoir's sets emphasize a world of enclosures', set design repeatedly evokes the permeability of Mme Lanlaire's socialised stage.[43] In the garden, a cleft ruptures the wall that is meant to separate the Lanlaires' garden from that of Captain Mauger, who mocks the Lanlaires and readily courts Célestine.

Furthermore, recalling the *haute bourgeoisie* in *La Règle du jeu*, the Lanlaires' vain endeavour to preserve what Massey refers to as 'a moment and a form where they had a power' is challenged over the course of the narrative by repeated assaults on the opulent décor that bolsters Mme Lanlaire's sense of propriety.[44] Because the physical décor of the residence is crucial to the preservation of Mme Lanlaire's regime, Captain Mauger's breaking of the glass windows that house the Lanlaires' flower beds is not merely an act of vandalism. It represents the active dismantling of the *haute bourgeoisie*'s values, which are already undergoing gradual dissolution. By exploiting the breached wall separating Mauger's garden from that of the Lanlaires, he freely transgresses the wall that surrounds the Lanlaires' garden. He even demonstrates his ability to accurately aim a stone at the Lanlaires' glasshouse from the comfort of his own garden. The breaking of glass suggests a relentless, immediately apparent, and fundamentally irreversible march of time. Viewed in temporal terms, it explicitly represents the rupturing of the embodied past, an additional *fêlure* in Renoir's cracked crystal. Moreover, Mauger transgresses the property twice, physically mocking M. Lanlaire, who reacts only by futilely chasing Mauger with the same gun that he refuses to load, leaving himself open to Mauger's Chaplinesque physical effrontery. M. Lanlaire recalls Robert de la Chesnaye's fastidious demand for 'no rabbits, no fences', but is even more ineffectual, for he fails to punish those who do enter and thus leaves Mme Lanlaire's regime subject to subversion. If the Lanlaires' system is 'defeated anyway', as Durgnat suggests, it is not only because Mauger is free to deface their property, but also because M. Lanlaire refrains from appropriately punishing him.[45]

The progressive disintegration of Mme Lanlaire's distinctly theatrical setting culminates in the staging of the anti-Bastille Day celebrations. An opulent marble fireplace, silverware laid out within the room, and windows resembling proscenium arches testify to the importance of theatrical routine and complementary décor to the spatio-temporal continuity of her anachronistic vision. The room's aura is ruptured when M. Lanlaire, in his sole act of revolt, opens the window to allow the march played by the Bastille Day music band to invade the carefully composed setting. The destruction of Mme Lanlaire's stage features once more in the climactic brawl in the greenhouse between Joseph and Georges as the latter's hands break through the greenhouse in an attempt to prevent Joseph from escaping with Célestine. The shattering of glass is particularly pertinent in this case since, as already discussed, Georges's dissatisfaction within the home partly stems from his disdain for his mother. That Georges's hands shatter the glass in the closed door of the greenhouse further suggests the usurpation of the family's stubbornly maintained social position from within is as radical an attack on the foundations of the Lanlaire household as Joseph's removal of the family silver. Braudy rightly locates 'some new openness in personal relations' in the 'emergence of conflict from the shroudings of class and society', stating that Georges's own shattering of the greenhouse during the fight indicates Georges's 'new sense of connection'.[46] This reprise of the motif of broken glass represents the final stage in a series of physical manifestations that erode the partial temporal stasis imposed by Mme Lanlaire's *mise en scène*.

Diary of a Chambermaid is at once like and unlike the films analysed in the previous three chapters. Although it shares the preoccupation with theatre which is exhibited most saliently by Renoir's urban narratives and Front populaire output, *Diary* mobilises costume design, set design, and characterisation to foreground the role of spectacle in the imposition and simultaneous dissolution of the Lanlaires' crumbling regime, whereas Renoir's characteristic staging of multiple events in depth no longer assumes an important role in his portrayal of open space-time. Although *Diary* therefore challenges the primacy of *profondeur de champ* in Deleuze's philosophy, the film aligns with Deleuze's assertion that in the cinema, 'the image may be flat, without depth, and through this very fact, assumes all the more dimensions or powers which go beyond space'.[47] Bazin, perhaps understanding the semiotic value of the techniques that he had earlier denigrated, later revised his scathing review of the film:

> It is also undoubtedly with *Diary* that Renoir extricates himself entirely this time from the 'realism' of his French work. [. . .] Perhaps it is also here that Renoir's dread of the theatre finds its source. [. . .] Perhaps for the first time in Renoir's work, we no longer discern theatre, but theatricality in a pure state.[48]

Echoing Braudy's observation that *Diary of a Chambermaid* presents us with a Renoir who is 'already closer to the attitude toward the past he will have in the 1950s', this theatricality and its overt emphasis on the relationship between class and spectacle would resurface in their most self-consciously artificial form six years (and three films) later in *The Golden Coach*.[49]

The Golden Coach (1952)

Given this chapter's general emphasis on theatricality, it is worth noting that Deleuze lavishes more praise on *The Golden Coach* than on any other instalment in Renoir's post-war corpus, remarking that it is in this film that the Renoirian tension between 'theatricality in a pure state' (Deleuze cites Bazin's revised review of *Diary of a Chambermaid*) and a coexisting reality existing beyond the crystal 'will be brought to its highest point [. . .]'.[50] This exchange is all the more prominent for those who have read Prosper Mérimée's *Le Carrosse du Saint-Sacrement* (1829) since Renoir sacrificed much of Mérimée's source text, foregrounding the protagonist's problematic attempts to distinguish between the theatre and 'real life' within both the world of the *commedia dell'arte* troupe and that of the Spanish court. In the play, Camilla, the lead actress, has already established her reputation in a Spanish colony in Peru. Mérigeau's entire drama is confined to the viceroy's quarters where he is informed by his servant of Camilla's romantic involvement with other men in the colony including a matador and a captain, and of the allegedly subversive nature of her performances. Over the course of the play, Camilla meets with the viceroy to defend herself and, eventually, to request a coveted golden coach purchased by the viceroy. Much of Mérimée's narrative revolves around their disputes and provisional reconciliations, and the viceroy's eventual appeasement of Camilla through the gift of the titular coach, which she finally renounces to the church.

Renoir's adaptation not only elaborates on Camilla's (played by Anna Magnani) relationships with the viceroy (Duncan Lamont), the captain (Paul Campbell), and the matador (Riccardo Rioli), but also portrays Camilla's arrival in the colony. Furthermore, Renoir juxtaposes the theatrical sets constructed by the *commedia dell'arte* troupe with the ideologically charged spectacle embodied by the Spanish court within their opulently designed palace. Renoir's sets underscore the theatricality inherent to each of these strata by setting the entire narrative on a stage, bookending the story with shots of a proscenium arch that circumscribes the spatial and temporal limits of the characters' world.

'A few rules . . .': theatre as 'the opposite of dialogue'

Although theatre is a 'formalised game' (to use Elsaesser's term) for both Camilla's troupe and the court, each stratum characterises one particular aspect of spectacle, the second component of theatre elucidated by Elsaesser. On the one hand, the Spanish court performs by drawing on social etiquette, lavish décor, and costumes with a repetitive, socially regressive ritual that demands no target audience other than themselves in an effort to reassure their members of their own hegemony and to externalise any potentially intrusive elements that do not correspond with the colonial identity that they actively perform.

On the other hand, Camilla and the troupe employ the visual appeal of theatre to extend her community beyond the physical space circumscribed by the theatre to members of the audience, regardless of their class. The camera frames the communal, democratic social space created by Camilla's professional theatrical displays. Even before the troupe's opening night, her first lines on the newly constructed proscenium arch at the innkeeper's residence are 'my dear public, my dear public'. The camera later emphasises the relationship between Camilla and her spectators during the troupe's first public performance. As one of the troupe's child-performers bows at the front edge of the stage, the camera recedes to allow the audience to enter the frame, illustrating a relationship between the audience and the performers that we are never granted during the court's dance in the palace. During Camilla's performance before the general public, the camera further emphasises this relationship by photographing the audience from Camilla's point of view (Figure 4.2), pitting

Figure 4.2 An audience gathers in front of the stage on the troupe's opening night

Figure 4.3 Camilla and the viceroy discuss material wealth at his palace

the footlights located in the foreground with the audience to emphasise what Elsaesser terms the 'rules and conventions recognized as binding together performer and audience'.[51] This framing differentiates Camilla's brand of theatre from the self-indulgent spectacle of the court which, corresponding with the obverse aspect of Elsaesser's dichotomy, 'require[s] no particular audience (other than us, the film spectators)'.[52]

The latter is made manifest during the scenes following the actors' first performance at the palace. Shortly after this performance, Camilla arrives on a balcony in the foreground to speak to the viceroy whilst the other members of the court retreat to the parlour in the background where they proceed to dance (Figure 4.3). This parlour is visible through three doors adorned by curtains that emphasise the theatricality of the dance unfolding in the background. The court's performance of pre-assigned movements demands no audience, and is devoid of the spontaneity that thrills Camilla's spectators: their gestures are mechanical responses that conform to social etiquette and the rhythm of the music that plays, engendering their *rôles morts*. During a conversation with Camilla on the balcony, the viceroy himself reduces the court's activities to 'a few tricks of speech, a few gestures now and then. A few rules', recalling Debord's conception of societies of spectacle as those demanding 'absolute conformism in existing social practices', whilst the staging of the palace interiors in depth conveys Camilla's obligation to remain distanced from the space striated by the court's performance.[53]

The different brands of theatre engendered through the troupe's and the court's respective social practices in this scene are illustrated by each stratum's costumes: whereas the deep multicoloured hues of the *commedia dell'arte* costumes worn by Camilla and the troupe testify to a rich cultural legacy and distinguish the characters from the palatial setting, the golden clothes worn by the viceroy, the duke, the marquise, and various other members of the court during the troupe's dramatisation signal the court's general preoccupation with opulence that forms a core part of their everyday performance. The avarice implied by the golden designs acquires a distinctly colonialist dimension during this scene as the viceroy wearily curses his country's agenda before Camilla: 'We're here only for this treacherous gold. No-one dreams of anything else. And where gold commands, laughter vanishes.' The extravagant veneer sported by the court provides what Hayward terms 'literally a *mise en scène* and performance of wealth'.[54] However, unlike Camilla's enactments, which consolidate new public relations amongst different strata, their self-indulgent opulence and repetitive etiquette aim to exclude lower strata, in accordance with Debord's manifesto, through 'an irreversible relation to the very centre which maintains their isolation'.[55]

Off-screen space is essential to our understanding of the relationship between the court's externalisation of undesired elements of the colony and the simultaneous petrifaction of the court's own roles. The fact that this process of externalisation affects the future of the colony encourages us to read Renoir's *mise en scène* in temporal terms. The court is content to play out its roles and to ignore turbulent colonial issues unfolding beyond the palace, particularly the conflict between Spanish troops and Peruvian natives at a colonial outpost in Cusco.[56] The real violence of Cusco is reduced to comments that are both menacing and deceptively comic in tone. The first reference is spoken by the exploitative innkeeper who threatens Felipe when the latter accosts him: 'Better not cause any trouble here or it's Cusco for you. [. . .] Cusco, the army, they're trapped by Indians there and not too particular about how they get replacements, so be careful.' A short time later, as Camilla grants her first performance to the public, the viceroy, the marquise, and her father play cards in a parlour. When the marquise doubts the sincerity of the viceroy's love for her, she declares, 'I stood by you loyally when you ordered my poor husband to Cusco. A general commanding an outpost like that . . . [. . .]. Since those beastly Indians made me a poor defenceless widow. . . .' The viceroy insists that her husband 'died a hero' and ignores talking about the war until he later exploits it as a pretext for retaining the coach as a personal asset. In fact, when Felipe later declares to Don Antonio (Odoardo Spadaro) that 'I've been offered a captaincy in this war they're fighting here', it marks the first time that the conflict in Cusco is defined as a war by any of the characters.

In fact, we are completely unaware of the severity of the colonial conflict until the viceroy attempts to justify both his purchase of the coach and his demand for contributions from the nobility towards the war effort: the viceroy remarks that whereas the coach was bought during a time of peace, Spanish colonial rule is now at war with rebelling Mexican natives. The viceroy's allusion to the war, made without any reaction of surprise from his counsel, implies that the strife has been escalating out of control for at least a short period of time prior to this discussion, and Hayward convincingly suggests that the decreased wealth of the court is already suggested by the understated arrival of the coach in the beginning of the film.[57] Yet the colony remains decidedly insulated from the off-screen horrors reported by the characters, which are evoked solely through verbal reference and our pre-existing knowledge of the court's interest in Cusco's resources. The court's refusal to negotiate directly with the colonised indigenous people in favour of attempting to sustain its manifestly extravagant lifestyle blinds its members to the conflict and signals the potential dissolution of colonial rule.

Social threats, once relegated beyond the walls of the colony, are reassuringly invisible. Within the walls of the colony, however, they pose an immediately apparent threat. Thus, rather than prioritise the war, the nobility exploits the coach as a fulcrum to purge Camilla from the palace and only offers contributions to the war effort on condition that the viceroy permit them to use the coach and ratify a decree prohibiting entry to the palace of anyone not descended from at least eight lines of noble ancestry. The court's general vigilance is more broadly exemplified by its male members, who peer obtrusively through curtains and doors around the palace and, in the case of members of the nobility, wear eye-glasses around their necks. This concern for homogenised social space within the palace is most notably evidenced after their performance when the chief justice suspiciously asks, 'Who knows what lies behind those masked faces?' as he urges his superior to reconsider holding a personal meeting with any of the actors. However, this vigilance is problematically circumscribed by the walls of the palace. All of the windows that separate the palace from the colony are covered either with blinds or criss-crossing shutters. This allows the court to mute the presence of the impoverished society beyond the windows but, by approaching the windows more closely, to witness events such as the arrival of the golden coach when desired.

This enclosure and the colonisers' quest for gold and silver also prevent them from arriving at an understanding of the 'beastly Indians' (as the marquise labels the native South Americans) later befriended by Felipe who, during his captivity, realises that 'They're not savages. They helped me discover a truth and kindness and beauty. [. . .] They're much better than we are. That's what I've discovered. [. . .] I'm leaving this civilisation that's making us brutal and dishonest.' Their preoccupation with the war stems primarily from five silver mines located west of Cusco that fuel the lifestyle displayed so opulently during the dance sequence on the veranda and disparaged by the viceroy himself in the very same scene.

The palace, recalling Wintersborn, La Colinière, and the Lanlaire residence, lends Renoir's crystal an architectural structure that hosts the *rôles morts* engendered through the court's myopic, deliberate self-enclosure and self-indulgent spectacle enforced by its members' xenophobic social protocol. At the end of the film, the war is still looming beyond the confines of the palace, a fact that we should not ignore despite the visual beauty of the palace and costumes that lure the spectator as much as the colonisers into focusing on Camilla's confinement onstage.

'Any platform, any public place . . .': Camilla's social confinement

Emphasising Camilla's isolation on a proscenium arch in the film's closing scene, Deleuze argues that Camilla alone remains entrapped within the world of the theatre at the end of the film: 'At the end of *The Golden Coach*, three characters will have found their living role, whereas Camilla will remain within the crystal, but to try more roles there, one of which may allow her to discover the true Camilla.'[58] Because the social stratification of the Spanish court's palace is beyond the scope of Deleuze's analysis, he fails to address the extent to which Camilla's audience – an aspect that distinguishes her brand of the theatre from that of the court – contributes to Camilla's confinement.

Crucially, the ending of Renoir's film deviates notably from the conclusion of Mérimée's play. In the latter, Camilla returns to the viceroy with the coach, accompanied by the bishop, and the bishop announces to all present that she has granted the coach to the church. Order has been restored. Renoir's conclusion begins similarly, presenting Camilla on the stage ascending the stairs with the bishop, who remarks to all present that Camilla has returned the coach. After the bishop has invited everyone to the church ceremony featuring Camilla, the jubilant troupe emerges from the lower floor, playing music as they climb the stairs. The nobility, Camilla's lovers, the people of the colony, and Camilla herself all walk towards the balustrade to watch the musicians as they play. Don Antonio raises his arm, the actors bow towards their audience, and a curtain falls. Don Antonio declares that he wanted to present 'a new melodrama in the Italian style, but Camilla is still missing'. He calls Camilla onstage and she obligingly enters from the right-hand wing of the stage. Don Antonio warns Camilla against the folly of engaging with reality:

> Don't waste your time in the so-called real-life. You belong to us, the actors, acrobats, mimes, clowns, mountebanks! Your only way to find real happiness is on any stage, any platform, any public place, during those two little hours when you become another person, your true self.

A red curtain falls between Camilla and the remainder of the troupe. She now shares the stage only with Don Antonio, trapped on the stage of life by other people's expectations of her, robbed of her suitors:

> CAMILLA: Felipe, Ramon, the Viceroy. Disappeared. Gone. Don't they exist any more?
> DON ANTONIO: Disappeared. Now they are a part of the audience. Do you miss them?
> CAMILLA: [*pauses*] A little.

Camilla's silent display of emotion represents grief, humility, and, above all, a degree of nuance hitherto absent from her behaviour. We should therefore consider that Camilla is emoting what she truly feels. Camilla remains an actress by profession, but she is not exhibiting her grief with a view to eliciting applause. Therefore, although Janet Bergstrom rightly asserts that Camilla 'speaks of her suitors with warmth and regret', Bergstrom's proposal that '[Camilla] decides to give up her three suitors and remain with the troupe. The decision is her own' is less convincing.[59] Rather than focus exclusively on Camilla's isolation on the proscenium arch, we must remember two significant points. Firstly, the fall of the curtains is not pure happenstance. It occurs after the renunciation of the coach, thus implying that the audience present during the reception of Camilla's act is directly implicated in her imprisonment. Whether Camilla is giving a conscious performance or making a sincere 'act of true charity', as the bishop suggests, her confinement results from what the people surrounding her at this point in time believe, especially since Camilla's theatre, unlike that of the court, relies on a diegetic audience. Even if her act of charity is genuine, Camilla's act remains a performance because the court and townspeople who have hitherto constituted her audience (and who now share the stage with her) only appreciate it as such. Don Antonio's determination to direct a new melodrama immediately after Camilla's alleged triumph selfishly devalues the real emotion felt by the grieving Camilla, and fixes her status as a performer.

Secondly, the stage marks the confluence of social forces operating in the Spanish colony including the Church and the nobility, which both define themselves in part through theatricality. As an emphatically socialised theatre, the stage is in no way disconnected from the rest of the theatrically defined hierarchised space of the colony: when the curtain falls, the characters who have now 'disappeared' and become 'part of the audience' according to Don Antonio all remain on the stage, divided only by two curtains that fall in succession on the stage. Deleuze's assertion that Camilla's lovers have escaped the crystal risks simplifying both the film's dissection of social spaces of theatre and Don Antonio's remark that Felipe, Ramon, and the viceroy are part of the audience. Just as Don Antonio insists that Camilla must exploit 'any stage, any platform, any public place' that happens to be available, 'the audience' to whom he refers does not designate any particular physical space, least of all the seats in front of the proscenium arch photographed in the prologue and epilogue, but rather the spectators themselves who enter into a social contract (to borrow Elsaesser's term) with the performers in any given physical space. Even though the characters are part of Camilla's audience, the falling curtain does not necessarily mean that her sacrifice has liberated them from their own *rôles morts*. Such a view is supported by an earlier draft of Don Antonio's speech:

> Noble sirs and gentle ladies! See where destiny has led the characters of this comedy in the Italian style. How do they find their happy endings? (*Medium shot: Antonio stands to one side and the curtain rises to show Ramon and a bull.*) . . . Ramon, the bullfighter . . . Ramon, the man of uncomplicated passions! Here he is – once again united with his noisy reality . . . (*The curtain is lowered and raised to reveal Felipe surrounded by Indians.*) . . . Felipe, the nature lover . . . pioneer – has finally found his true destiny. (*The curtain is lowered and raised to show the viceroy and the marquise.*) . . . The viceroy . . . in all his greatness and misery! Misery of noble courts, meshes of intrigue, the necessary nourishment of this unhappy race, bound from their tenderest infancy in the tinsel of royal palaces . . . (*The curtain is lowered and raised again for Camilla.*)[60]

Although it would be misguided to allow the previous draft to dictate an interpretation of the finished film, this version does indicate a conception of the world as a theatre in which people are at once spectators of Camilla and, either by virtue of their profession or their class, performers trapped in roles that stultify social agency. The complexity of the filmed version of this sequence lies in the decision to progressively isolate Camilla from her peers through two curtains whilst suggesting, as in the previous draft, that they all still remain on a single, all-encompassing stage that signifies this inherent theatricality. Far from embodying potential escape from the crystal as Richard Rushton suggests, the characters are all entrapped within the theatre, either through the attraction of the stage or the appeal of the spectacle flaunted by the court.[61] Crucially, Camilla's spectators also remain trapped in their own roles on the theatre of life, and it is implied that none will find the role that will liberate them. Felipe, through his experience of captivity under the Indians, is the only character who appears to approach a new future devoid of theatrical shackles. This off-screen space, deprived of any roads that could accommodate Camilla's coach and resisting enslavement under the Spanish, arguably represents the only true *ligne de fuite* from any of the characters' shared plight. However, insofar as Felipe's own experience is concerned, there is a sharp irony in his retention of his military uniform following his experience in the economically impoverished milieu, and the narrative implies that such a pursuit requires a complete rejection of the colonial structures that stratify the Americas.

The Golden Coach arguably demonstrates the extent to which society is capable of nullifying the potential of space as a precondition for the temporal more clearly than any other Renoir film, with the possible exception of *La Grande Illusion*. Through the *surcroît de théâtralité* that emerges from combinations of characterisation, costume design, set design, and a complex interplay between off-screen and on-screen space, the film intimately demonstrates that the potential for escape from any role assigned by hegemonic powers deploying social spectacle is but a fantasy with no bearing on the reality that is theatre, echoing Debord's regret for the development of a world within which 'all that was once directly lived has become mere representation'.[62]

Eléna et les hommes (1956)

Further developing the stylistic and political motifs that feature in *Diary of a Chambermaid* and *The Golden Coach*, *Eléna et les hommes* exploits ideologically imbued décor to foreground theatricality, specifically exploring the influence of military spectacle on volatile nationalist sentiment in the public space of *belle époque* Paris. Renoir himself called attention to the film's emphasis on artifice in an interview granted on 30 November 1955, when shooting was just beginning: 'My story [. . .] is far too fantastical for anyone to lend it any appearance of reality. It is better to begin by saying that it is a false story.'[63] Discussing his reliance on in-studio décor, Renoir observed:

> The action in this film of artificial appearance would not readily accommodate realistic décor. The reds and the blues clash with one another without any transition. Claude Renoir filmed some shots of stormy landscapes which directly evoke images designed for children. Ingrid Bergman, who played the main role, got by with her

> characteristic genius and succeeded in creating a character as unbelievable as the settings.[64]

Eléna features a myriad of interwoven relations, competing political plots, economic interests, and hidden motives, not to mention a central heroine whose complexity renders her own precise outlook difficult to elucidate. Eléna Sokorowska (Ingrid Bergman) is an impoverished Polish princess pursued by the elderly Martin-Michaud (Jacques Jouanneau), an industrial shoe-manufacturer who also seeks to secure a marriage between his son and the daughter of an industrialist manufacturing rubber products. During Bastille Day celebrations, Eléna is separated from Martin-Michaud and accidentally meets Henri de Chevincourt (Mel Ferrer). He introduces her to General Rollan (Jean Marais), who is inspecting the troops at the Paris garrison that day. When a French surveillance balloon accidentally lands in Germany and its soldiers are imprisoned as spies, Rollan is encouraged by his advisers to issue an ultimatum. The release of the soldiers transforms Rollan into a national hero, and the French call for him to become president. Fearing that Rollan will establish a dictatorship, the President of the Republic places him under house arrest. Driven by their own interests, Rollan's advisers ask Eléna to convince Rollan to break free and seize power. Although Rollan initially agrees out of love for Eléna, he departs with his mistress, Paulette (Elina Labourdette), in the wake of his election as president, renouncing the French military and his prospective political career. Meanwhile, Eléna foregoes a pre-arranged marriage of convenience to Martin-Michaud and remains with Henri.

'Vive Rollan!': *nationalist spectacle and the French public*

There is a moment during the Bastille Day celebrations that open the film when Eléna is tossed from one part of the ecstatic crowd to another. Many are waving or selling flags and all are equally eager to catch a glimpse of General Rollan as he conducts the military review at the Paris garrison. At first, Eléna does not even know who Rollan is, and responds 'Rollan? Who is that?' ('Qui ça, Rollan?') to a man who asks if she has come to see the general. Yet by the next shot, she is loudly crying, 'Long live Rollan!' ('Vive Rollan!'). When she accidentally bumps into Henri for the first time two shots later, she is insisting that she wants to see Rollan in person. Carrying the child of a mother who prefers to direct her energy towards cheering enthusiastically for Rollan, Eléna is swept away by the crowd once more and happens upon a man who offers her the chance to look through a periscope in a vain effort to witness Rollan. During her acquisition of the periscope, Eléna loses both her umbrella and the child, all in her effort to see this figurehead whom she has never even heard of until now.

The periscope, patriotically adorned with the French tricolour, is hopelessly impractical: because both apertures are located on the same side of the periscope, Eléna must turn her back to the events at hand in order to view them. In doing so, she must also redirect her attention towards the limited view offered by the periscope of a select area above the crowd, and risks being buffeted by the crowd that now eludes her gaze. The impracticality and patriotic design of the periscope within this scene metaphorises the distortive and socially volatile perspective engendered through nationalism that consumes the crowd: the narrow view offered by fervently patriotic perspectives is unreliable because it is restricted and is liable to leave patriots open to assault whilst their backs remain turned.

The threat posed by this crowd's unconditional support is exposed as the Bastille Day celebrations continue into the night. Soldiers and members of the general public alike sing 'L'Artilleur de Metz' ('The Artilleryman of Metz') in praise of the French military and join in the singing of 'La Chanson de Roland' ('The Song of Roland'), a ballad that elevates Rollan to the legendary status of Roland (homonymous with Rollan) and which is heard repeatedly throughout the remainder of the narrative. Later during the celebrations, Henri and Eléna raise a glass to Rollan; a man sitting in the bar shouts, 'Down with Rollan!' in response. After Eléna flees the conflict, the same man declares, 'Down with Rollan, down with dictators!'[65] This anonymous man's scepticism regarding Rollan's suitability as a French political figure, as we shall see, is justified in part by Rollan's susceptibility to the ulterior motives of his influential advisers. That an opinion opposed to the one articulated by the majority of French citizens is accepted only as an insult rather than a topic for discussion signals the myopic perspective of the majority of the French public and the dangerous failure of the patriotic crowd to accommodate deviating opinions. Clearly, 'Vive Rollan!' not only expresses support for a single figure who embodies what they consider the French political ideal, but also articulates the failure of the nationalist majority to accommodate alternative opinions in a place where support for Rollan, however ubiquitous, is not unanimous. As Colin Davis notes, the celebration 'may in fact involve nothing better than mindless, proto-fascist conformism'.[66] Renoir himself recollected that 'I constructed a satire around [the woman, Eléna]. I toyed with political stories, stories of generals. I tried to demonstrate the futility of human enterprises including the enterprise which we call patriotism [. . .]', and these sequences could well be read as a microcosm of the entire film's incisive portrayal of the impact of spectacle on popular political sentiment.[67]

Rollan and his corps politique

As in the cases of *Diary of a Chambermaid* and *The Golden Coach*, the narrative's satirical exploration of the relationship between society and spectacle is critical to our integration of temporality into our analysis of space in *Eléna*. Central to the tension between *rôles morts* and the possibility of entering what Deleuze calls 'decanted reality' is Rollan's public identity, which is instrumentalised by his associates in their endeavour to stoke the already fervent nationalism with a view to furthering their own political goals. Renoir's *mise en scène* of the military review taking place during the Bastille Day celebrations makes it clear that the review itself is partly a ploy to ignite public enthusiasm, for the proceedings themselves are startlingly anticlimactic when juxtaposed with the throngs that congregate in the streets of Paris, a fact echoed by a woman who sarcastically declares, 'They call that a parade!'[68] In a wide shot, Rollan arrives on his horse and dismounts to inspect the underwhelming number of soldiers lined up. Reds, whites, and blues of the military uniforms dominate the frame. Surprisingly, we witness little of this event that marks a climax for the local newspaper, *Le Petit Journal*: just as Rollan begins his review, the camera cuts to Eléna and Henri who are discussing Rollan's future. The camera does not cut back to the review until the review is complete and Rollan's associates are congratulating him: '120,000 people, it is a record.'[69] Far less important than the anticlimactic scale of the review are the numbers accumulating outside the garrison, which testify to Rollan's growing popularity. The sober framing of the formalities, dominated by static long shots and medium shots of small groups of characters, lends scope to the superficial spectacle of their colourful and detailed costumes, counterposing the review with the kinetic dynamic that proliferates in the crowd scenes (Figure 4.4).

At this point, it is worth reiterating Renoir's distinction between *la vérité intérieure* and *la vérité extérieure*, as *Eléna*'s narrative presents us with two obverse aspects of Rollan's character: firstly, the Rollan adored by the Parisian public whose routines are measured by the emphatic theatricality implied by *mise en scène*; secondly, the Rollan who is incapable of acting of his own accord and whose inability to make decisions renders it increasingly difficult for the spectator to determine how he ever became a general in the first place, much less the object of national admiration.

Figure 4.4 Eléna (far right) watches Rollan (centre, in military regalia) as he talks to his coterie

Debord states that 'the imposed image of the good envelops in its spectacle the totality of what officially exists, and is usually concentrated in one man, who is the guarantor of totalitarian cohesion. Everyone must magically identify with this absolute celebrity or disappear.'[70] Such is the case of Rollan who, like Debord's star (*vedette*) of spectacle, 'has renounced all autonomous qualities in order to identify with the general law of obedience to the course of things', sacrificing his own agency in order to channel the crystallising capacity of nationalist discourse.[71] The colourful costumes and set design of the military review appeal to members of the public who are eager for a masculine personification of French identity and military prowess, but emphasise Rollan's presence as a superficial nationalist image lacking agency. As Daniel Serceau accurately remarks, Rollan is '[a] canvas for all projections' and 'has no [. . .] consistency other than to furnish an object for a desire that pre-exists him'.[72] Rollan constantly refuses to develop his own authority, and remains a superficial nationalist spectacle, deployed by his own associates in their endeavour to stimulate the French public's desire for a strong, autocratic leader and, by extension, to satisfy their own political ambitions.

The contrasting hues of the costumes worn by Rollan and his advisers at the review accentuate the constructedness of his public image. Rollan's advisers are all discreetly dressed in grey suits whereas Rollan wears elaborate military regalia adorned with golden designs, a feathered hat, and a light blue uniform which distinguish him from his associates, the visitors, and other soldiers present. Henri introduces Rollan's coterie to Eléna as 'le corps politique du général'. Interestingly, *le corps* may be translated not only as Rollan's corps (as suggested by the Criterion DVD) but also as a body. Henri proceeds to assign each man the function of a particular corporeal organ, suggesting that Rollan himself is merely an ideologically infused image whose trajectory is entirely dictated by these five men in both the public space of Paris and in the media: 'Duchêne, the brain; Fleury, the eyes; Lisbonne, the heart; and Buchez, the mind. [. . .] And here is the indispensable Isnard, former running champion.'[73] The remarks that follow further reinforce such an interpretation: Henri remarks that Lisbonne began as a theatre publicist, to which the latter proudly remarks, 'Without me, Sarah Bernhardt would still be at the Comédie Française.'[74] It is Lisbonne who declares, after their collective introduction to Eléna, 'A good headline: "The Princess and the General"', which hints towards Lisbonne's power to mould the general's image in the newspapers.[75] Furthermore, that Isnard is associated with movement and deemed 'essential' by Henri suggests that Rollan's own trajectory would grind to a halt without his *corps*.

Their influence visibly informs Rollan's activities over the course of the narrative. It is they who pull Rollan aside from his conversation with Eléna regarding her daisy mere moments after their introduction, and warn him that an important government representative is now present, thus ensuring that he maintains essential relations with official members of the government. When Vidauban, an officer in the military, accidentally lands a hot-air balloon in German territory and is imprisoned, the advisers realise that the country will need a leader to deal with the crisis. In particular, they require someone who can simultaneously serve as a visually convincing mouthpiece and allow them to engineer the political machine to their own ends. Tellingly, Rollan presents himself to his public from his balcony following the release of Vidauban (Figure 4.5) and, later, during a promotional appearance, smiling and waving silently each time whilst his eager coterie waits discreetly behind him, separated by a door. The staging of Rollan's visually muted advisers behind the general – invisible to the public but nonetheless present – provides a metaphor for the social forces operating through the spectacle embodied by Rollan.

Their influence as puppet masters of Rollan's fate remains salient throughout the remainder of the narrative. When the advisers later conclude that Rollan must perform a *coup d'état*, Duchêne remarks that Rollan may not even accept, underscoring their own importance in determining Rollan's political trajectory. When they realise that Eléna is needed to motivate Rollan towards a *coup d'état*, Fleury succeeds in learning of Eléna's entire marriage schedule, the reasons for which the

Figure 4.5 Rollan's advisers watch as he greets the general public

wedding will be delayed for one month (incidentally, to take place at the same time as her future son-in-law's wedding), and her current location at the château de Maisonvilliers. These are but a few examples that demonstrate that Rollan the human being is startlingly ill-equipped to perform his own role of general and that, as O'Shaughnessy writes of the crowd, 'spectacle's sensual appeal is the main form of influence upon this non-reflective mass'.[76] No one realises this better than Rollan's *corps*. Rollan is a colourful ideological instrument whose military uniform precedes any coherent corporeality. His rise to prominence evidently results from the skilful scheming of his coterie, whose fingers are placed on the pulse of the French nation at a time when the majority of the French public is predisposed towards any figure offering potential opportunities to elevate France's grandeur. The crowd idolises the image of Rollan propagated by his coterie rather than Rollan the human being, about whom they know surprisingly little. If they scraped beyond the *vérité extérieure* projected by his advisers, it is unlikely that they would wish for him to take office at all, much less in a *coup d'état*.

Rollan's core flaws may well be his indecisiveness, his submission to authority, and his apparent lack of interest in his political career as Serceau suggests.[77] However, these failings stem from a general lack of willpower that imprisons him within his *rôle mort*. For much of the film, Rollan remains in docile imprisonment under the orders of the president, or leaves himself open to the persuasion of his colleagues and Eléna (herself under the influence of Rollan's ambitious colleagues), unwilling to exercise his authority.

Figure 4.6 From the natural surroundings of Martin-Michaud's hunting grounds . . .

Furthermore, the military manoeuvres near Martin-Michaud's residence that provide us with our sole view of Rollan on the battlefield are reduced to a hollow, self-aggrandising farce. Despite the proximity of Martin-Michaud's castle and the location of the manoeuvres, the *mise en scène* of the landscape in each is radically different: as Henri and Eléna ride in the château's grounds, the camera pits them against a natural forest beneath the blue sky (Figure 4.6). Conversely, when Eléna and Henri are escorted to Rollan's base, the emphatically false décor used to construct these outdoor surroundings is bathed in a red light that reduces the manoeuvres to a spectacular caricature (Figure 4.7). After Eléna offers Rollan a daisy to aid him in his future decisions, one of Rollan's officers informs him that one of the on-field commanders has given the order to attack. 'Under enemy fire, in a real war', remarks an incredulous Rollan, 'he would have massacred his men'.[78] Both Rollan and the army are, in the final analysis, ineffectual. As Eléna and Rollan navigate Martin-Michaud's castle in subsequent scenes, various items of military regalia encased in glass or draped on mannequins like museum pieces are present in various rooms. These displays suggest that the roles inhabited by Rollan and his men are, no less than the identities inhabited by Boëldieu and von Rauffenstein, 'condemned because they are already doomed to become memories'.[79]

Renoir's satire of Rollan's image arguably stems from his own intimate romanticisation of late nineteenth-century armies as a child through his collection of lead soldiers which, according to Renoir, 'were an important matter for all of the children of my generation'.[80] Renoir remarked that 'some of them were quite beautiful' and elaborated on his childhood

Figure 4.7 . . . to the visible artifice of Rollan's training grounds

impressions of the spectacle of warfare: 'For me, war, with its real miseries, with its real misfortunes, did not exist in epochs of beautiful costumes. This realistic war had begun with the grubby costumes of the end of the 19th century [. . .].'[81]

As in *Diary of a Chambermaid*, the tension between the *vérité intérieure* and the *vérité extérieure* invoked by costume design is crucial to our understanding of the imprisoning capacity of the socially assigned roles satirised by Rollan's regalia. Unlike Célestine and Joseph, whose defiant attitudes contrast with their official roles and serve to hold their potential futures in tension with the imposing force of the past, Rollan's submissive boredom dismisses the potential creation of a new future beyond the current role designated by his costume.

To agree with Durgnat's suggestion that Rollan, 'through his love for Eléna, realises the emptiness of power' would be to flatter the general.[82] Rather, Rollan's disinterest in the army wavers little as the film progresses, but he gradually realises that he can use it to appeal to Eléna, who insists on catalysing his relationship with the French public in order to encourage him to seize power. Rollan finally casts aside his role and escapes towards a new future but only by renouncing both his military career and Eléna. Furthermore, when he finally escapes the influence of his cohorts in the closing scene, it is only because his mistress has persuaded him to travel with her to the south of France instead of taking the train bound for Paris in the wake of his election. The front page of a newspaper closes the film, announcing that both are spending their honeymoon in Venice and that Rollan has retired. Thus, Rollan is definitively detached from the French military, his *corps*' agenda, and his *rôle mort* as their political instrument. Elsewhere in the film, however, Rollan's refusal to exercise his own agency assimilates him within the hollow spectacle that structures the entire film and crystallises social relations within a city, where the public sacrifices its agency to such superficial images, and remains susceptible to spectacles that prevent it from questioning the efficacy of national institutions.

'I love the crowd . . .': Eléna, men, and social mobility

The power of spectacle to induce 'paralysis of history and memory'[83] is especially interesting in the case of Eléna because she eventually sacrifices her agency to the appeal of spectacle, despite embodying what Hayward rightly recognises as a progressive portrayal of the *belle époque* woman by displaying 'a great sense of freedom far in excess of the reality of the times' and making independent choices in ways that are 'undoubtedly more myth than fact'.[84] Indeed, Eléna herself refuses to commit to any man (Martin-Michaud provides little more than a convenient financial buttress) until she finally falls for Henri, preferring to provide moral support for professional projects of the men she meets. Although she has no fixed assets by her own estimation, she does not even capitalise on the success of the men whom she has nurtured to success such as the budding composer whose opera has been accepted for performance thanks to Eléna's support. Renoir himself claimed that Eléna 'does not know what money is. She has never known. She doesn't care about it. It does not count. Moreover, she would be as happy a beggar as a millionaire.'[85] Indeed, once at the Bastille Day celebrations, she recklessly loses one item of clothing after another (a parasol, a small handbag, a glove) and buoyantly discards her hat in favour of developing a rapport with the crowd of revellers.

Eléna's affinity with the crowd is suggested on numerous occasions and initially appears harmless. When she first travels to the city streets with Martin-Michaud, the crowd is visible from her carriage through a small window. When the carriage ceases to move, Eléna readily descends, leaving her fiancé behind in favour of mixing with citizens of lower social ranking than herself: to Martin-Michaud, the crowd is a threat; to Eléna, it is an invitation. 'Ah princess, are we mixing together today?' one man asks. 'That is why you stormed the Bastille!'[86] she responds. This rapport is underscored by her intercultural appropriation of the everyday habits of her new homeland. The red and white colours that adorn Eléna's apartment, as Hayward observes, initially suggest Eléna's strict allegiance to Poland.[87] However, Eléna continues to develop a strong rapport with

French populace, as evidenced by her drinking of wine (despite her self-professed love of Polish vodka), her fluent French, her support of Rollan, and her eventual commitment to his cause (or rather, that of his coterie). Eléna herself repeatedly declares, 'I love the crowd' as she drinks with Henri during the Bastille Day celebrations,[88] suggesting her desire to be carried along by the social dynamic rather than being subjugated either by her own romantic desires or by those of any one man.

Yet Eléna's affinity with the crowd is problematic, since her nascent support for Rollan marks her as the personification of its nationalist fervour which subjugates both Eléna and the broader public to Rollan's brain-trust: like them, she supports Rollan enthusiastically on Bastille Day before she even sees him, and when she does finally meet him, she is easily duped by his superficial image. Eléna's susceptibility to the appeal of spectacle is later evidenced when Fleury suggests that Rollan escape to Paris on a train. Disappointed by the escape plan, she admits, 'I would have preferred battle. It is more glorious. But the end justifies the means.'[89] This penchant for spectacle leads her to make two significant errors of judgement which together lead to her confinement within the crystal without her knowledge. First of all, her attraction to the nationalist spectacle projected by Rollan discourages her from discerning that Rollan is far less interested in national duty than in her love and from attempting to determine whether or not Rollan and his policies would benefit international relations. As social tensions mount in Paris in the wake of the imprisonment of the French soldiers in Germany, Rollan issues an ultimatum to the Germans but later admits to Eléna at Martin-Michaud's residence that he sent the ultimatum out of love for her rather than out of political discernment; however, this prompts no realisation on Eléna's part, even when Rollan tellingly refers to his career as 'the cause that you make me hate'.[90] Secondly, as a result of her failure to comprehend Rollan's fundamental indifference to his military career, Eléna fails to realise that she is being exploited by both Rollan's coterie, whose members encourage her to convince Rollan to act on their desired course of action, and by her own ageing fiancé, who has bartered Eléna's favours in return for the imposition of protectionist tariffs that will benefit his show-manufacturing business. Eléna sacrifices her own agency by insisting upon crystallising the ambitions and ideals of the image of 'le général Rollan' instead of attempting to understand Rollan's own indifference towards the goals set by his associates.

Henri represents Eléna's only hope for escape from the metaphorical crystal which is constituted by her affinity with the French public and misplaced devotion to Rollan. Unlike Eléna, Henri remains critically distanced from the political atmosphere, only attending the Bastille Day celebrations because Rollan is his personal friend and only shouting 'Vive Rollan!' in an effort to impress Eléna in front of one of Rollan's few detractors. When Eléna asks Henri to disclose his main goal in life, he responds, 'To do nothing. My dream is to achieve perfect idleness. Unfortunately, these days it is almost impossible. [. . .] Universal idleness for both the poor and the rich. What a goal!'[91] Eléna initially spurns Henri's apparent lack of ambition, ignoring the potential value of adhering to ideals that are detached from dominant ideology, and continues in her efforts to persuade Rollan to seize power. Unlike any other character, Henri deftly negotiates a middle ground between Eléna's sense of duty to the French political machine and her growing interest in Henri himself. At the end of the film, when escape becomes imperative for Rollan, Henri dons Rollan's uniform, stands at a dimly lit window with Eléna, and pretends to kiss her romantically in order to detract attention from Rollan who escapes through the crowd gathered outside. The crowd is only pacified by the example of love set by Henri and Eléna's masquerade whose popularity among the crowd further testifies to the superficial demands of the popular masses. Eléna accepts Henri's kiss as a primal form of nationalism, itself associated with Henri's understanding of France's cultural legacy:

> The French respect matters pertaining to love. [. . .] When it comes to digging for oil or choosing our governments or the manufacturing of explosives, perhaps we do not quite come in first place. But when it comes to the art of living, you can bank on the French.[92]

This kiss offers a perfect compromise between Eléna's support for French patriotic icons and her own desire to aid Rollan's escape. Love (or the illusion of love) can distract both the crowd and Eléna from Rollan's public appeal. By closing their eyes for one another and encouraging the public to follow suit, they also close their eyes to the spectacle of Rollan, freeing all present from the unconditional patriotism inspired by their theatrical surroundings. In the end, Eléna is free to gaze beyond the window with Henri as they break free of their *jeu de rôle* in front of the otherwise preoccupied crowd. Through this *deus ex machina*, which constitutes what is rightly announced in the credits as *une fantaisie musicale*, society is liberated from its petrifying reverence for Rollan. It is important to note, however, that as in the case of *Diary of a Chambermaid*, the heroine is subject to a double bind, and remains subjugated to Henri: although the molar line imposed by spectacle has disintegrated, patriarchal dominance crystallises around Eléna's *ligne de fuite*, precluding her entry into a social configuration in which she is entirely free to determine her own future.

Conclusion: Society and Spectacle

Hayward astutely observes that the textual richness of Renoir's economical storytelling in *Eléna* is 'an effect of set design as much as camera-work'.[93] The same could be said of any of the three films discussed in this chapter, which rely on sets and costumes to characterise individuals and their societies, all of which are often viewed through a static frame that enhances the *surcroît de théâtre* featuring in all three. Each film portrays worlds where what Christopher Faulkner refers to as Renoir's 'socialization of space' is inextricably connected with the passage of time.[94] However, if we are to interpret each film's *mise en scène* temporally, spectacle must be recognised as an ideologically imbued construct and, in the case of the ruling classes, as a composite of molar lines that 'never cease to seal, plug, block the lines of flight'.[95]

Furthermore, all three are surprisingly pessimistic works that portray cunning human attempts to nullify the 'juxtapositions yet to flower into interaction', particularly among members of lower social classes: in all three films, the ruling classes seek to entrench their *sociétés du spectacle* in the very 'chains of meaning which embed [space] with closure and stasis',[96] entailing diverse ramifications regarding the nature of Renoir's crystal, some of which intersect with the characteristics associated by Deleuze with Visconti's *mise en scène* of temporality.

In particular, *Diary of a Chambermaid* and *The Golden Coach* evoke an artificially constructed 'synthetic crystal' ('cristal synthétique'), which is 'inseparable from a process of decomposition which eats away at them from within'.[97] Aligning with Deleuze's discussion of this crystalline state, their worlds are subject to major historical developments that prevent potential salvation from arriving on time. Moreover, the hegemonic strata in each embody 'a vanished past' by endeavouring to preserve a precise moment in space-time through spectacular décor and antiquated social practices. New social configurations usurp Mme Lanlaire's theatre from within, specifically the rise of the *nouveaux riches*, which Deleuze considers a core characteristic of Visconti's work, and which is embodied by Joseph in *Diary*. Similarly, the Spanish colonial forces of *Coach* are under increased pressure from the looming off-screen violence in Cusco. Worse still, when the Spanish court does realise that it is imbricated in a costly conflict, its morally corrupt members remain primarily preoccupied with Camilla and the coach. Camilla ultimately remains entrapped within the colonial *société du spectacle*, and the prospect of a genuinely new future that corresponds with the heroine's desired terms remains unlikely. Even in *Diary of a Chambermaid* and *Eléna et les hommes*, where the heroines emerge from a stultifying social configuration, the prospect of a genuinely new future that corresponds with either of the heroines' desired terms remains unlikely.

Renoir's women are, as Sumit Ghose observes, 'often present as the key agents for the resolution of the problems that both arise in the discourse and affect the lives of the male characters' because the heroines' own agency in each of the films analysed is subjugated, however inadvertently, by their male counterparts who endeavour to actualise their own desires, lending credence to Roger Viry-Babel's assertion that 'all [Renoirian spaces] express the notion of enclosure or dependency, on Others in general, and on Man in particular. There is no place or space in which the woman may isolate herself.'[98] Space, through its imbrication in temporality, is open to becoming, but the openness of that process of becoming is inevitably conditioned by gender. Thus, as Viry-Babel rightly observes, such a space can only exist 'outside the limits of the field and out-of-field, in an eternally inaccessible future'.[99] It is undoubtedly true that Renoir's male protagonists fare little better than his heroines analysed within this chapter. However, the men in each of these three films are given the opportunity to implement the future on their own terms rather than basing their projected trajectory on the demands of the women who surround them.

Stanley Cavell usefully distinguishes between the counterfeit and the artificial, that is to say, between cases where *mise en scène* is 'meant to fool the camera into thinking that what is revealed to it is reality' and cases where the explicit artifice of a visual setting is interpreted by the spectator as '*competing* with our sense of reality'.[100] The films discussed within this chapter, particularly *The Golden Coach* and *Eléna et les hommes*, clearly belong to the latter category. As a result, they provide an interesting response to broader debates surrounding the representation of temporality in *Cinéma 2*. Deleuze himself hints at the relevance of colour, spectacle, and the qualities of Renoir's *crises anti-réalistes* during his discussion of 'powers of the false' ('les puissances du faux'), stating that we see crystalline description 'in a diverse range of areas, the flat views, and flat tints of colour in the musical comedy [. . .]'.[101] The relationship between the *mise en scène* of social space and temporality within these three *crises anti-réalistes* can be best understood if we first consider the material genealogy of Deleuze's crystal and, building on this, examine how socially stultifying ideological discourse is lent visual, symbolic form. Both *profondeur de champ* and *images planes* emphasise the material spectacles that stratify the worlds in each film, portraying the settings as milieux susceptible to the ideologically manipulative force of spectacle, which imposes what Debord terms *le temps gelé* and, by extension, the *rôles morts* linked by Deleuze with theatricality.

Deleuze arguably provides the most lucid albeit indirect dissection of the impact of Renoir's *crises anti-réalistes* on the director's socialisation of space: Deleuze writes that truth 'must be created in every domain' and that it is a fallacy to even believe in any definitive kernel of truth since 'to say "the truth is a creation" implies that the truth is produced by a series of processes that mould its substance, literally through a series of falsifications'.[102] Although Debord insightfully reduces alleged ideological facts to '[a] deformed consciousness of realities', visibly false realities constitute the only tangible truths in each of the three films discussed and, by virtue of this, serve as 'real factors which, in return, instigate real deforming acts'.[103] As Éric Rohmer notes of *Eléna*, Renoir 'works less on a noble reality than on the caricature that it has sustained'.[104] By going beyond ontological understandings of realism for their terms of reference, these films construct their own truths regarding reality of spectacle and its ideological influence in a world where 'all that was directly lived has receded into a representation', pushing Bazin's assertion that 'realism in art can only be achieved through artifice' to its limit and demonstrating Renoir's own assertion that 'life is a tissue of deception'.[105]

Conclusion

This book began with two central aims: firstly, to develop a framework that would allow us to integrate temporality into our analysis of Renoir's *mise en scène* of space with due consideration of the construction of social space, developments in filmmaking technology, and shifts in Renoir's ideological outlook; secondly, to argue that Renoir frames the mutually affective relationship between physical and social space at each stage of his career, producing an image of open space-time in which the possibility for change remains constant. Building on three key shortcomings of Deleuze's reading of Renoir, individual chapters specifically sought to emphasise the import of Renoir's recurring narrative settings, his attitude towards the French Left, and his deployment of spectacular costume design and décor towards his portrayal of open space-time. This Conclusion briefly summarises the ways in which the preceding analysis permits us to arrive at a more comprehensive appreciation of what Leo Braudy refers to as Renoir's 'open world' and to constructively reconceptualise the process of crystallisation portrayed by Renoir's films.[1]

In *L'Évolution créatrice*, Bergson observed that 'our perception manages to solidify into discontinuous images the fluid continuity of the real', inaccurately condensing periods of evolution into a stable perspective that '*is only a snapshot view of a transition*'.[2] Renoir's cinema contests such perspectives, so one can see why Deleuze lauds Renoir's work, even if, as Colin Davis rightly notes, Deleuze's conceptualisation of Renoir's work 'is questionable in detail and in general, as the director's entire output is made to fit into a single category which does little justice to it'.[3] Clearly, what obscures the relevance of Deleuze's philosophical framework is less its infeasibility than its application within Deleuze's own *Cinéma* volumes. The spatio-temporal ontology of Renoir's work is constructed around a range of ideological, technological, and plastic components, many of which are rendered legible by Deleuze and Guattari's spatial thought and by other spatial theories, most notably Doreen Massey's treatise on space-time. By integrating *Mille Plateaux* into our analysis and demonstrating its relevance to the fluctuating spatial politics of Renoir's films, this book fulfilled two methodological aims: first, to demonstrate the possibility of interpreting the theatre as a composite of molar lines; second, to distinguish between the *point de fuite* (the visible possibility for change within the world viewed) and the *ligne de fuite* (the visible emergence of new interrelations in space-time) in Renoir's work and, by extension, to emphasise the susceptibility of *points de fuite* and *lignes de fuite* to 'microfascisms simply waiting to crystallise'.[4] If, as Patricia Pisters notes, 'one of the most challenging aspects of "applying" Deleuze is to highlight the relation of the cinema books to concepts that he developed elsewhere, mostly together with Guattari', then the resulting frameworks are also some of the most rewarding.[5]

By reading Deleuze and Guattari's vision of space through Massey's theorisation of spatial politics, the spectator is in a position to examine how the mutual implication of space and time is conveyed by Renoir's *mise en scène* across various narrative settings including urban streets, rural fields, domestic interiors, and realms of memory. This framework also allows us to lend special attention to characteristically Renoirian elements discussed by Deleuze (ranging from *profondeur de champ* to plastic aspects of *mise en scène* such as theatres and rivers) as well as techniques such as montage, which lend themselves less readily to orthodox readings of Renoir's work. Off-screen space has emerged from this analysis not only as one of the key challenges of integrating time into our vision of Renoir's social space, but also as a key component of Renoir's crystal. Echoing Bazin, Gilberto Perez writes that 'Renoir establishes [the off-screen world] socially as a concrete milieu of human and material interconnections'.[6] Renoir plays upon our expectations of more to transgress the frame, our sense that the information within the frame is incomplete and, like the unstable, oscillatory social relations viewed, remains open to drastic reconfiguration. Although this study has foregrounded the importance of Renoir's signature techniques to narrative space-time in his films, it has also sought to emphasise the importance of considering the combinations through which they interact with classical techniques as well as other visual and aural elements of *mise en scène*. Where films such as *Diary of a Chambermaid* (1946) are concerned, such combinations may initially appear crudely incoherent and antithetical to commonly held understandings of Renoir's narrative style upon initial viewings. However, as Andrew Sarris ecstatically wrote in *The American Cinema*, 'there is nothing crude about Renoir's technique once its purposes have been fully understood. Only when style is confused with meaningless flourishes does Renoir's economy of expression seem inadequate for textbook critics.'[7]

This book's four individual chapters allow us to draw three more specific conclusions regarding space-time in Renoir's films. First of all, all four chapters demonstrate that Renoir's *mise en scène* of space-time essentially implies that societies are produced within ongoing processes of spatialisation, itself a fundamentally open process imbued in temporality. Across Renoir's silent works, landmark films of the 1930s, Hollywood output, and post-war *crises anti-réalistes*, Renoir's directorial style clearly displays the import of centralised social practices such as capitalism and colonialism towards the homogenisation of society, but firmly situates these practices within a space of coeval spatial politics. This is not merely a space in which social analysis is performed by the camera (as suggested by Faulkner's emphasis on Renoir's 'socialization' of space[8]) or where characters may visibly implement radical political change (as suggested by O'Shaughnessy's Deleuzian analysis of 'chronological depth' in Renoir's work[9]), but a manifestly dynamic, inherently heterogeneous product of the fluctuating interrelations between physical and social space, whose sheer extensiveness and imbrication in time challenge any attempt by characters or spectators to determine 'how such chaos might be ordered, how juxtapositions may be regulated, how space might be coded, how the terms of connectivity might be negotiated'.[10] This particular point is critical to our understanding of the relationship between Renoir's camera techniques and the milieux photographed, for it acknowledges that spatialisation is the product not only of human intervention (even if this is a salient aspect of films as diverse as *Le Bled* [1929] and *Le Crime de Monsieur Lange* [1936]), but also of the physical space that they navigate (as in *La Chienne* [1931] and *The Southerner* [1945]), which actively alters the spatio-temporal trajectories of Renoir's characters. Crucially, the characters' fates are not exclusively determined by their own agency, but often feature as a by-product of the Parisian cityscape or the deceptively inert rural landscape. With the notable exception of *The River* (1951), an understanding of the manifest heterogeneity and simultaneity of the power relations that striate space demands that we consider the broader ideological context in which the films were produced. In *The River*, on the other hand, spectators must detach themselves from such political and economic coordinates, and develop a primarily philosophical approach to the spatial memories portrayed.

Secondly, Renoir's unfilmed *Ida* (1935) suggests the importance of situating the community projects featuring in Renoir's Front populaire output in relation to other coeval powers that striate space. By extension,

Renoir's Front populaire output encourages us to view *La Règle du jeu* (1939) as a culmination of Renoir's longstanding concern for the increased likelihood of war.

Thirdly, a complete appreciation of the relationship between space and time in the emphatically theatrical settings of Renoir's *crises anti-réalistes* demands that we distinguish between the various kinds of theatre featuring within each narrative and examine the stultifying ideological role that theatricality engenders for the strata that deploy it. The rigidly stratified patriarchal societies that condition space-time in all three narratives usefully remind the spectator of the impact of gender on the production of *points de fuite* and the pursuit of *lignes de fuite*.

The importance of a fundamentally open social space within which class barriers are negotiated and social change is possible evidently remains a consistent characteristic of Renoir's *mise en scène* throughout his varied career in silent filmmaking, in his most famous works of the 1930s, during his wartime Hollywood exile, and in his post-war *crises anti-réalistes*. Contrary to Deleuze's optimistic approach to Renoir's work, Renoir sometimes portrays self-destructive societies in which change cannot be envisioned in positive terms. However, Renoir constantly frames space as an ongoing process rather than a static container. Tellingly, this approach even informs *La Règle du jeu*, filmed on the eve of war as Marcel Carné was filming the foreboding apogee of poetic realism, *Le Jour se lève* (1939). It is worth briefly comparing the structurally opposed styles that each director deployed on the eve of war. Referring to Braudy's distinction between open and closed worlds, Ben McCann argues the latter film 'can be unequivocally placed in the "closed" film column'.[11] Interestingly, even in what Renoir himself described as a 'war film', he refuses to portray the *haute bourgeoisie*'s irrevocable fate within formally static compositions in which the fluctuating qualities of space recognised by Massey, Deleuze and Guattari have been nullified.[12] Rather, Renoir insists on conceptualising a fluid space and on defining the inevitability of the impending war through the manifest coevalness of differing ideological perspectives in Paris, and the liberty (albeit deceptive) experienced by a vanishing class amidst the landscapes of la Sologne. Even Renoir's fatalism finds its greatest expression in movement rather than in stasis and in a refusal to allow the dramatic force of society's *danse macabre* to supplant a recognition of the inextricable relationship between space and time.

The chronological breath and aesthetic diversity of this corpus has enabled us to reassess canonised landmarks (*La Grande Illusion*, 1937; *La Règle du jeu*) and to revisit works that remain underappreciated (*Diary of a Chambermaid*) and which even risk being forgotten (*Le Bled*), despite the prestige that Renoir's name lends to their titles. Therefore, it is hoped that this book will stimulate further analysis of his under-discussed works and encourage others to bring them into dialogue with his most acclaimed films.

Reconstituting the Cracked Crystal

Deleuze's analysis of Renoir's work, like any attempt to impose a single framework on a diverse corpus, obviously has its limits. In addition to the criticism noted in the Introduction, two further points regarding Deleuze's reading of Renoir's cracked crystal have been elucidated by the preceding analysis and may inform future applications of Deleuze's concepts. First of all, as noted in the analyses of *La Règle du jeu* and *The Golden Coach* (1952), Renoir's crystalline state is not consistent from film to film. Such possibilities for deviations from the crystalline states assigned by Deleuze have already been signalled by Lucio Angelo Privitello's argument that Visconti's *Il Gattopardo* (1963) exemplifies Federico Fellini's seed-crystal rather than the crystal in dissolution.[13] Such caution towards Deleuze's categories should remain central to any appropriation of Deleuze's taxonomy. Secondly, the state perceived within an individual film is not necessarily consistent from shot to shot: *Le Crime de Monsieur Lange* and *The Southerner* alternate between moments depicting optimistic *lignes de fuite* (as when the cooperative is formed, and when Sam acquires his land) and moments in which mobility in space-time is impeded (the image of la Cagoule in *Lange* and Devers's physically insulated ranch in *The Southerner*). Such cases exemplify Ronald Bogue's insightful (albeit undeveloped) suggestion that films may be interpreted as though the crystal contained facets of different qualities.[14]

Renoir's work frequently portrays characters who endeavour to actualise new possibilities as well as characters who are beset by forces beyond their control, with which they must repeatedly contend. Renoir's framing (particularly within his Front populaire output and *crises anti-réalistes*) suggests that the new sets of circumstances invoked by qualitative changes in space, no matter how radically differentiated from those embodied by the past, are not sufficient to stave off the inevitable re-emergence of spatialising forces. This is true of the entire body of work examined within this book. History should be understood not only in the sense of the major wars that menace the *haute bourgeoisie* of *La Règle du jeu* or the Spanish colonisers in *The Golden Coach*, but also within the context of the everyday lives portrayed within much of Renoir's French, American, and 'transnational' work: across all of Renoir's narratives, if characters actualise a genuinely new future beyond predetermining elements, this state of being inevitably materialises in the form of a fleeting present moment which rarely corresponds with the imagined ideal, and its transience has no currency in the irresistible *jaillissement* of the present. As such, it is important to note that Renoir's work exhibits another potential crystalline state which cannot be characterised by a single crystal, but rather by the endless formation of flawed crystals. When Renoir's characters pursue their own goals, they must constantly vie to escape the embodied past and locate yet another *point de fuite*, lest they remain petrified within the theatre of *rôles morts* that stultifies society. As Jean Epstein once wrote (evidently under Bergson's influence), 'crystals become larger, growing on top of one another, smoothly uniting [. . .]'.[15]

It is worth noting that when discussing the four crystalline states, Deleuze employs a register that is inquisitive inasmuch as it is uncertain, and which therefore signals the potential existence of alternative states beyond those discussed in the subsequent pages of *Cinéma 2*. Two such examples are immediately apparent: before discussing Fellini's crystal, Deleuze remarks that 'There is *perhaps* another, third state'; and before describing Visconti's crystal in dissolution, Deleuze states that 'The last state to be considered *could be* the crystal in dissolution.'[16] Deleuze's cautious use of the of the conditional form in the latter instance suggests that he remains uncertain regarding the signs that he locates in the cinema and the criteria that he is establishing to interpret them. An elucidation and appreciation of such ambiguities in Deleuze's philosophical discourse remains a rewarding avenue of enquiry towards a stronger appreciation of the rich textures of Renoir's narratives and Deleuze's film philosophy.

It should be emphasised that the Deleuzian framework advanced by the present study offers but one means of integrating temporality into our analysis of space in Renoir's films. In an insightful analysis of Christine de la Chesnaye's misinterpretation of Robert and Genevieve's farewell embrace as a germinating love affair, Jill Forbes reminds us that 'although the interpretation it allows her to place on their current relationship is false, it simultaneously allows her to make sense of the past in a way that would not otherwise have been possible'.[17] The same could be said for the methodology employed by this book. Indeed, Deleuze and Renoir hardly represent the only test cases available for time and philosophy, but the productive dialogue between the two provides a fascinating way of showing how film allows us to examine space-time in the world around us.

Renoir *auteur*(?)

Although this study understands each of the films analysed as products of cultural and ideological conditions beyond Renoir's control as well as the director's collaboration with members of his cast and crew, the present analysis proposes that Renoir's approach to space-time stems, in part at least, from his personal experience of warfare. Drawing on Thomas Elsaesser's distinction between 'recovered memory' (present in the forms of manifest, unambiguous traces) and 'recovered referentiality' (a trauma that must be found, rather than being given by the text),[18] Davis convincingly argues that post-war identity is consistently embedded in the form of 'recovered referentiality' in Renoir's post-1939 output, in which events disturb the inner cohesion of communities, 'laying bare violent antagonisms which otherwise might be more or less successfully concealed'.[19]

Whereas Davis focuses on the psychological impact of the Second World War and its impact on the films Renoir directed after the outbreak of war in 1939, I would propose that Renoir's crystalline narratives derive from his prior experience as a Great War veteran. More specifically, although the socio-political, economic, and technological factors affecting Renoir's portrayal of space-time may continue to be debated, there is certainly an argument to be made for Renoir's scission of time representing 'recovered referentiality'. Renoir spent his formative years in an era of increased mobility and geographic anxiety owing to the impact of war and revolutionary technological advances on perceptions of spatial borders and divisions. Robert T. Tally observes that whereas time-focused discourse before the First World War 'served to mask the underlying spatial realities' operating in society, the true nature of such spaces reasserted its importance in the critical consciousness after the two world wars.[20] This was already becoming clear after the First World War, whose opaque goals, mechanised massacre, and seemingly ceaseless tug of war dismantled nineteenth-century interpretations of time as a linear teleology geared towards social progress and produced what Jean-Jacques Becker describes as France's 'great mutation'.[21] Such was the impact of the war on Renoir's vision of space and time that he directed *La Grande Illusion*, which remains one of the cinema's most significant examples of 'recovered memory' of the First World War and, more interestingly, also constitutes one of the French film industry's few exceptions to the 'silent memory' of the French film industry, which 'as a whole [. . .] abstained from screening the period'.[22] Renoir, who was nineteen when war broke out and twenty-four when it drew to a belated close, asserted decades later in his 1974 autobiography that 'if our species does not entirely disappear and if historians still exist in a few hundred years, they will be able to divide our history into two parts: before and after 1914'.[23] Echoing Renoir's assertion, John Horne writes that 'World War I was not an end, but rather a beginning, and the forces and quarrels that it unleashed – and transformed – continued to destabilize the world.'[24] Regardless of our perspective on the variety of socio-political, economic, and cultural factors that conditioned Renoir's evolution as a filmmaker, the fact remains that Renoir's portrayal of the bifurcation of time transcends changes in his narrative style, production contexts, and shifts in his ideological outlook.

Final Remarks: Keys and Ideas

Criticising the pessimism and violence of *La Règle du jeu*, Deleuze remarks that the film 'is one of Renoir's finest films, but does not give us the key to the others' because it runs contrary to Renoir's 'complete idea', defined by Deleuze as a cinematographic world in which, 'without the need for violence and through the development of experimentation, something will escape from the crystal'.[25] In doing so, Deleuze hints towards the question of whether or not any single film encapsulates the essence of Renoir's *mise en scène* of open space-time. Having already emphasised the complexity and diversity of Renoir's most deceptively similar films, it would appear that the very possibility of selecting a single key Renoir work becomes ever more elusive, even impossible.

At this point, it is more appropriate to refer to how the preceding analysis corresponds with Renoir's own comments on his approach to filmmaking. Discussing his portrayal of the French Revolution in *La Marseillaise* (1938) during an interview with the editors of *Cahiers du Cinéma*, Renoir stated:

> History [*L'Histoire*] with a capital H is created by historians, who are very useful, because they present a synthesis without which we could not understand it. But in a film, one can try to make people understand this uneven, erratic, and unforeseen aspect of life during major events.[26]

With or without a capital H, the French *histoire* should be understood in the dual sense of 'history' and 'story'. For if, as Perez observes, Renoir's art entered 'the arena of what is, and developed the means for rendering and interpreting the world's situations in their concrete complexity',[27] it is because Renoir intimately frames the significance of deceptively minor interactional events within the broader context of an inherently relational space that is imbued in temporality: Lulu and Legrand's happenstance meeting in *La Chienne* is just as pivotal and symbolic an event as Harriet's mental flight towards the grove in *The River*, the colonial war ignored by the Spanish court in *The Golden Coach*, and the transgression of the Swiss border in *La Grande Illusion*. Simple acts such as walking in the street, tilling a field, and dwelling within interior space are no less important to our understanding of society and space than the colonising process or the confinement of another country's citizens within a prison camp. All potentially bolster or erode ideological values that are constantly in flux, and all constantly subject space, itself a volatile matrix of 'loose ends and missing links', to radical revision.[28] Eliciting what Perez calls Renoir's 'sympathy combined with detachment', all are lent equal dramatic weight and are contextualised within broader networks of inherently interconnected territories.[29]

To say that every shot of each film expresses the spatio-temporal qualities discerned by the framework developed in the Introduction would be a tenuous claim at best. What is proposed by this study, however, is that the range of visual and aural elements marshalled by Renoir's narratives interact with one another over the course of each film to express these qualities, thus corresponding with Éric Rohmer's assertion that 'the director must [. . .] shoot not only the contents of every shot in relation to a certain conception of spatiality, but the totality of the filmed space'.[30] If, as Bazin puts it, Renoir 'brought his lens before reality like a telescope, concealing or revealing things as he wished', he never loses sight of reality itself.[31] Space, in its transformative capacity and intrinsic relationship with time, remains the central object of Renoir's vision from one film to the next. Even when Renoir presents us with the close-ups of *Diary of a Chambermaid* or the tenebrous confines of *Les Bas-fonds* (1936), our focus is never restricted to a delimited character or set of objects. Rather, our gaze searches beyond the parameters of the camera's frame within the dynamic Whole of space-time, absorbing Renoir's cinematographic images of a transient world that is fundamentally incomplete, necessarily imbalanced, and imbued with as many possibilities as the societies in which we live. Whether or not Renoir himself was entirely aware of this precise continuity within his work when he wrote his autobiography is subject to debate. However, his approach to the integral relationship between space and time is probably best encapsulated by the words that entitle Renoir's own chapter on his favoured approach to *mise en scène*: 'Forming part of a whole'.[32]

Appendix: Corpus Breakdown

Whereas the filmography features a complete list of films referenced over the course of this book, the final column in this table ('discussed by book') refers exclusively to the twelve films that provide the book's core focus.

	Black and white	Colour	Discussed by Deleuze	Discussed by book
Silent films				
Catherine (co-dir. Albert Dieudonné, 1924)	•			
La Fille de l'eau (1925)	•			
Nana (1926)	•		1	
Sur un air de Charleston (1927)	•			
Marquitta (1927)	•			
La Petite Marchande d'allumettes (1928)	•		2	
Tire-au-flanc (1928)	•			
Le Tournoi dans la cité (1928)	•			
Le Bled (1929)	•			•
Sound films				
On purge bébé (1930)	•			
La Chienne (1931)	•			•
La Nuit du carrefour (1932)	•			
Boudu sauvé des eaux (1932)	•		2	•
Chotard et cie (1933)	•			
Madame Bovary (1934)	•			
Toni (1935)	•			
Le Crime de Monsieur Lange (1936)	•		1	•
La Vie est à nous (1936)	•			
Partie de campagne (1936)	•		2	
Les Bas-fonds (1936)	•			•
La Grande Illusion (1937)	•		2	•
La Marseillaise (1938)	•		2	
La Bête humaine (1938)	•		1	
La Règle du jeu (1939)	•		1 + 2	•
Swamp Water (1941)	•			
This Land is Mine (1943)	•			
Salute to France (co-dir. Garson Kanin, 1944)	•			
The Southerner (1945)	•			•
Diary of a Chambermaid (1946)	•		1	•
Woman on the Beach (1947)	•			
The River (1951)		•	2	•
The Golden Coach (1952)		•	2	•
French Cancan (1954)		•	2	
Eléna et les hommes (1956)		•		•
Le Testament du Docteur Cordelier (TV, 1959)	•			
Le Déjeuner sur l'herbe (1959)		•	2	
Le Caporal épinglé (1962)	•			
Le Petit Théâtre de Jean Renoir (TV, 1970)		•	2	

Notes

Preface

1. West-Pavlov, *Temporalities*, p. 41.
2. Ibid., p. 41.
3. Bakhtin, 'Forms of Time', p. 84.
4. Epstein, '*Photogénie* and the Imponderable', p. 189.
5. Epstein, *Le Cinéma du diable*, p. 101: 'si [. . .] le cinéma inscrit la dimension dans le temps avec la dimension dans l'espace, il démontre aussi que toutes ces relations n'ont rien d'absolu, rien de fixe'.
6. Epstein, *Esprit de cinéma*, p. 18: 'de la variance de toutes les relations dans l'espace et dans le temps, de la relativité de toute mesure, de l'instabilité de tous les repères, de la fluidité de l'univers'; Bakhtin, 'Forms of Time', p. 250.

Introduction

1. Deleuze, *L'Image-temps*, p. 117: 'C'est Renoir qui avait une vive conscience de l'identité de la liberté avec un avenir, collectif ou individuel, avec un élan vers l'avenir, une ouverture d'avenir.'
2. Panofsky, cited in Kracauer, *From Caligari to Hitler*, p. 6.
3. Bazin, 'L'Évolution', p. 78: 'le secret d'un récit cinématographique capable de tout exprimer sans morceler le monde, de révéler le sens caché des êtres et des choses sans en briser l'unité naturelle'.
4. Renoir, *Ma vie*, p. 260: 'Lorsqu'un fermier français se trouve à diner à la même table qu'un financier français, ces deux Français n'ont rien à se dire. Ce qui intéresse l'un laisse l'autre parfaitement indifférent. Mais si nous imaginons une réunion entre notre fermier français et un fermier chinois, ils auront des tas de choses à se raconter. Ce thème du rassemblement des hommes par métiers ou par intérêts communs m'a poursuivi toute ma vie et me poursuit encore. C'est le thème de *La Grande Illusion*. Il figure plus ou moins dans chacun de mes ouvrages.'
5. O'Shaughnessy, *Jean Renoir*, p. 2.

6. Renoir, *Pierre-Auguste Renoir*, p. 66: 'l'argent était déjà sans grand attrait'; p. 39: 'un ouvrier de la peinture'.
7. The servants' contribution to household tasks such as pacifying the young Jean and cooking a weekly *pot-au-feu* is noted in Mérigeau, *Jean Renoir*, p. 35.
8. O'Shaughnessy, *Jean Renoir*, pp. 6, 5.
9. Renoir, *Ma vie*, p. 55.
10. Narboni et al., *Jean Renoir*, p. 98.
11. See Ogle, 'Technological and Aesthetic Influences', pp. 51–2; Allen and Kuhn, 'Deep-focus', p. 149.
12. Crisp, *The Classic French Cinema*, pp. 9–10; Hayward, *French National Cinema*, p. 135.
13. McCann, *Ripping Open the Set*, p. 142.
14. Brunius, cited in Comolli, 'Technique et idéologie', p. 211: 'ce n'est qu'à grand peine que nous pûmes nous procurer des objectifs anciens considérés comme fossiles'; Brunius, *En marge du cinéma français*, p. 95: 'de devancer les prétendus innovateurs de près de dix ans'.
15. Renoir, 'Souvenirs . . .', p. 148: 'plus j'avance dans mon métier, plus je suis amené à faire de la mise en scène en profondeur par rapport à l'écran. Plus ça va, plus je renonce aux confrontations entre deux acteurs placés sagement devant l'appareil comme chez le photographe.'
16. Narboni et al., *Jean Renoir*, p. 284.
17. O'Brien, 'Relocating Renoir's Sound and Music', p. 37.
18. Narboni et al., *Jean Renoir*, p. 338: 'J'ai procédé énormément avec des objectifs assez fermés et donnant une grande profondeur de champ, de façon à ne jamais perdre de vue derrière mes personnages, les champs.' Note that by the word 'closed' ('fermé'), Renoir was referring to the aperture of the lens, hence my translation of 'objectifs' (lenses) as 'apertures': the narrower the aperture, the greater the depth of field available to the camera.
19. Sesonske, 'The River Runs', p. 109.
20. Giddens and Sutton, *Sociology*, p. 485.
21. Ibid., p. 322.
22. Bourdieu, *Distinction*, p. 96.
23. Ibid., p. 104.
24. Murdoch, 'Middle-class Territory?', p. 360.
25. Bazin, 'L'Évolution'. An abridged version of this article is reprinted in Bazin, *Jean Renoir*, pp. 69–84.
26. Bazin, 'Renoir français', p. 74: 'suppose[nt] le respect de la continuité de l'espace dramatique et naturellement de sa durée'.
27. See especially: Bazin, 'L'Évolution', pp. 75–80. See also Bazin, *Orson Welles*, pp. 70–80.
28. Rhode, *A History of the Cinema*, p. 325; Faulkner, *The Social Cinema*, p. 50.
29. Faulkner, *The Social Cinema*, pp. 49–50.
30. Ibid., p. 50. See also ibid., p. 63.

31. Braudy, *The World in a Frame*, p. 46.
32. The table printed provides a summary of the salient aspects of each style. For Braudy's complete discussion of the attributes of each style, see ibid., pp. 46–51.
33. Balázs, *Theory of the Film*, pp. 145–7.
34. Deleuze, *L'Image-temps*, p. 354: 'un présent successif suivant un rapport extrinsèque de l'avant et de l'après'.
35. Ibid., p. 355: 'ce n'est plus le temps qui est subordonné au mouvement, c'est le mouvement qui se subordonne au temps'.
36. Deleuze, *Le Bergsonisme*, p. 54: 'Le passé et le présent ne désignent pas deux moment successifs, mais deux éléments qui coexistent, l'un qui est le présent, et qui ne cesse de passer, l'autre, qui est le passé, et qui ne cesse pas d'être, mais par lequel tous les présents passent.'
37. Deleuze, *L'Image-temps*, p. 108: 'l'opération la plus fondamentale du temps'.
38. Ibid., p. 106: 'Le présent, c'est l'image actuelle et *son* passé contemporain, c'est l'image virtuelle.' Deleuze's italics. See also ibid., pp. 108–9.
39. Ibid., pp. 92–3: 'l'image biface, actuelle et virtuelle à la fois'.
40. Deleuze, *L'Image-temps*, pp. 111–13.
41. Ibid., pp. 111–12.
42. Ibid., p. 113: 'n'est jamais pur et parfait, il y a une faille, un point de fuite, un « crapaud »'.
43. Ibid., p. 113: 'toujours fêlé'; p. 117: 'se donne un avenir'.
44. Ibid., p. 116: 'rôles gelés, figés, tout faits, trop conformes'; p. 117: 'déjà voués au souvenir'.
45. Ibid., p. 114: 'une réalité décantée'.
46. Deleuze employs the French term, *profondeur de champ*, which may be translated as depth of field (a product of deep focus technology) or deep space (also known as deep staging). David Bordwell and Kristin Thompson distinguish between deep staging and deep focus: 'Depth of field should not be confused with the concept of deep space [. . .]. *Deep space* is a term for the way the filmmaker has staged the action on several different planes, *regardless of whether all of these planes are in focus.* [. . .] Deep space is a property of *mise en scène*, the techniques that affect what is placed in front of the camera. Depth of field depends on the camera itself, with the lens determining what layers of the *mise en scène* are in focus. [. . .] In Hollywood during the 1940s, partly due to the influence of *Citizen Kane* [1941], filmmakers began using faster film, short-focal-length lenses, and more intense lighting to yield a greater depth of field. The contract-signing scene from *Citizen Kane* offers a famous example. This practice came to be called deep focus.' See Bordwell and Thompson, *Film Art*, pp. 172–3. Renoir employed deep staging throughout his career rather than deep focus. Discussing Renoir's films of the 1930s, Charles H. Harpole observes that 'the scenes are obviously set up with perspective, movements, and extensive spaces to allow

room for the simultaneous juxtaposition of people (and/or things) within the same frame [. . .] and everything visible is equally in focus. However, real "deep focus" is not in evidence since highly focused detail – high definition – is just not there, is just not a part of the visual information from the screen.' See Harpole, 'Ideological and Technological Determinism', p. 19. Similarly, Barry Salt asserts: 'For the last time, there is *no* "deep focus" in Jean Renoir's films, just extensive use of staging in depth, sometimes beyond the limits of sharp focus.' See Salt, *Film Style and Technology*, p. 226. In light of these sources, this book refers to Renoir's use of deep space and deep staging. Where discussions concern both deep staging and deep focus, this book employs the more inclusive French term, *profondeur de champ*.

47. Deleuze, *L'Image-temps*, pp. 113–14: 'rend évident que le cristal est là pour que quelque chose en fuie, dans le fond, par le fond'.
48. Ibid., p. 117: 'en fonction d'une dimension d'avenir'.
49. Ibid., p. 117: 'C'est Renoir qui avait une vive conscience de l'identité de la liberté avec un avenir, collectif ou individuel, avec un élan vers l'avenir, une ouverture d'avenir. C'est même la conscience politique de Renoir, la manière dont il conçoit la Révolution française ou le Front Populaire.' Deleuze's use of the term *élan* is strongly reminiscent of Bergson's conceptualisation of the *élan vital* ('life force' or 'vital impulse'). Bergson develops this idea in *L'Évolution créatrice* (1907) to explain the complex, spontaneous, and organised development of organisms. For Bergson, the *élan vital* originates in 'an original impulse [*élan*] of life' (Bergson, *L'Évolution créatrice*, p. 88: 'un élan originel de la vie'). This impulse results in the ongoing development of 'reality [as] a perpetual growth, a creation pursued without end', and leads to the evolution of species (ibid., p. 240: 'la réalité est une croissance perpétuelle, une création qui se poursuit sans fin'). In *Le Bergsonisme*, Deleuze describes the *élan vital* as 'a virtuality in the process of being actualised' ('une virtualité en train de s'actualiser'). See Deleuze, *Le Bergsonisme*, p. 96. See also Bergson, *L'Évolution créatrice*, pp. 88–98.
50. Bowie, *Psychoanalysis and the Future of Theory*, p. 23.
51. Deleuze, *L'Image-temps*, p. 115: 'dans ses moments pessimistes'.
52. Ibid., p. 115.
53. Deleuze, *L'Image-mouvement*, p. 7.
54. Davis, *Critical Excess*, p. 78.
55. Deleuze, *Pourparlers*, p. 83: 'des concepts propres au cinéma'; 'des concepts venus du dehors'.
56. Davis, *Critical Excess*, p. 77; Badiou, *Deleuze*, p. 27.
57. Deleuze, *L'Image-temps*, p. 116: 'l'ensemble des rôles'; p. 115: 'ne vaut que comme recherche d'un art de vivre'.
58. Ibid., p. 293: 'l'image visuelle montre la structure d'une société, sa situation, ses places et ses fonctions, les attitudes et les rôles, les actions et réactions des individus, bref la forme et les contenus'.

59. Colman, *Deleuze and Cinema*, p. 148.
60. Deleuze, *L'Image-temps*, p. 115: 'retrouve le fil de l'eau en sortant du théâtre intime et renfermé du libraire où il a essayé beaucoup de rôles'.
61. Ibid., p. 117.
62. Ibid., p. 114: 'Sans qu'il y ait besoin de violence, et par le développement d'une experimentation'; p. 117: 'insensiblement'.
63. Ibid., p. 117: 'l'essai des rôles est indispensable'.
64. O'Shaughnessy, 'Shooting in Deep Time', pp. 23–4.
65. Deleuze, *L'Image-temps*, pp. 138–46.
66. Deleuze, *L'Image-mouvement*, p. 42: 'un plan de longue durée fixe ou mobile [. . .] avec profondeur de champ'.
67. Ibid., p. 28.
68. Ibid., p. 28: 'l'alternative de Bazin, cache ou cadre'.
69. Bazin, 'Renoir français', p. 26.
70. Deleuze, *L'Image-temps*, p. 30. Deleuze oddly omits any direct reference to Burch's text in this instance, but refers to *Praxis du cinéma* (the French edition of *Theory of Film Practice*, in which this model appeared) multiple times in *Cinéma 2*, specifically on pp. 36–7 and p. 260.
71. Burch, *Theory of Film Practice*, pp. 21, 24.
72. See Kuhn, 'Classic Hollywood Narrative', pp. 45–6.
73. Bazin, 'L'Évolution', p. 72.
74. Thompson, *Breaking the Glass Armor*, p. 219. See pp. 218–44 for Thompson's complete analysis of interlocking classical and nonclassical modes of narration in *La Règle du jeu*.
75. Deleuze, *L'Image-temps*, p. 143: 'Il y a des images-temps qui se créent par suppression de la profondeur'; p. 113: 'moins visible'; p. 113: 'l'image plane, comme dans *Le Carrosse d'or*'.
76. Bogue, *Deleuze on Cinema*, p. 124.
77. Deleuze, *L'Image-temps*, p. 114: 'pessimiste'.
78. Williams, 'The Deep Focus Question', pp. 73–9. See Ogle, 'Technological and Aesthetic Influences', for a closer examination of the impact of film technology and aesthetic influences such as painting and photography on the development of *profondeur de champ*.
79. Comolli, 'Technique et idéologie', p. 203: 'la question de son utilité [. . .] (à quoi sert-il) soit totalement recouverte par celle de son utilisation (comment s'en servir)'.
80. Deleuze, *L'Image-mouvement*, p. 196: 'est simplement ceci: des milieux et des comportements, des milieux qui actualisent et des comportements qui incarnent'.
81. Ibid., p. 284.
82. Deleuze, *L'Image-temps*, p. 113: 'On hésitera d'autant plus à lui donner le rôle que voulait Bazin, d'une pure fonction de réalité. La profondeur a plutôt pour fonction de constituer l'image en cristal, et d'absorber le réel qui passe ainsi dans le virtuel autant que dans l'actuel.' For an analysis

of correspondences between Bazin and Deleuze's respective approaches to *profondeur de champ*, see Arnaud, 'From Bazin to Deleuze', pp. 85–94.

83. Deleuze, *L'Image-temps*, p. 101: 'le plan des images-mouvement est un bloc d'espace-temps'; p. 101: 'une perspective temporelle'.
84. Ibid., p. 28: 'espaces vides'; p. 28: 'espaces déconnectés'.
85. Ibid., p. 169: 'seulement des Puissances et de Qualités pures, indépendamment des états de choses ou des milieux qui les actualisent'.
86. Ibid., p. 169: 'un champ de forces, des oppositions et tensions entre ses forces'; 'des lois qui renvoient à la distribution des *centres de forces* dans l'espace'. Deleuze's italics.
87. Ibid., p. 169: 'leurs caractères ne peuvent pas s'expliquer de façon seulement spatiale'.
88. Ibid., p. 169: '[des] espaces, vides, amorphes, qui perdent leurs coordonnées euclidiennes'; 'les espaces cristallisés'; 'les espaces deviennent hallucinatoires dans un milieu qui ne retient plus que des germes cristallins et des matières cristallisables'.
89. Deleuze and Guattari, *Mille Plateaux*, pp. 592–625.
90. Ibid., p. 12: 'le monde a perdu son pivot'.
91. Ibid., p. 593: 'n'existent en fait que par leurs mélanges l'un avec l'autre'.
92. Ibid., p. 273: 'ne cessent pas de colmater, de boucher, de barrer les lignes de fuite'.
93. Deleuze and Guattari, *Mille Plateaux*, p. 268: 'ne cesse pas d'être animé de toutes sortes de mouvement de décodage et de déterritorialisation qui affecte des « masses », suivant des vitesses et des allures différentes. Ce ne sont pas des contradictions. Ce sont des fuites.'
94. Ibid., p. 16: 'On fait une rupture, on trace une ligne de fuite, mais on risque toujours de retrouver sur elle des organisations qui restratifient l'ensemble, des formations qui redonnent le pouvoir à un signifiant, des attributions qui reconstitutent un sujet – tout ce qu'on veut, depuis les résurgences oedipiennes jusqu'aux concrétions fascistes. Les groupes et les individus contiennent des micro-fascismes qui ne demandent qu'à cristalliser.'
95. Flaxman, 'Transcendental Aesthetics', p. 176.
96. Doel, 'A Hundred Thousand Lines of Flight', p. 421.
97. Lefebvre, *La Production de l'espace*, p. 40: 'chaque société (donc chaque mode de production [. . .]) produit un espace, le sien'; p. 102: 'inhérent aux *rapports de propriété* (la propriété du sol, de la terre, en particulier), et d'autre part lié aux *forces productives* (qui façonnent cette terre, ce sol)'.
98. Ibid., p. 88: 'enveloppe les choses produites, comprend leurs relations dans leur coexistences et leur simultanéité'; Massey, *For Space*, p. 107.
99. Ibid., pp. 95, 151–2.
100. Ibid., p. 12.
101. Ibid., p. 89.
102. Ibid., p. 48.

103. Deleuze, *L'Image-temps*, p. 109: 'le jaillissement du temps comme dédoublement, comme scission'.
104. Massey, *For Space*, p. 89.
105. Deleuze, *L'Image-temps*, p. 117: 'en fonction d'une dimension d'avenir'.
106. O'Shaughnessy, *Jean Renoir*, p. 59.
107. Renoir, *Correspondance*, p. 111: 'beaucoup plus un auteur de film qu'un metteur en scène'.
108. Renoir, 'Propos Rompus', pp. 24–5: 'au fond, j'ai tourné un film, je continue à tourner un film depuis que j'ai commencé, et c'est le même. J'y ajoute des choses, je vois des choses que je n'avais pas dites avant et qu'il faut que je dise.'
109. Davis, *Scenes of Love and Murder*, pp. 7–8.
110. Rushton, 'A Deleuzian Imaginary', p. 253.
111. Ibid., pp. 253–8.
112. Ibid., p. 248.
113. O'Shaughnessy, 'Shooting in Deep Time', p. 21. O'Shaughnessy reiterates this argument in O'Shaughnessy, 'Between the "I" and the "We"', p. 44.
114. O'Shaughnessy, 'Shooting in Deep Time', pp. 31, 26.
115. Ibid., p. 28.
116. Ibid., p. 30.
117. Ibid., p. 29.
118. Ibid., p. 29.
119. Ibid., pp. 25, 20.
120. The films noted here do not indicate the entire list of projects involving Renoir and each of the named collaborators. Rather, I have included those films that will be studied in depth in this book in each instance.
121. Andrew, *Mists of Regret*, p. 293.
122. Wollen, *Signs and Meanings in the Cinema*, pp. 144–5.
123. Deleuze, *L'Image-temps*, p. 94: 'est le caractère objectif de certaines images existantes, doubles par nature'.
124. Ibid., p. 94: 'se fait seulement « dans la tête » de quelqu'un'; 'une illusion objective'.
125. Bazin, 'L'Évolution', pp. 65–6: 'n'est pas dans l'image, il en est l'ombre projetée, par le montage, sur le plan de conscience du spectateur'.

Chapter 1

1. Baudelaire, Les Fleurs du mal, p. 111: 'Le vieux Paris n'est plus (la forme d'une ville. Change plus vite, hélas! que le coeur d'un mortel . . .).'
2. Calvino, *Invisible Cities*, pp. 139–40.
3. Renoir, *Ma vie*, pp. 13–29.
4. Williams, *The Country and the City*, p. 289.
5. Newby, 'Locality and Rurality', p. 209.
6. Massey, *For Space*, p. 140.

7. Lury and Massey, 'Making Connections', p. 231.
8. Massey, *For Space*, p. 169.
9. Certeau, *L'Invention du quotidien*, p. 60: 'une maîtrise du temps par la fondation d'un lieu autonome'; 'l'action calculée'; 'le terrain qui lui est imposé'.
10. Ibid., p. 142.
11. Williams, *The Country and the City*, pp. 165, 89.
12. Kracauer, *Theory of Film*, p. 28.
13. Ibid., p. 62.
14. Ibid., p. 303.
15. Nowell-Smith, 'Cities: Real and Imagined', p. 99.
16. Hayward, 'The City as Narrative', p. 29.
17. Ibid., p. 26.
18. Ibid., p. 33.
19. Donald, *Imagining the Modern City*, p. 92.
20. Ibid., p. 27.
21. Massey, *For Space*, p. 89; Certeau, *L'Invention du quotidien*, p. 144: '[une] condition de possibilité'.
22. Burgin, *In/different Spaces*, p. 28.
23. Rojex, cited in Bell, 'Variations on the Rural Idyll', p. 155.
24. Urry, cited in Emerson, *Regarding Manneken Pis*, p. 126.
25. Turim, 'The Displacement of Architecture', pp. 28–9.
26. Flinn, *The Social Architecture of French Cinema*, p. 5.
27. Massey, *For Space*, p. 156.
28. Hussey, *Paris*, p. xv.
29. See Fouchardière, *La Chienne*, pp. 9–11; Mouézy-Éon, *La Chienne*, p. 5.
30. 'Un grand drame social'; 'vous prouvera que le vice est toujours puni'.
31. 'Nous allons avoir l'honneur de vous présenter une comédie à tendances morales.'
32. 'Mesdames et messieurs, n'écoutez pas ces braves gens. La pièce que nous allons vous montrer n'est ni un drame ni une comédie. Elle ne comporte aucune intention morale et elle ne vous prouvera rien du tout.'
33. 'S'est fait une culture intellectuelle et sentimentale au-dessus du milieu où il évolue, de telle sorte que dans ce milieu il a exactement l'air d'un imbécile.'
34. Davis, *Scenes of Love and Murder*, p. 29.
35. 'Elle est toujours sincère. Elle ment tout le temps.'
36. 'Le môme Dédé, et rien de plus.'
37. Burch, *Theory of Film Practice*, pp. 21, 24.
38. Davis, *Scenes of Love and Murder*, p. 28.
39. 'Les personnages n'en sont ni des héros ni des sombres traîtres. Ce sont de pauvres hommes comme moi, comme vous.'
40. In the case of Braudy, see Braudy, *Jean Renoir*, pp. 68–9.
41. Bazin, *Jean Renoir*, pp. 26–7: 'une recherche systématique de l'effet de cadre-cache intérieur au plan'.
42. Burch, *Theory of Film Practice*, p. 19. Burch's italics.

43. Sesonske, *Jean Renoir*, p. 89.
44. Ibid., p. 84.
45. Ibid., p. 84.
46. O'Shaughnessy, *Jean Renoir*, p. 77.
47. Hayward, 'The City as Narrative', p. 30.
48. Certeau, *L'Invention du quotidien*, p. 149: 'privilégient, muent ou délaissent des éléments spatiaux'; p. 150: 'une articulation conjonctive et disjonctive de places'.
49. Massey, *For Space*, p. 173.
50. Sennett, *The Fall of Public Man*, p. 39; Pratt and San Juan, *Film and Urban Space*, p. 55.
51. Massey, *For Space*, p. 11.
52. Hewitt, 'Shifting Cultural Centres', p. 45.
53. O' Brien, *Cinema's Conversion to Sound*, p. 161. For a graph representing the average shot lengths of thirty-one films directed by Renoir between 1925 and 1970, see O'Brien, 'Relocating Renoir's Sound and Music', p. 37.
54. Bauman, *Liquid Modernity*, p. 96. Bauman's italics.
55. Ibid., p. 96. Bauman's italics.
56. Bauman, *Postmodern Ethics*, p. 149.
57. Ibid., p. 150.
58. Ibid., p. 150.
59. O'Shaughnessy, *Jean Renoir*, p. 77.
60. For an in-depth analysis of the interplay between windows, the spectator's gaze, and the camera's frame over the course of *La Chienne*, see Nevin, 'Paris vs Providence'.
61. Faulkner, *The Social Cinema*, p. 24. Jean-Louis Leutrat remarks, without referring to Deleuze, that the song creates 'a "crystal" of space-time' ('un « cristal » d'espace-temps') by binding multiple moments unfolding in interior and exterior spaces together and regards this scene as the centre of the film for its treatment of space and time. However, Leutrat ignores the relationship between the present and the past within Deleuze's definition of the crystal. See Leutrat, *« La Chienne »*, p. 45.
62. 'Il aurait bien pu me dire bonjour, surtout que j'ai des lettres pour Madame Pelletier.'
63. Faulkner, *The Social Cinema*, p. 26.
64. Braudy, *Jean Renoir*, p. 72.
65. Deleuze, *L'Image-temps*, p. 116: 'Tout ce qui est passé retombe dans le cristal, et y reste: c'est l'ensemble des rôles gelés, figés, tout faits, trop conformes, que les personnages ont essayés tour à tour, rôles morts ou de la mort, la danse macabre des souvenirs dont parle Bergson, comme dans le château de *La Règle du jeu* [. . .].'
66. Deleuze, *L'Image-temps*, p. 115: 'retrouve le fil de l'eau en sortant du théâtre intime et renfermé du libraire où il a essayé beaucoup de rôles'; Perez, *The Material Ghost*, p. 74.

67. Braudy, *Jean Renoir*, p. 49.
68. 'Mes pipeaux sont fatigués.'
69. Deleuze, *L'Image-temps*, pp. 50–1.
70. See Certeau, *L'Invention du quotidien*, p. 149.
71. Deleuze, *L'Image-mouvement*, pp. 47–8: 'des rapports binaires qui constituent un *montage alterné parallèle*'; p. 56: '*l'intervalle aussi bien que le tout prennent un nouveau sens*'. Deleuze's italics.
72. 'De grosses lettres.'
73. Kracauer, *Theory of Film*, p. 72.
74. Ibid., p. 72.
75. Massey, *For Space*, p. 59.
76. Bourdieu, *Le Sens pratique*, pp. 441–61.
77. Donald, 'This, Here, Now', p. 197.
78. Bourdieu, 'The Forms of Capital'.
79. Flinn, *The Social Architecture of French Cinema*, p. 80.
80. 'Un bon coup de pied dans le derrière'; 'n'est plus rien pour moi'.
81. Perez, *The Material Ghost*, p. 74.
82. See Sesonske, *Jean Renoir*, pp. 393–5; Reader, *La Règle du jeu*, pp. 29–41.
83. Curchod and Faulkner, *La Règle du jeu*, p. 249.
84. Ibid., p. 260.
85. The Place du Trocadéro is located in the sixteenth *arrondissement*, on the opposite side of the Seine, but the apartment's distance from the monuments suggests that it is located opposite the Place du Trocadéro rather than adjacent to it. I am indebted to Keith Reader for these observations.
86. Junyk, 'The Face of the Nation', p. 98.
87. Sesonske, *Jean Renoir*, p. 394.
88. Peer, cited in Junyk, 'The Face of the Nation', p. 98.
89. Ibid., p. 102.
90. Ibid., pp. 109–10.
91. Nora, 'Between Memory and History', p. 7.
92. Ibid., p. 7.
93. Renoir, *Écrits*, p. 174: 'il s'agissait d'un guide de l'Exposition de 1900, oublié dans un coin de ma bibliothèque'.
94. Ibid., p. 174: '*la science à la portée de tous*'. Renoir's italics.
95. Renoir, letter to Albert André, 12 July 1941: 'un peu déçu et attristé de me retrouver au milieu de cette espèce d'exposition '37 qu'est la ville de Hollywood'.
96. Massey, *For Space*, p. 19.
97. Certeau, *L'Invention du quotidien*, p. 150: 'a [. . .] pour fonction d'implanter l'autre relatif à ce « je » et d'instaurer ainsi une articulation conjonctive et disjonctive des places'.
98. Sesonske, *Jean Renoir*, p. 394.
99. Massey, *For Space*, pp. 94–5.
100. Amin, 'The Nation', p. 9.

101. Ibid., p. 10.
102. Reader, *La Règle du jeu*, p. 14.
103. Amin, 'The Nation', p. 11.
104. 'La mère de la Chesnaye avait un père qui s'appelait Rosenthal et qui arrivait tout droit de Francfort.'
105. Sesonske, *Jean Renoir*, p. 415.
106. Durgnat, *Jean Renoir*, p. 208.
107. 'Pauvre Christine. Je la plains parce qu'elle est étrangère'; 'obligée de vivre ici à Paris, au milieu de gens qui ne parlent même pas sa langue'.
108. 'Christine est restée très de son pays. Une Parisienne comprendrait. Elle, pas.'
109. Curchod and Faulkner, *La Règle du jeu*, p. 246.
110. Massey, *For Space*, p. 169.
111. Lourié, *My Work in Films*, p. 67.
112. O'Shaughnessy, *Jean Renoir*, p. 150.
113. Massey, *Space, Place, and Gender*, p. 169.
114. Ibid., p. 169.
115. Ibid., p. 12.
116. O'Shaughnessy, *Jean Renoir*, p. 149.
117. Narboni et al., *Jean Renoir*, p. 292: 'Mais quel plan! Je crois que c'est le meilleur plan que j'aie fait de ma vie. Ah! C'est fantastique. Le mélange d'humilité et d'orgueil, de réussite et de doute. . . .'
118. GENEVIÈVE: Partons ensemble, Robert!
ROBERT: Où ça? Ici je suis chez moi. Je ne vais tout de même pas tout abandonner.
GENEVIÈVE: Oh ce que vous êtes agaçant avec votre sens de la propriété. Comme si ça avait de l'importance, une maison!
ROBERT: Faut d'abord que je parle à Christine.
119. 'Les oiseaux de l'armurerie ont un peu souffert, et puis j'ai trouvé une balle dans une porte. Bien entendu, je ne parle pas de la verrerie.'
120. Deleuze, *L'Image-temps*, p. 114: 'qui casse le circuit, qui fait éclater le cristal fêlé et en fait fuir le contenu, à coups de fusil'.
121. Ibid., p. 124: 'un cristal synthétique'; p. 125: 'inséparables d'un processus de décomposition qui les mine du dedans'.
122. Massey, *For Space*, p. 67; Certeau, *L'Invention du quotidien*, p. 61: 'n'a [. . .] pas la possibilité de se donner un projet global ni de totaliser l'adversaire dans un espace distinct, visible et objectivable'.
123. Deleuze, *L'Image-mouvement*, pp. 185–6: 'la répétition du passé est matériellement possible, mais impossible spirituellement, de par le Temps'.
124. Deleuze, *L'Image-temps*, p. 125: 'l'Histoire gronde à la porte'.
125. Renoir, *Ma vie*, p. 156: 'C'est un film de guerre, et pourtant, pas une allusion à la guerre n'y est faite.'
126. Deleuze, *L'Image-temps*, p. 126.
127. Massey, *For Space*, p. 107.

128. Narboni et al., *Jean Renoir*, p. 299: 'Le monde ne vit que de sacrifices, alors il faut tuer des gens pour apaiser les dieux. Là, cette société va continuer encore quelques mois, jusqu'à la guerre et même plus tard, et cette société va continuer parce que Jurieux a été tué, Jurieux est l'être qu'on a sacrifié sur l'autel des dieux pour la continuation de ce genre de vie.'
129. 'Une nouvelle définition du mot « accident ».'
130. 'Ce la Chesnaye ne manque pas de classe et ça devient rare, mon cher Saint-Aubin, croyez moi, ça devient rare.'
131. Harris, 'Renoir's Paris', pp. 93, 85.
132. Donald, 'The Citizen', p. 171.
133. Sennett, *The Fall of Public Man*, p. 264; Donald, *Imagining the Modern City*, p. 96.
134. Harris, 'Renoir's Paris', p. 93.

Chapter 2

1. Perez, *The Material Ghost*, p. 91.
2. Narboni et al., *Jean Renoir*, p. 337: 'cette terre, ces champs jouent un rôle'.
3. Williams, *The Country and the City*, p. 1; DuPuis, 'Landscapes of Desires?'; Short, 'Idyllic Ruralities'; Bell, 'Variations on the Rural Idyll'.
4. Hayward, 'Filming the (Post-)Colonial Landscape', p. 163. Hayward notes three exceptions including Marcel Pagnol's Marseilles works, Claude Berri's remakes of these films, and Bresson's austere portraits of rural life.
5. Perez, *The Material Ghost*, p. 218.
6. Ibid., p. 218.
7. Deleuze, *L'Image-temps*, p. 115: 'étrangement proche de Lawrence'; p. 116: 'proche de Maupassant'.
8. Ibid., pp. 115–16: 'une façon dont le théâtre s'ouvre à la vie, se déverse dans la vie, entraînant Nini dans une eau courante agitée'. Deleuze's imagery is reminiscent of Pierre-Auguste's oft-cited remark that 'one must let oneself go through life like a cork on a stream of water' ('il faut se laisser aller dans la vie comme un bouchon dans le courant d'un ruisseau'). Cited in Renoir, *Pierre-Auguste Renoir*, p. 44.
9. Harper and Rayner, 'Introduction', p. 18.
10. Newby, 'Locality and Rurality', p. 209; Williams, *The Country and the City*, p. 1.
11. Massey, *For Space*, p. 9.
12. Harvey, *The Limits to Capital*, p. 416.
13. Harper and Rayner, 'Introduction', p. 19.
14. See Chapter 4 for a discussion of Deleuze's analysis of the formal and thematic characteristics of *The Golden Coach*.
15. Deleuze, *L'Image-temps*, p. 117: 'en fonction d'une dimension d'avenir'.
16. *Les Éditions du Centenaire de l'Algérie*, cited in Hodeir and Pierre, *L'Exposition*

coloniale, p. 30: 'la mémoire des soldats de France qui, il y a cent ans, ont libéré l'Algérie du joug barbaresque, puis l'ont rendue à ses justes destinées en y instaurant la « paix française »'.

17. Durgnat, *Jean Renoir*, p. 58; Sesonske, *Jean Renoir*, p. 68. For further information on the film's production context and Renoir's own attitude towards colonialism, see Nevin, 'Jean Renoir's *Le Bled*', pp. 1–4.
18. Dine, *Images of the Algerian War*, p. ix.
19. Fanon, *Les Damnés*, p. 300: 'pas seulement domination, mais à la lettre décision de n'occuper somme toute qu'un terrain'.
20. For a comprehensive assessment of the reasons underlying critical neglect of *Le Bled*, see Nevin, 'Jean Renoir's *Le Bled* (1929)', pp. 2–4.
21. Mérigeau, *Jean Renoir*, p. 126: 'a été écœuré par la manière qu'avaient les Français de considérer et de traiter les Algériens'.
22. Durgnat, *Jean Renoir*, p. 58; 'un pays d'une prodigieuse activité industrielle et commerciale'.
23. Fanon, *Les Damnés*, p. 300: 'la brousse, les moustiques, les indigènes et les fièvres'; 'l'inexistence politique et économique de l'indigénat'.
24. Pierre-Auguste's comments on his experience of painting Algeria are transcribed by Jean in Renoir, *Pierre-Auguste Renoir*, pp. 253–5.
25. Fanon, *Les Damnés*, p. 300: 'le panorama, la toile de fond *naturelle* de la présence humaine française'. Fanon's italics.
26. Ibid., p. 70: 'ce monde coupé en deux [. . .] habité par des espèces différentes'.
27. Abel, *The First Wave*, p. 159.
28. 'Allons! Bon. Aujourd' hui, il s'est habillé en zouave.'
29. 'Il y a cent ans, nos devanciers n'ont trouvé ici que des marécages.'
30. 'Et, avant de les transformer en champs fertiles, des milliers de colons sont morts à la tache . . . Pendant qu'ils y étaient nos grand-pères auraient bien dû faire de meilleurs chemins. On t'attendait pour celà mon garçon.'
31. Fanon, *Les Damnés*, p. 82: 'le colon [qui] fait l'histoire'; pp. 81–2: 'Il est le commencement absolu: « Cette terre, c'est nous qui l'avons faite. » Il est la cause continuée: « Si nous partons, tout est perdu, cette terre retournera au Moyen Âge. »'
32. Massey, *For Space*, p. 95.
33. Bazin, *Jean Renoir*, p. 20: 'un perpetuel contresens technique: sa mise en scène étant très souvent conçue en profondeur de champ cependant que Renoir s'entête à utiliser des objectifs lumineux donnant une photo très douce mais aucune netteté des arrière-plans'.
34. Deleuze, *L'Image-temps*, p. 140: 'une profondeur [. . .] *dans* le champ'; 'une profondeur *de* champ'. Deleuze's italics. For a more descriptive analysis of both categories of deep staging as they feature in *Le Bled*, see Nevin, 'Jean Renoir's *Le Bled*', pp. 11–12.
35. Benali, *Le Cinéma colonial au Maghreb*, p. 64: 'le marqueur principal de l'achèvement du processus d'appropriation du territoire algérien'.

36. 'C'est honteux, ce que nous avons fait. Cette chasse est trop barbare.'
37. 'Je passerais volontiers toute ma vie ici.'
38. Pulju, *Women and Mass Consumer Society*, p. 104.
39. Slavin, *Colonial Cinema and Imperial France*, p. 154.
40. Benali, *Le Cinéma colonial au Maghreb*, p. 91.
41. O'Shaughnessy, *Jean Renoir*, pp. 64–5.
42. Badger, *The New Deal*, pp. 163, 182, 182.
43. Ibid., pp. 168, 299.
44. Ibid., p. 189.
45. Ibid., p. 302.
46. Narboni et al., *Jean Renoir*, p. 338: 'J'ai procédé énormément avec des objectifs assez fermés et donnant une grande profondeur de champ, de façon à ne jamais perdre de vue derrière mes personnages, les champs. Car en réalité cette terre que mon héros voulait absolument cultiver, et sur laquelle il compte pour devenir indépendant, cette terre, ces champs jouent un rôle. C'est aussi un personnage du film, alors il faut le voir. C'est la raison pour laquelle j'ai employé ces objectifs qui me donnent de la profondeur et qui permettent de rester en contact avec le fond, alors que l'on est cependant intéressé, je l'espère, par ce que peut raconter le personnage du premier plan.' Note that by the word 'closed' ('fermé'), Renoir was referring to the aperture of the lens: the narrower the aperture, the greater the depth of field available to the camera.
47. Little, cited in Massey, *For Space*, p. 181.
48. Ibid., pp. 47, 85.
49. Deleuze, *L'Image-temps*, p. 115: 'les remous de la rivière conflée sous l'orage et piquée par la pluie'.
50. Harper and Rayner, 'Introduction', p. 16.
51. DuPuis, 'Landscapes of Desires?', p. 126.
52. Deleuze, *L'Image-temps*, pp. 124–6.
53. Braudy, *Jean Renoir*, p. 140.
54. O'Shaughnessy, *Jean Renoir*, p. 170; Massey, *For Space*, p. 85.
55. Deleuze, *L'Image-temps*, p. 117: 'en fonction d'une dimension d'avenir'.
56. Cauliez, *Jean Renoir*, p. 118: '*contraignent* des éléments plus ou moins épars à se rassembler dans un montage à la fois ramassé et harmonieux'. Cauliez's italics.
57. For further information regarding the film's reception, see Durgnat, *Jean Renoir*, pp. 283–4. Bazin's defence is printed in Bazin, *Jean Renoir*, p. 107.
58. Lourié, *My Work in Films*, p. 162.
59. Renoir, letter to Mr Schlamm dated 14 April 1949. Box 9, Folder 7. *Jean Renoir Papers*.
60. Massey, *For Space*, p. 129.
61. Deleuze, *L'Image-temps*, p. 115: 'abrités dans une sorte de cristal ou de kiosque hindou essaient des rôles, dont certains tournent au tragique, dont meurt tragiquement le petit frère'.

62. Ibid., p. 117 : 'sera sauvé parce qu'elle saura renoncer au rôle de son premier amour'.
63. See Deleuze, *L' Image-temps*, pp. 67–75, 92.
64. For example, when Harriet is told to wear shoes outside: '"Oh, well!" she said, and sighed again and her mind went off on a rapid Harriet canter of its own, too rapid for stops. Will-I-get-hookworm-you-get-all-kinds-of-worms-in-India-and-diseases-too-there-is-a-leper-in-the-bazaar-no-nose-and-his-fingers-dropping-off-him-if-I-had-no-fingers-I-couldn't-learn-music-could-I-no-March-of-the-Men-of-Harlech. She looked at her own fingers [. . .].' Cf. Godden, *The River*, p. 3.
65. Renoir, letter to Claude Renoir Jr dated 22 September 1950. Correspondence Files: Box 10, Folder 13. *Jean Renoir Papers.*
66. Renoir, 'Jean Renoir [document handwritten by Renoir, dated December 1948]'. Correspondence Files: Box 9, Folder 3. *Jean Renoir Papers.*
67. Renoir, letter to Kenneth McEldowney dated 1 August 1949. Correspondence Files: Box 9, Folder 11. *Jean Renoir Papers.* For an in-depth discussion of the technical issues encountered by Renoir's crew in India, see Sesonske, 'The River Runs', pp. 105–31.
68. Bachelard, *La Poétique de l'espace*, p. 11: 'l'espace saisi par l'imagination [. . .] est vécu, non pas dans sa positivité, mais avec toutes les partialités de l'imagination'.
69. Deleuze, *L'Image-temps*, p. 112: 'le dédoublement du temps, qui fait passer tous les présents et les fait tendre vers le cirque comme vers leur avenir, mais aussi qui conserve tous les passés'.
70. Ibid., p. 140: 'explorer chaque fois une région du passé, un continuum'.
71. Ibid., p. 143: 'un certain type d'image-temps direct, qu'on peut définir par la mémoire, les régions virtuelles de passé [. . .]. Ce serait moins une fonction de réalité qu'une fonction de mémoration, de temporalisation: non pas exactement un souvenir, mais « une invitation à se souvenir ».'
72. Ibid., p. 132: 'des nappes de passé'.
73. Ibid., p. 142: 'les aspects ou éléments *optiques* empruntés aux différents plans en interaction'; 'un ensemble de liaisons non-localisables, toujours d'un plan à un autre, qui constitue la région de passé ou le continuum de durée'. Deleuze's italics.
74. Ibid., p. 142: 'plus exigeante, plus contraignante, en quelque sorte *théorématique*'. Deleuze's italics.
75. Ibid., p. 117: 'en fonction d'une dimension d'avenir'.
76. Younger, '*The River*', p. 173.
77. Ibid., p. 172.
78. Deleuze, *L'Image-temps*, p. 144: 'les nappes virtuelles du passé qu'on explore pour y retrouver le souvenir cherché'.
79. Ibid., p. 113: 'au fond, en profondeur, par le troisième côté ou la troisième dimension, par la fêlure'.

80. Ibid., pp. 130–1: 'la coexistence de toutes les nappes de passé'.
81. Ibid., pp. 129–30: 'la mémoire n'est pas en nous, c'est nous qui nous mouvons dans une mémoire-Être, dans une mémoire-monde'.
82. Doane, 'The Voice in the Cinema', p. 324. Doane's italics.
83. Ibid., p. 324.
84. Deleuze, *L'Image-temps*, pp. 109–10: 'le point d'indiscernabilité'.
85. Doane, 'The Voice in the Cinema', p. 324.
86. Deleuze, *L'Image-temps*, p. 306: 'renvoie [. . .] au Tout qui s'exprime dans les ensembles, au changement qui s'exprime dans le mouvement, à la durée qui s'exprime dans l'espace, au concept vivant qui s'exprime dans l'image, à l'esprit qui s'exprime dans la matière'.
87. Ibid., p. 306: 'en actes de parole très spéciaux, réflexifs et non plus interactifs (voix qui évoque, qui commente, qui sait, douée d'une toute-puissance ou d'une forte puissance sur la suite des images)'.
88. Turim, *Flashbacks in Film*, pp. 1, 11.
89. Ibid., p. 12.
90. Deleuze, *Foucault*, p. 127: 'tel qu'il se condense au dedans, dans le rapport avec soi'.
91. Ibid., p. 127: 'Penser le passé contre le présent, résister au présent, non pas pour un retour, mais « en faveur, je l'espère, d'un temps à venir » (Nietzsche), c'est-à-dire en rendant le passé actif et présent au dehors, pour qu'arrive enfin quelque chose de nouveau, pour que penser, toujours, arrive à la pensée.'
92. Deleuze, *L'Image-temps*, p. 115: 'quelque chose se forme à l'intérieur du cristal, qui réussira à sortir par la fêlure et à s'épanouir librement'.
93. Ibid., p. 115: 'C'était déjà le cas de Boudu, qui retrouve le fil de l'eau en sortant du théâtre intime et renfermé du libraire où il a essayé beaucoup de rôles. Ce sera le cas d'Harriet dans le film grandiose « *Le fleuve* », où les enfants abrités dans une sorte de cristal ou de kiosque hindou essaient des rôles [. . .] dont la jeune fille va faire son apprentissage, jusqu'à ce qu'elle y trouve la puissante volonté de vie qui se confond avec le fleuve et le rejoint au dehors.'
94. Deleuze and Guattari, *Mille Plateaux*, p. 36. English lyrics cited are Deleuze and Guattari's own.
95. Deleuze, *L'Image-temps*, p. 115.
96. Deleuze draws on Bachelard to emphasise that images can only be deemed virtual through their relationship with corresponding actual images and vice versa in ibid., p. 94.
97. Bachelard, *L'Eau et les rêves*, p. 29: 'Les « images » dont l'eau est le prétexte ou la matière n'ont pas la constance et la solidité des images fournies par la terre, par les cristaux, les métaux et les gemmes.'
98. Ibid., p. 22: 'L'eau gonfle les germes et fait jaillir les sources. [. . .] La source est une naissance irrésistible, une naissance *continue*. De si grandes images marquent à jamais l'inconscient qui les aiment.' Bachelard's italics.

99. Ibid., p. 107: 'l'eau emporte au loin, l'eau passe comme les jours. [. . .] Chacun des éléments a sa propre dissolution, la terre a sa poussière, le feu a sa fumée. L'eau dissout plus complètement. Elle nous aide à mourir totalement.'
100. Ibid., p. 13: 'L'être voué à l'eau est un être en vertige. Il meurt à chaque minute, sans cesse quelque chose de sa substance s'écoule.'
101. Deleuze, *L'Image-temps*, p. 109: 'le jaillissement du temps comme dédoublement, comme scission'.
102. Ibid., p. 109: 'une seule matière a tout pris. « Tout est dissous. »'
103. Ibid., p. 113: 'un vertige, une oscillation'.
104. Turim, *Flashbacks in Film*, p. 12.
105. Harper and Rayner, 'Introduction', p. 20.
106. Harvey, *The Limits to Capital*, p. 416; Murdoch, 'Middle-class Territory?', p. 373.
107. Harper and Rayner, 'Introduction', p. 19.
108. Perez, *The Material Ghost*, p. 218.
109. Harper and Rayner, 'Introduction', p. 18.

Chapter 3

1. Massey, *For Space*, p. 61.
2. Leenhardt, cited in Gauteur, *D'un Renoir l'autre*, p. 43: 'Notre grand Jean, s'il a eu le coeur à gauche, n'avait pas la tête politique.'
3. Deleuze, *L'Image-temps*, p. 117: 'une vive conscience de l'identité de la liberté avec un avenir, collectif ou individuel'; 'la conscience politique de Renoir, la manière dont il conçoit la Révolution française ou le Front Populaire'.
4. Andrew and Ungar, *Popular Front Paris*, p. 322.
5. Reader, '*Toni*', p. 452.
6. Date provided in ibid., p. 253.
7. Bowles, 'Renoir under the Popular Front', p. 406.
8. Chardère, *Premier Plan*, p. 166: 'Faudra-t-il décidément rétablir le générique: *Le Crime de Monsieur Lange* – un film du Groupe Octobre – assistant technique Jean Renoir.'
9. Gauteur, *D'un Renoir l'autre*, pp. 60–1.
10. Buchsbaum, *Cinema Engagé*, p. 185.
11. Spaak, cited in Courtade, *Les Malédictions*, p. 137: 'qui à ce moment-là flirtait beaucoup avec les communistes, a reçu des observations: il n'était pas question de prendre des libertés avec Gorki'.
12. Renoir, 'Gorki en celluloïd', p. 27.
13. Reported by Aveline, 'Apropos the Prix Louis Delluc', p. 262.
14. Leenhardt, 'Les Arts', p. 833: 'pour opposer au Grand Prix du Cinéma, académique et bien-pensant, un jugement exempt de conformisme artistique, patriotique et moral'.

15. Duclos, cited in Courtade, *Les Malédictions*, p. 137: 'au nom du Parti communiste, le grand metteur en scène dont le talent magnifique a donné des œuvres qui resteront'; 'le grand ami du people qui nous a donné le beau film *La Vie est à nous*'.
16. O'Shaughnessy, *La Grande Illusion*, p. 25.
17. Ory, 'De « Ciné-liberté » à *La Marseillaise*', p. 163: '*le* film du Front Populaire'. Ory's italics; Renoir, cited in Andrew and Ungar, *Popular Front Paris*, p. 154.
18. Sesonske, *Jean Renoir*, pp. 323–5.
19. O'Shaughnessy, *Jean Renoir*, p. 234.
20. Jeancolas, *Le Cinéma des Français*, p. 196; Ousselin, 'Film and the Popular Front', p. 956.
21. Marie, 'Renoir and the French Communist Party', p. 328.
22. Andrew, *Mists of Regret*, p. 217.
23. Buchsbaum, *Cinéma Engagé*, p. 161.
24. Marie, 'Renoir and the French Communist Party', p. 331. These articles are reprinted in Renoir, *Écrits*, pp. 132–244.
25. Mérigeau, *Jean Renoir*, pp. 238–9.
26. Gauteur, *D'un Renoir l'autre*, p. 30.
27. Leenhardt, 'Les Arts', p. 834: 'le metteur en scène de génie des gauches'.
28. Renoir, *Ma vie*, p. 114: 'Il fut un moment où les Français crurent vraiment qu'ils allaient s'aimer les uns les autres. On se sentait porté par une vague de générosité.'
29. Reader, 'Renoir's Popular Front Films in Context', p. 40.
30. Strebel, 'Jean Renoir and the Popular Front', p. 76; Gauteur, *D'un Renoir l'autre*, p. 9: 'Saint Renoir n'existe pas, ni n'a jamais existé. [. . .] Jean Renoir fut un homme, avec toute la force et les faiblesses qu'implique l'humaine condition.'
31. Poulle, *Renoir 1938*, p. 18: 'il y avait plusieurs couleurs politiques chez Renoir'.
32. Braunberger, cited in Mérigeau, *Jean Renoir*, p. 257: 'Sur l'échiquier politique, il se situait plutôt à droite. [. . .] Il était social sans être socialiste. [. . .] Je l'encourage vivement à accepter [la proposition des communistes] comme une tâche ingrate, lui expliquant qu'il a l'opportunité de trouver, enfin, un vrai public.'
33. Spaak, cited in ibid., p. 257: 'oubliait que marxisme et nazisme n'étaient pas synonymes'; 'le traître intégral'.
34. Gauteur, *D'un Renoir l'autre*, p. 49: 'en tournant à l'étranger, on trahit à la fois la France et le cinéma'.
35. Carné, *Ma vie à belles dents*, p. 102.
36. Bowles, 'Renoir under the Popular Front', p. 399.
37. Sesonske, *Jean Renoir*, p. 441.
38. Mérigeau, *Jean Renoir*, p. 440: 'choisira par la suite de taire, préférant situer

sa décision de filmer *Tosca* après que la guerre avec l'Allemagne eut été déclarée'.

39. O'Shaughnessy, *Jean Renoir*, p. 16.
40. Renoir, *Œuvres de cinéma inédites*, p. 66.
41. Renoir, '*Ida*', p. 10: 'en quelques années son autorité n'était plus discutée et on pouvait dire que c'était une espèce de Mussolini ou de Hitler de la forêt'.
42. Renoir, '*Ida*', p. 18: 'la plus vilaine maison en pierres meulières que l'on puisse imaginer'; 'mentalité simple et harmonieuse'.
43. Renoir, '*Ida*', p. 19: 'Cette maison du boucher m'entraîne bien loin mais il faut qu'on en parle. Ce sont ces horreurs qui ont déshonoré la banlieue de Paris et aussi les alentours de toute grande ville.'
44. Renoir, '*Ida*', p. 19: 'En Allemagne on fait HITLER, en Italie on fait MUSSOLINI, en France la même catégorie de petit bourgeois arrogants fait des maisons en pierres meulières et c'est presque aussi dangereux.' Renoir's capital letters.
45. Renoir, '*Ida*', p. 1: 'Cette minuscule agglomération de deux cents habitants sera le centre de l'histoire que je vais essayer de transcrire. Naturellement je change le nom du pays et des indigènes. Quelqu'un pourrait se reconnaître et se vexer. Mais, mes noms de remplacement ne sont pas faux. Ils sont empruntés à des gens et à des lieux réels qui auraient très bien pu être les acteurs et former le cadre d'un drame analogue.'
46. Deleuze and Guattari, *Mille Plateaux*, p. 16: 'on fait une rupture, on trace une ligne de fuite'; 'les groupes et les individus contiennent des micro-fascismes qui ne demandent qu'à cristalliser'; 'on risque toujours de retrouver sur elle des organisations qui restratifient l'ensemble'.
47. Ibid., p. 36.
48. Massey, *For Space*, pp. 100, 95, 107.
49. Narboni et al., *Jean Renoir*, p. 324: 'un essai de lien des fonds et du premier plan, par le même plan'.
50. Bush, 'Feminine Narrative and the Law', p. 58.
51. Massey, *For Space*, p. 107.
52. Sesonske, 'Jean Renoir as Moralist', pp. 8, 8–9.
53. Faulkner, 'Paris, Arizona', p. 31.
54. Massey, *For Space*, pp. 162, 12.
55. O'Shaughnessy, 'Shooting in Deep Time', p. 26. O'Shaughnessy reiterates this argument elsewhere, observing a 'clear solidarity between the camera and the group'. See O'Shaughnessy, 'Between the "I" and the "We"', p. 52.
56. Parry, 'Counter Revolution by Conspiracy', p. 161.
57. Blatt, 'The Cagoule Plot'.
58. Bourdrel, *La Cagoule*, p. 20.
59. Ibid., pp. 33–4.
60. Renoir, cited in Gauteur, *D'un Renoir l'autre*, p. 60: 'ce vieux Berlin était une ville paisible avec de bons bourgeois qui fumaient leur pipe et qui discutaient des élections comme on aurait discuté d'élections normales [. . .]

et voilà que le lendemain de l'élection, une autre partie de la population – à moins que ce ne soit la même – était déchainée'.

61. Andrew and Ungar, *Popular Front Paris*, p. 339.
62. O'Shaughnessy, 'Between the "I" and the "We"', p. 54.
63. Deleuze and Guattari, *Mille Plateaux*, p. 16: 'des micro-fascismes qui ne demandent qu'à cristalliser'.
64. Deleuze, *L'Image-temps*, p. 116: 'rôles morts ou de la mort'.
65. Deleuze and Guattari, *Mille Plateaux*, p. 16: 'des organisations qui restratifient l'ensemble'.
66. Massey, *For Space*, p. 19; Deleuze, *L'Image-temps*, p. 124.
67. For other interpretations of the pan, see the following, who all restore a politics of collectivity to the camera movement: Sesonske, *Jean Renoir*; Strebel, 'Jean Renoir and the Popular Front'; Tifft, 'Theatre in the Round'; O'Shaughnessy, *Jean Renoir* and 'Breaking the Circle'; Ousselin, 'Film and the Popular Front.
68. Davis, *Scenes of Love and Murder*, p. 67
69. Ibid., p. 67. Davis's italics.
70. O'Shaughnessy, 'Breaking the Circle', p. 37.
71. Ibid., pp. 32, 32, 37.
72. Massey, *For Space*, pp. 89, 106–7.
73. Reader, 'The Circular Ruins?', p. 297.
74. Bazin, *Jean Renoir*, p. 42: 'l'expression spatial pure de toute la mise en scène'; Massey, *For Space*, p. 153.
75. Conley, 'Cartographies in Deep Focus', p. 50.
76. See especially Deleuze, *L'Image-mouvement*, pp. 114–16.
77. Faulkner, 'Paris, Arizona', p. 28.
78. Durgnat, *Jean Renoir*, p. 142.
79. 'Tu oublies que je suis le patron ici et que tu me dois le respect.'
80. Gorky, *Les Bas-fonds*, p. 14.
81. Braudy, *Jean Renoir*, p. 122.
82. Sesonske, *Jean Renoir*, p. 278.
83. Deleuze, *L'Image-temps*, p. 116: 'la danse macabre des souvenirs'.
84. Sesonske, *Jean Renoir*, p. 259.
85. Nevin, '"Prochainement: Arizona Jim contre Cagoulard"', p. 8.
86. Sesonske, *Jean Renoir*, p. 262.
87. 'Les ivrognes ne sont pas toujours ivres, les voleurs pas toujours en prison.'
88. Sesonske, *Jean Renoir*, p. 266.
89. O'Shaughnessy, *Jean Renoir*, p. 122.
90. 'Nous sommes tous aussi fautifs que Pépel.'
91. 'Moi aussi, j'ai donné des coups'; 'c'est les bas-fonds qui l'ont tué mais pas plus Pépel qu'un autre'.
92. Note that Renoir published an enthusiastic review of *Modern Times* on 20 May 1936. See Renoir, *Écrits*, pp. 109–11.
93. Faulkner, *The Social Cinema*, pp. 82–3; Andrew, *Mists of Regret*, p. 292.

94. 'Venez, c'est sérieux. L'acteur s'est pendu . . . Ce soir, c'est fini de chanter.'
95. Gorky, *Les Bas-fonds*, p. 123.
96. O'Shaughnessy, *Jean Renoir*, p. 122; Andrew, *Mists of Regret*, p. 292; Bowles, 'Renoir under the Popular Front', p. 412.
97. Bowles, 'Renoir under the Popular Front', p. 413.
98. Cavell, *The World Viewed*, p. 188.
99. Deleuze, *L'Image-temps*, p. 114: 'la profondeur rend évident que le cristal est là pour que quelque chose en fuie, dans le fond, par le fond'.
100. Ibid., p. 117: 'sont déjà voués au souvenir'; 'Les deux évadés seront sauvés par le sacrifice de l'autre.'
101. 'On doit aboutir dans un jardin, derrière les bâtiments que tu vois là-bas. C'est en pleine campagne.'
102. 'On l'a attrapé dans les jardins derrière les bâtiments et on l'a tiré dessus.'
103. Macdonald, *In Search of* La Grande Illusion, p. 38.
104. 'D'un côté, des enfants qui jouent au soldat – et de l'autre, des soldats qui jouent comme des enfants.'
105. O'Shaughnessy, *La Grande Illusion*, pp. 83–4.
106. Massey, *For Space*, p. 85.
107. Foucault, *Surveiller et punir*, p. 229: 'le regard partout est en éveil'.
108. Ibid., p. 233: 'aménage des unites spatiales qui permettent de voir sans arrêt de reconnaître aussitôt'.
109. Howard, *The First World War*, p. 9.
110. Ibid., pp. 18–19.
111. Und ob mein Herz im Tode bricht,
wirst du doch drum ein Welscher nicht.
Reich, wie an Wasser deine Flut,
ist Deutschland ja an Heldenblut.
Lieb Vaterland, magst ruhig sein,
lieb Vaterland, magst ruhig sein,
Fest steht und treu die Wacht, die Wacht am Rhein.
Fest steht und treu die Wacht, die Wacht am Rhein.
112. O'Shaughnessy, *La Grande Illusion*, p. 84.
113. Lourié, *My Work in Films*, pp. 11–12, 21. Lourié's italics.
114. Ibid., p. 28.
115. Deleuze and Guattari, *Mille Plateaux*, p. 16: 'les groupes et les individus contiennent des micro-fascismes qui ne demandent qu'à cristalliser'.
116. Deleuze, *L'Image-temps*, p. 116: 'l'eau gelée'.
117. 'Mettre fin à cette putain de guerre.'
118. Deleuze, *L'Image-temps*, p. 117: 'se donne un avenir'.
119. See Deleuze, *L'Image-temps*, p. 115: 'We are born in a crystal, but the crystal only retains death'/'On naît dans un cristal, mais le cristal ne retient que la mort [. . .].'
120. O'Shaughnessy, 'Shooting in Deep Time', pp. 28–9.
121. Ibid., p. 32.

122. Massey, *For Space*, p. 93.
123. O'Shaughnessy, 'Shooting in Deep Time', p. 30.
124. Discussed by Renoir in Narboni et al., *Jean Renoir*, p. 298: 'Nous dansons sur un volcan.'
125. Ibid., p. 207: 'Le 6 février 1934, le jour où il y a eu ces bagarres place de la Concorde, je déjeunais dans un petit restaurant qui était peut-être à cinquante mètres de l'endroit où ça se passait. Et il se passait pas mal de choses. Eh bien, c'est en rentrant chez moi que j'ai rencontré un ami qui m'a appris ce qui avait eu lieu pendant mon déjeuner! On croit toujours qu'un événement est immédiatement et universellement perçu. On croit même qu'il est immédiatement et universellement compris. Ce n'est pas vrai. L'événement reste souterrain ou isolé pendant très longtemps. Ce n'est que peu à peu qu'il émerge, ce n'est qu'après coup qu'il prend son sens.'
126. Massey, *For Space*, p. 63.

Chapter 4

1. Letter from Flaubert to George Sand dated 29 April 1871, cited in Bourdieu, *Les Règles de l'art*, p. 91: 'Tout était faux: faux réalisme, faux crédit et même fausses catins [. . .].'
2. Baudrillard, *Les Stratégies fatales*, p. 200: 'Ce qui vous fait exister, ce n'est pas la force de votre désir [. . .], c'est le jeu du monde et de la séduction, c'est la passion de jouer et d'être joué, c'est la passion de l'illusion et des apparences [. . .].'
3. Braudy, *Jean Renoir*, p. 148.
4. Hayward, *French Costume Drama of the 1950s*, p. 17.
5. Narboni et al., *Jean Renoir*, p. 314: '*Le Journal d'une femme de chambre* correspond à une de mes crises anti-réalistes.'
6. Ibid., p. 314: 'Il y a des moments où je me demande si la seule vérité n'est pas la vérité intérieure et si la vérité des maquillages, des costumes, des apparences, des meubles, la vérité extérieure, si vraiment nous ne devons pas la négliger pour avancer un tout petit peu plus en avant vers cette vérité intérieure. *Le Journal d'une femme de chambre* correspond à cette préoccupation.'
7. Bazin, '*Le Journal d'une femme de chambre*': 'Par quelle aberration mentale, par quelle absence d'esprit auto-critique, ou par quel goût dangereux du paradoxe, Renoir a-t-il voulu tourner précisément en Amérique le sujet qui lui dentait le plus à cœur et surtout qui pouvait le moins se traiter hors de France ? [. . .] On sent les sunlights sur les rosiers de Burgess Meredith, le film entier baigne dans cette lumière d'aquarium caractéristique des studios hollywoodiens et tout – les acteurs compris – y fait figure de fleur japonaise dans un bocal.' For a more comprehensive review of the reception of *Diary of a Chambermaid*, see Vitanza, 'Rewriting the Rules of the Game', pp. 172–87.

8. Renoir, *Correspondance*, p. 268: 'quelques plans d'atmosphère dans un pays d'Amérique latine'.
9. The film even divided *Cahiers* critics. Jacques Doniol-Valcroze embraced the work. See Doniol-Valcroze, 'Camilla et le don'. Other critics reacted negatively to Renoir's visibly artificial décor: Herman G. Weinberg criticised Renoir for saturating the visuals at the expense of believability. See Weinberg, 'Lettre de New-York', p. 35.
10. Deleuze, *L'Image-temps*, p. 113: 'l'image plane, comme dans *Le Carrosse d'or*'; 'c'était moins visible'.
11. Ibid., p. 116: 'une nouvelle réalité qui ne préexistait pas'; 'des rôles gelés, figés, tout faits, trop conformes'.
12. Elsaesser, 'Theatricality and Spectacle', p. 240.
13. Ibid., p. 240. On the meaning of the term *élan vital*, see note 49 to the Introduction.
14. Elsaesser, 'Theatricality and Spectacle', p. 240.
15. Debord, *La Société du spectacle*, p. 16: 'un rapport social entre des personnes, médiatisé par des images'.
16. See especially ibid., pp. 27–8.
17. Ibid., p. 20: 'Le spectacle se présente comme une énorme positivité indiscutable et inaccessible. Il ne dit rien de plus que « ce qui apparaît est bon, ce qui est bon apparaît ». L'attitude qu'il exige par principe est cette acceptation passive qu'il a déjà en fait obtenue par sa manière d'apparaître sans réplique, par son monopole de l'apparence.'
18. Ibid., p. 23: 'échappe à la reconsidération et à la correction'.
19. Ibid., p. 133: 'La raisonnement sur l'histoire est, inséparablement, *raisonnement sur le pouvoir*'; p. 156: '*fausse conscience du temps*'; 'la paralysie de l'histoire et de la mémoire'. Debord's italics.
20. Ibid., p. 129: 'sociétés froides'; 'ont ralenti à l'extrême leur part d'histoire'; 'une structure définitive a exclu le changement'; p. 192: 'la pseudo-histoire [. . .] à tous les niveaux de la consommation de la vie'; 'le temps gelé'.
21. Massey, *For Space*, p. 89.
22. Differences between Mirbeau's novel and Renoir's adaptation are discussed in this analysis where appropriate. For an extensive list of differences between each, consult Tesson, 'Autour du *Journal d'une femme de chambre*'.
23. Gilcher, 'Jean Renoir in America', p. 307.
24. Rivette and Truffaut, 'Entretien avec Jean Renoir', p. 19: 'd'une façon extrêmement romantique'; Narboni et al., *Jean Renoir*, p. 313.
25. Renoir, *Correspondance*, p. 62.
26. Rivette and Truffaut, 'Entretien avec Jean Renoir', p. 19: 's'est trouvé entièrement modifié, étant donné que je l'ai réalisé au commencement de cette période ou je voyais les scènes d'une façon plus concentrée, plus théâtrale, avec moins de champs et de contre-champs'.
27. See Chapter 1 and Chapter 3 for discussions of La Colinière and Hallbach respectively.

28. Mirbeau, *Le Journal d'une femme de chambre*, p. 173.
29. Massey, *Space, Place, and Gender*, p. 169.
30. Deleuze, *L'Image-temps*, p. 116: 'rôles gelés, figés, tout faits, trop conformes'.
31. Ibid., p. 97: 'le cristal est une scène'.
32. Ibid., p. 97: 'rend actuelle l'image virtuelle du rôle, qui devient visible et lumineux. [. . .] Mais plus l'image virtuelle du rôle devient actuelle et limpide, plus l'image actuelle de l'acteur passe dans les ténèbres et devient opaque.'
33. Ibid., p. 98: '[la] double face de l'acteur'.
34. Renoir, *Ma vie*, p. 123: 'mettre le public en contact avec un être humain'.
35. Narboni et al., *Jean Renoir*, pp. 314–15.
36. Ibid., p. 352; p. 314: 'J'ai évidemment pensé en le tournant à la *commedia dell-arte*, j'ai pensé – c'est très pretentieux – à la tragédie classique. La tragédie classique se passe avec les mêmes costumes comme pour la *commedia dell'arte*, ça n'a pas empêché ces deux genres de traiter des sujets extrêmement importants, extrêmement profonds, que ce soit de la comédie ou du drame. En réalité, est-ce que l'être humain n'est pas gêné par les apparences plutôt qu'aidé? Voilà la question.'
37. Renoir, *Ma vie*, p. 247: 'la vérité intérieure se cache souvent derrière un environnement purement artificiel'.
38. Braudy, *Jean Renoir*, p. 148.
39. Narboni et al., *Jean Renoir*, pp. 358–9: 'À l'origine et, je crois, également dans sa réalisation, le film est une espèce de course vaine de la part de gens représentant une société déjà morte; c'est une course de fantômes. Ces gens représentent une bourgeoisie qui n'existe plus, car la bourgeoisie qui les a remplacé est une bourgeoisie d'affaires, une bourgeoisie active, une bourgeoisie qui fait de l'argent [. . .].'
40. Braudy, *Jean Renoir*, p. 148.
41. Golsan, 'A Hollywood Fairytale', pp. 56–7.
42. Deleuze and Guattari, *Mille Plateaux*, p. 16: 'des micro-fascismes qui ne demandent qu'à cristalliser'.
43. Braudy, *Jean Renoir*, p. 92.
44. Massey, *Space, Place, and Gender*, p. 169.
45. Durgnat, *Jean Renoir*, p. 254.
46. Braudy, *Jean Renoir*, pp. 92, 92, 93.
47. Deleuze, *L'Image-temps*, p. 34: 'l'image peut être plane, sans profondeur, et prendre par là d'autant plus de dimensions ou puissances excédant l'espace'.
48. Bazin, '*The Diary of a Chambermaid*': 'C'est aussi sans doute avec *Le Journal* que Renoir se dégage totalement cette fois du « réalisme » de son oeuvre française. [. . .] Aussi bien est-ce peut-être ici que prendra source la hantise du théâtre de Renoir [. . .]. C'est peut-être pour la première fois que nous discernons dans l'œuvre de Renoir, non plus le théâtre, mais la théâtralité à l'état pur.'

49. Braudy, *Jean Renoir*, p. 148.
50. Deleuze, *L'Image-temps*, p. 113: 'une « théâtralité à l'état pur »'; 'seront portés au plus haut point [. . .]'.
51. Elsaesser, 'Theatricality and Spectacle', p. 239.
52. Ibid., p. 239.
53. Debord, *La Société du spectacle*, p. 129: 'le conformisme absolu des pratiques sociales existantes'.
54. Hayward, 'Design at Work', p. 92.
55. Debord, *La Société du spectacle*, p. 30: 'un rapport irréversible au centre même qui maintient leur isolement'.
56. The only reference to Cusco in the source text is when Camilla declares to the viceroy that her other suitors are of no concern: 'Should your highness have doubts, he may send the captain to Panama and the matador to Cusco!' ('Pour peu que Votre Altesse conserve des doutes, elle peut envoyer le capitaine à Panama, et le matador à Cuzco!') See Mérimée, 'La Carrosse du Saint-Sacrement', p. 33.
57. Hayward, 'Design at Work', p. 92.
58. Deleuze, *L'Image-temps*, p. 116: 'À la fin du *Carrosse d'or*, trois personnages auront trouvé leur rôle vivant, tandis que Camilla restera dans le cristal, mais pour y essayer encore des rôles dont l'un lui fera découvrir peut-être la vraie Camilla.'
59. Bergstrom, 'Jean Renoir's Return to France', p. 485.
60. Renoir, '*The Golden Coach.* Shooting script', Box 3, Folder 1. *Jean Renoir Papers*, pp. 203–4.
61. Rushton, 'A Deleuzian Imaginary', pp. 253–8.
62. Debord, *La Société du spectacle*, p. 15: 'tout ce qui était directement vécu s'est éloigné dans une représentation'.
63. Renoir, *Écrits*, p. 378: 'Mon histoire [. . .] est une histoire beaucoup trop fantaisiste pour que l'on puisse lui donner aucune apparence de réalité. Il vaut mieux partir en disant que c'est une histoire fausse.'
64. Renoir, *Ma vie*, p. 248: 'L'action, dans ce film d'apparence artificiel, s'accommoderait mal de décors réalistes. Les rouges et les bleus s'y affrontent sans transition. Claude Renoir a tourné quelques plans de paysages orageux qui nous ramènent directement vers l'imagerie pour enfants. Ingrid Bergman, qui jouait le rôle principal, s'en tira avec son génie habituel et réussit à donner un personnage aussi invraisemblable que les décors.'
65. 'À bas Rollan!'; 'À bas Rollan, à bas les dictateurs!'
66. Davis, *Postwar Renoir*, pp. 76–7.
67. Narboni et al., *Jean Renoir*, p. 152: 'Autour de [la femme, Eléna], j'ai construit une satire, je me suis amusé avec des histoires politiques, des histoires de généraux. J'ai essayé de montrer la futilité des entreprises humaines, y compris l'entreprise qu'on appelle le patriotisme [. . .].'
68. 'Ils appellent ça un défilé!'
69. '120, 000 personnes, c'est un record.'

70. Debord, *La Société du spectacle*, p. 59: 'L'image imposée du bien, dans son spectacle, recueille la totalité de ce qui existe officiellement, et se concentre normalement sur un seul homme, qui est le garant de sa cohésion totalitaire. À cette vedette absolue, chacun doit s'identifier magiquement, ou disparaître.'
71. Ibid., p. 56: 'a renoncé à toute qualité autonome pour s'identifier lui-même à la loi générale de l'obéissance au cours des choses'.
72. Serceau, *Jean Renoir: la sagesse du plaisir*, p. 54: 'support de toutes les projections'; 'n'a [. . .] d'autre consistance que de fournir un objet à un désir qui lui préexiste'.
73. 'Duchêne, le cerveau; Fleury, les yeux; Lisbonne, le coeur; et Buchez, l'esprit. [. . .] Et voici l'indispensable Isnard, ancien champion de course à pied.'
74. 'Sans moi, Sarah Bernhardt serait encore à la Comédie Française.'
75. 'Bon sujet d'article: « La Princesse et le Général ».'
76. O'Shaughnessy, *Jean Renoir*, p. 205.
77. Serceau, *Jean Renoir: la sagesse du plaisir*, p. 55.
78. 'Sous les feux de bataille, dans une vraie guerre, il ferait massacrer tous ses hommes.'
79. Deleuze, *L'Image-temps*, p. 117: 'condamnés, parce que déjà voués au souvenir'.
80. Renoir, *Écrits*, p. 32: 'étaient une grande chose pour tous les enfants de ma génération'.
81. Ibid., p. 32: 'il y en avait de très beaux'; 'Pour moi, la guerre, avec ses vraies misères, avec ses vrais malheurs, n'existait pas aux époques de beaux costumes. Cette guerre réaliste avait commencé avec les costumes crasseux de la fin du XIXe siècle [. . .].'
82. Durgnat, *Jean Renoir*, p. 316.
83. Debord, *La Société du spectacle*, p. 156: 'la paralysie de l'histoire et de la mémoire'.
84. Hayward, *French Costume Drama of the 1950s* , p. 383.
85. Renoir, *Écrits*, p. 384: 'ne sait pas ce que c'est que l'argent, elle ne l'a jamais su. Elle s'en fiche, ça ne compte pas; d'ailleurs, elle serait aussi heureuse mendiante que millionnaire.'
86. 'Ah princesse, on se mélange?'; 'C'est pour ça que vous avez pris la Bastille!'
87. Hayward, 'Design at Work', p. 101.
88. 'J'aime la foule.'
89. 'J'aurais préféré la bataille. C'est de plus glorieux. Mais la fin justifie la moyenne.'
90. 'La cause que vous me faites haïr.'
91. 'De ne rien faire. Mon idéal est d'atteindre à la parfaite paresse. Malheureusement de nos jours, c'est presque impossible. [. . .] La paresse universelle pour les pauvres, comme pour les riches. Quel but!'
92. 'Les Français ont un respect pour les choses de l'amour. [. . .] En ce qui

concerne le forage des puits de pétrole ou le choix de nos gouvernements ou la fabrication des explosifs, nous sommes peut-être légèrement d'à côté. Mais quand il s'agit de l'art de vivre, vous pouvez faire confiance aux Français.'

93. Hayward, 'Design at Work', p. 103.
94. Faulkner, *The Social Cinema*, p. 50.
95. Deleuze and Guattari, *Mille Plateaux*, p. 273: 'ne cessent pas de colmater, de boucher, de barrer les lignes de fuite'.
96. Massey, *For Space*, pp. 11, 19.
97. Deleuze, *L'Image-temps*, p. 124; p. 125: 'inséparable d'un processus de décomposition qui les mine du dedans'.
98. Ghose, 'Treatment of Women', p. 8; Viry-Babel, 'Les Images de la femme', p. 302: 'tous [les espaces Renoiriens] traduisent la notion d'enfermement et de dépendance, aux Autres en général, et à l'Homme en particulier. Il n'y a pas de lieu, d'espace où la femme puisse s'isoler.'
99. Viry-Babel, 'Les Images de la femme', p. 302 : 'hors des limites du champ et du hors-champ, dans un futur toujours inaccessible'.
100. Cavell, *The World Viewed*, p. 196. Cavell's italics.
101. Deleuze, *L'Image-temps*, p. 165: 'dans les domaines les plus divers, les vues plates et les aplats de couleurs de la comédie musicale [. . .]'.
102. Deleuze, *Pourparlers*, p. 172: 'est à créer dans chaque domaine'; 'dire « la vérité est une création » implique que la production de vérité passe par une série d'opérations qui consiste à travailler une matière, une série de falsifications à la lettre'.
103. Debord, *La Société du spectacle*, p. 203: 'la conscience déformée des réalités'; 'des facteurs réels exerçant en retour une réelle action déformante'.
104. Rohmer, 'Les singes et Vénus', p. 39: 'travaille moins sur une réalité noble que sur la caricature qu'elle a suscitée'.
105. Debord, *La Société du spectacle*, p. 15: 'tout ce qui était directement vécu s'est éloigné dans une représentation'; Bazin, 'Le Réalisme cinématographique', p. 269: 'le réalisme en art ne saurait [. . .] ne procéder que d'artifices'; Renoir, *Ma vie*, p. 27: 'la vie est un tissu de déceptions'.

Conclusion

1. Braudy, *The World in a Frame*, pp. 46–51.
2. Bergson, *L'Évolution créatrice*, p. 302: 'notre perception s'arrange pour solidifier en images discontinues la continuité fluide du réel'; '*n'est qu'un instantané pris sur une transition*'. Bergson's italics.
3. Davis, *Critical Excess*, p. 78.
4. Deleuze and Guattari, *Mille Plateaux*, p. 16: 'des micro-fascismes qui ne demandent qu'à cristalliser'.
5. Pisters, *The Matrix of Visual Culture*, p. 9.
6. Perez, *The Material Ghost*, p. 138.

7. Sarris, *The American Cinema*, p. 74.
8. Faulkner, *The Social Cinema*, pp. 49–50. See also 'Jean Renoir: *l'exception glorieuse*' in the Introduction.
9. O'Shaughnessy, 'Shooting in Deep Time'. See also under 'Reading Deleuze on Renoir: Critical Opinions' in the Introduction.
10. Massey, *For Space*, pp. 151–2.
11. McCann, *Le Jour se lève*, p. 36.
12. Renoir, *Ma vie*, p. 156: 'film de guerre'.
13. Privitello, 'The Incompassable Language of Natural Aristocracy'.
14. Bogue, *Deleuze on Cinema*, p. 124.
15. Epstein, '*Photogénie* and the Imponderable', p. 189.
16. Deleuze, *L'Image-temps*, p. 117: 'Il y a *peut-être* encore un troisième état'; p. 124: 'Le dernier état à considérer *serait* le cristal en décomposition'. My italics.
17. Forbes, '*La Règle du jeu*', p. 89.
18. Elsaesser, 'Postmodernism as Mourning Work', pp. 9–10.
19. Davis, *Postwar Renoir*, p. 8.
20. Tally, *Spatiality*, pp. 12–13.
21. Becker, *La France en guerre, 1914–1918: la grande mutation.*
22. Sorlin, 'France: The Silent Memory', p. 134.
23. Renoir, *Ma vie*, p. 35: 'si notre espèce ne disparaît pas entièrement et si, dans quelques centaines d'années, il existe encore des historiens, ils pourront diviser le récit de notre histoire en deux parties: avant 1914 et après'.
24. Horne, 'Introduction', p. xx.
25. Deleuze, *L'Image-temps*, p. 114: 'est un des plus beaux films de Renoir, mais ne nous donne pas la clef des autres'; 'idée complète'; '[s]ans qu'il y ait besoin de violence, et par le développement d'une expérimentation, quelque chose sortira du cristal'.
26. Narboni et al., *Jean Renoir*, p. 207: 'L'Histoire avec un grand H est fabriquée par les historiens. Qui sont très utiles, car ils présentent une synthèse sans laquelle on ne comprendrait pas. Mais dans un film, on peut essayer de faire comprendre ce côté hâché, irrégulier, imprévu de la vie pendant les grands événements.'
27. Perez, *The Material Ghost*, p. 194.
28. Massey, *For Space*, p. 12.
29. Perez, *The Material Ghost*, p. 220.
30. Rohmer, 'Le Cinéma, art de l'espace', p. 42: 'ce n'est [. . .] pas seulement l'intérieur de chacun des plans que le réalisateur doit déterminer en fonction d'une certaine conception de la spatialité, mais la totalité de l'espace filmé'.
31. Bazin, *Jean Renoir*, p. 112: 'promenait sur la réalité la lunette d'approche de l'objectif, escamotant ou découvrant ce qu'il voulait'. Bazin is referring to the specific case of *The River*, but I feel his remark is relevant to each of the films analysed within this book.
32. Renoir, *Ma vie*, p. 156: 'Faire partie d'un tout'.

References

Primary Sources

Performing Arts Special Collections, Young Research Library, University of California, Los Angeles:

Jean Renoir Papers, 1915–1927

'Jean Renoir [document handwritten by Renoir, dated December 1948]'. Box 9, Folder 3. Production Files.

'*The Golden Coach*. Shooting script (mimeographed/offprint), 205 pages, annotated', n.d. Box 3, Folder 1. Production Files.

'*Ida*', Box 42, Folder 25. Production Files.

Letter from Renoir to Albert André, 12 July 1941. Box 2, Folder 2. Correspondence Files.

Letter from Renoir to Claude Renoir Jr dated 22 September 1950. Box 10, Folder 13. Correspondence Files.

Letter from Renoir to Kenneth McEldowney dated 1 August 1949. Box 9, Folder 11. Correspondence Files.

Letter from Renoir to Mr Schlamm dated 14 April 1949. Box 9, Folder 7. Correspondence Files.

Published Sources

Abel, Richard, *French Cinema: The First Wave, 1915–1929* (Princeton, NJ: Princeton University Press, 1984).

Allen, Michael and Annette Kuhn, 'Deep-focus', in Pam Cook (ed.), *The Cinema Book*, 3rd edn (London: BFI, [1985] 2007), pp. 149–50.

Amin, Samir, 'The Nation: An Enlightened or Fog-Shrouded Concept?', trans. Edward Ousselin, *Research in African Literatures* 28.4 (1997), pp. 8–18.

Andrew, Dudley, *Mists of Regret: Culture and Sensibility in Classic French Film* (Princeton, NJ: Princeton University Press, 1995).

——— and Steven Ungar, *Popular Front Paris and the Poetics of Culture* (Cambridge, MA: Harvard University Press, 2005).

Arnaud, Diane, 'From Bazin to Deleuze: A Matter of Depth', in Dudley Andrew (ed.), *Opening Bazin: Postwar Film Theory and Its Afterlife* (New York: Oxford University Press, 2011), pp. 85–94.

Aveline, Claude, 'Apropos the Prix Louis Delluc' (1939), in Richard Abel (ed.), *French Film Theory and Criticism, 1907–1939, Volume 2, 1929–1939* (Princeton, NJ: Princeton University Press, 1988), pp. 262–6.

Bachelard, Gaston, *L'Eau et les rêves: essai sur l'imagination de la matière*, 11th edn (Paris: Livre de Poche, [1942] 2011).

———, *La Poétique de l'espace*, 10th edn (Paris: Presses universitaires de France, [1957] 2011).

Badger, Anthony J., *The New Deal: The Depression Years, 1933–40* (Basingstoke: Macmillan, 1989).

Badiou, Alain, *Deleuze: « La clameur de l'Être »* (Paris: Hachette, 1997).

Bakhtin, Mikhail M., 'Forms of Time and of the Chronotope in the Novel: Notes toward a Historical Poetics', trans. Caryl Emerson and Michael Holquist, in Michael Holquist (ed.), *The Dialogic Imagination: Four Essays* (Austin: University of Texas Press, 1981), pp. 84–258.

Balázs, Béla, *Theory of the Film (Character and Growth of a New Art)* (London: Dennis Dobson, 1952).

Baudelaire, Charles, *Les Fleurs du mal*, 2nd edn (Paris: Gallimard, [1857] 1972).

———, 'Le Peintre de la vie moderne' (1863), in Francis Moulinat (ed.), *Écrits sur l'art*, 8th edn (Paris: Livre de poche, [1992] 2010), pp. 503–22.

Baudrillard, Jean, *Les Stratégies fatales* (Paris: Bernard Grasset, 1983).

Bauman, Zygmunt, *Liquid Modernity* (Cambridge: Polity Press, 2000).

———, *Postmodern Ethics* (Oxford: Blackwell, 1993).

Bazin, André, '*The Diary of a Chambermaid* (*Le Journal d'une femme de chambre*)', *Cahiers du Cinéma* 78 (1957), p. 81.

———, 'L'Évolution du langage cinématographique' (1950–55), in *Qu'est-ce que le cinéma?*, 18th edn (Paris: Cerf-Corlet, [1958–62] 2008), pp. 63–80.

———, *Jean Renoir*, ed. François Truffaut, 2nd edn (Paris: Ivrea, [1971] 2005).

———, '*Le Journal d'une femme de chambre*: une suite manqué à *La Règle du jeu*', *L'Écran Française*, 15 June 1948, p. 13.

———, *Orson Welles*, 3rd edn (Paris: Cahiers du cinéma, [1972] 2006).

———, 'Le Réalisme cinématographique et l'école italienne de la Libération' (1948), in *Qu'est-ce que le cinéma?*, 18th edn (Paris: Cerf-Corlet, [1958–62] 2008), pp. 257–85.

———, 'Renoir français', *Cahiers du cinéma* 8 (1952), pp. 9–29.

Becker, Jean-Jacques, *La France en guerre, 1914–1918: la grande mutation* (Brussels: Éditions Complexe, 1988).

Bell, David, 'Variations on the Rural Idyll', in Paul J. Cloke, Terry Marsden, and Patrick H. Mooney (eds), *Handbook of Rural Studies* (London: SAGE, 2006), pp. 149–60.

Benali, Abdelkader, *Le Cinéma colonial au Maghreb: l'imaginaire en tromp-l'œil* (Paris: Éditions du Cerf, 1998).

Bergson, Henri, *L'Évolution créatrice*, 12th edn (Paris: Presses universitaires de France, [1907] 2014).

Bergstrom, Janet, 'Jean Renoir's Return to France', *Poetics Today* 17.3 (1996), pp. 453–89.

Blatt, Joel, 'The Cagoule Plot, 1936–1937', in Kenneth Mouré and Martin S. Alexander (eds), *Crisis and Renewal in France, 1918–1962* (New York: Berghahn, 2002), pp. 86–104.

Bogue, Ronald, *Deleuze on Cinema* (New York: Routledge, 2003).

Bordwell, David and Kristin Thompson, *Film Art: An Introduction*, 8th edn (Boston: McGraw-Hill, [1979] 2008).

Bourdieu, Pierre, *Distinction: A Social Critique of the Judgement of Taste*, trans. Richard Nice, 2nd edn (Routledge, [1984] 2010).

———, 'The Forms of Capital' (1983), trans. Richard Nice, in John G. Richardson (ed.), *Handbook of Theory and Research for the Sociology of Education* (Westport, CT: Greenwood, 1986), pp. 243–8.

———, *Les Règles de l'art: genèse et structure du champ littéraire* (Paris: Éditions du Seuil, 1992).

———, *Le Sens pratique* (Paris: Éditions de Minuit, 1980).

Bourdrel, Philippe, *La Cagoule: histoire d'une société secrète du Front populaire à la Vè République* (Paris: Albin Michel, 1992).

Bowie, Malcolm, *Psychoanalysis and the Future of Theory* (Oxford: Blackwell, 1993).

Bowles, Brett, 'Renoir under the Popular Front: Aesthetics, Politics and the Paradoxes of Engagement', in Alastair Phillips and Ginette Vincendeau (eds), *A Companion to Jean Renoir* (London: Wiley-Blackwell, 2013), pp. 398–424.

Braudy, Leo, *Jean Renoir: The World of His Films* (London: Robson, 1977).

———, *The World in a Frame: What We See in Films*, 2nd edn (Chicago: University of Chicago Press, [1976] 2002).

Brunius, Jacques-B., *En marge du cinéma français*, ed. Jean-Pierre Pagliano, 2nd edn (Lausanne: Éditions l'Âge d'Homme, [1954] 1987).

Buchsbaum, Jonathan, *Cinema Engagé: Film in the Popular Front* (Urbana: Illinois University Press, 1988).

Burch, Noël, *Theory of Film Practice*, 2nd edn (Princeton, NJ: Princeton University Press, [1969] 1981).

Burgin, Victor, *In/different Spaces: Place and Memory in Visual Culture* (Berkeley: University of California Press, 1996).

Bush, Lyall, 'Feminine Narrative and the Law in Renoir's *Le Crime de M. Lange*', *Cinema Journal* 29.1 (1989), pp. 54–70.

Calvino, Italo, *Invisible Cities*, trans. William Weaver (London: Vintage, [1972] 1997).

Carné, Marcel, *Ma vie à belles dents* (Paris: L'Archipel, 1996).

Cauliez, Armand-Jean, *Jean Renoir* (Paris: Éditions Universitaires, 1962).

Cavell, Stanley, *The World Viewed: Reflections on the Ontology of Film*, 2nd edn (Cambridge, MA: Harvard University Press, [1971] 1979).

Certeau, Michel de, *L'Invention du quotidien*, 2nd edn (Paris: Gallimard, [1980] 1990).

Chardère, Bernard (ed.), *Premier Plan: Jean Renoir* 22–24 (1962).

Colman, Felicity, *Deleuze and Cinema: The Film Concepts* (Oxford: Berg, 2011).

Comolli, Jean-Louis, 'Technique et idéologie' (1971–2), in *Cinéma contre spectacle, suivi de Technique et idéologie (1971–1972)* (Lagrasse: Verdier, 2009), pp. 125–243.

Conley, Tom, 'Jean Renoir: Cartographies in Deep Focus', in *Cartographic Cinema* (Minneapolis: University of Minnesota Press, 2007), pp. 40–64.

Courtade, Francis, *Les Malédictions du cinéma français* (Paris: Alain Moreau, 1978).

Crisp, Colin, *The Classic French Cinema, 1930–1960* (Bloomington: Indiana University Press, 1993).

Curchod, Olivier and Christopher Faulkner (eds), *La Règle du jeu: scénario original de Jean Renoir* (Paris: Nathan, 1999).

Davis, Colin, *Critical Excess: Overreading in Derrida, Deleuze, Levinas, Žižek and Cavell* (Stanford, CA: Stanford University Press, 2010).

———, *Postwar Renoir: Film and the Memory of Violence* (New York: Routledge, 2012).

———, *Scenes of Love and Murder: Renoir, Film and Philosophy* (London: Wallflower Press, 2009).

Debord, Guy, *La Société du spectacle*, 3rd edn (Paris: Gallimard, [1967] 1992).

Deleuze, Gilles, *Le Bergsonisme*, 11th edn (Paris: Presses universitaires de France, [1966] 2011).

———, *Cinéma 1: L'Image-mouvement* (Paris: Éditions de Minuit, 1983).

———, *Cinéma 2: L'Image-temps* (Paris: Éditions de Minuit, 1985).

———, *Foucault*, 2nd edn (Paris: Éditions de Minuit, [1986] 2004).

———, *Pourparlers: 1972–1990*, 2nd edn (Paris: Éditions de Minuit, [1990] 2003).

——— and Félix Guattari, *Capitalisme et schizophrénie 2: Mille Plateaux* (Paris: Éditions de Minuit, 1980).

Dine, Philip, *Images of the Algerian War, 1954–1992* (Oxford: Clarendon, 1994).

Doane, Mary Ann, 'The Voice in the Cinema: The Articulation of Body and Space' (1980), in Leo Braudy and Marshall Cohen (eds), *Film Theory and Criticism: Introductory Readings*, 7th edn (New York: Oxford University Press, [1974] 2009), pp. 318–30.

Doel, Marcus A., 'A Hundred Thousand Lines of Flight: A Machinic Introduction to the Nomad Thought and Scrumpled Geography of Gilles Deleuze and Félix Guattari', *Environment and Planning D: Society and Space* 14.4 (1996), pp. 421–39.

Donald, James, 'The Citizen and the Man about Town', in Stuart Hall and Paul du Gay (eds), *Questions of Cultural Identity* (London: SAGE), pp. 170–90.

———, *Imagining the Modern City* (Minneapolis: Minnesota University Press, 1999).

———, 'This, Here, Now: Imagining the Modern City', in Sallie Westwood and John Williams (eds), *Imagining Cities: Scripts, Signs, Memory* (London: Routledge, 1997) pp. 179–99.

Doniol-Valcroze, Jacques, 'Camilla et le don', *Cahiers du Cinéma* 21 (1953), pp. 44–6.

DuPuis, E. Melanie, 'Landscapes of Desires?', in Paul Cloke, Terry Marsden, and Patrick Mooney (eds), *The Handbook of Rural Studies* (London: SAGE, 2006), pp. 124–32.

Durgnat, Raymond, *Jean Renoir* (Berkeley: University of California Press, 1974).

Elsaesser, Thomas, 'Postmodernism as Mourning Work', *Screen* 42.2 (2001), pp. 193–201.

———, 'Theatricality and Spectacle in *La Règle du jeu*, *Le Carrosse d'or*, and *Éléna et les hommes*', in Alastair Phillips and Ginette Vincendeau (eds), *A Companion to Jean Renoir* (London: Wiley-Blackwell, 2012), pp. 237–54.

Emerson, Catherine, *Regarding Manneken Pis: Culture, Celebration and Conflict in Brussels* (Oxford: Legenda, 2015).

Epstein, Jean, *Le Cinéma du diable* (Paris: Jacques Melot, 1947).

———, *Esprit de cinéma* (Paris: Jeheber, 1955).

———, '*Photogénie* and the Imponderable' (1935), trans. Richard Abel, in Richard Abel (ed.), *French Film Theory and Criticism, 1907–1939, Volume 2, 1929–1939* (Princeton, NJ: Princeton University Press, 1988), pp. 188–92.

Fanon, Frantz, *Les Damnés de la terre*, 2nd edn (Paris: Gallimard, [1961] 1991).

Faulkner, Christopher, 'Paris, Arizona; or the Redemption of Difference – Jean Renoir's *Le Crime de Monsieur Lange* (1935)', in Susan Hayward and Ginette Vincendeau (eds), *French Film: Texts and Contexts* (London: Routledge, 2000), pp. 27–41.

———, *The Social Cinema of Jean Renoir* (Princeton, NJ: Princeton University Press, 1986). Flaxman, Gregory, 'Transcendental Aesthetics: Deleuze's Philosophy of Space', in Ian Buchanan and Gregg Lambert (eds), *Deleuze and Space* (Edinburgh: Edinburgh University Press, 2005), pp. 176–88.

Flinn, Margaret C., *The Social Architecture of French Cinema, 1929–1939* (Liverpool: Liverpool University Press, 2014).

Forbes, Jill, '*La Règle du jeu*', in Jill Forbes and Sarah Street (eds), *European Cinema: An Introduction* (Basingstoke: Palgrave, 2000), pp. 81–94.

Foucault, Michel, *Surveiller et punir: naissance de la prison*, 3rd edn (Paris: Gallimard, [1975] 2013).

Fouchardière, Georges de la, *La Chienne* (Paris: Albin Michel, 1930).

Gauteur, Claude, *D'un Renoir l'autre*, 2nd edn (Paris: Le Temps des Cerises, [1980] 2005).

Ghose, Sumit, 'Treatment of Women in the Cinema of Jean Renoir', PhD dissertation (Ohio State University, 1997).

Giddens, Anthony and Philip W. Sutton, *Sociology*, 7th edn (Cambridge: Polity Press, [1989] 2017).

Gilcher, William Harry, 'Jean Renoir in America: A Critical Analysis of His Films from *Swamp Water* to *The River*', PhD dissertation (University of Iowa, 1979).

Godden, Rumer, *The River*, 2nd edn (London: Pan, [1946] 2004).

Golsan, Katherine, 'A Hollywood Fairytale: Renoir's *Diary of a Chambermaid*', *South Central Review* 25.2 (2008), pp. 45–62.

Gorky, Maxime, *Les Bas-fonds*, trans. Genia Cannac (Paris: L'Arche, 2009).

Harper, Graeme and Jonathan Rayner, 'Introduction – Cinema and Landscape', in Graeme Harper and Jonathan Rayner (eds), *Cinema and Landscape: Film, Nation and Cultural Geography* (Bristol: Intellect, 2010), pp. 13–28.

Harpole, Charles H., 'Ideological and Technological Determinism in Deep-Space Cinema Images: Issues in Ideology, Technological History, and Aesthetics', *Film Quarterly* 33.3 (1980), pp. 11–22.

Harris, Sue, 'Renoir's Paris: The City as Film Set', *South Central Review* 28.3 (2011), pp. 84–102.

Harvey, David, *The Limits to Capital* (Oxford: Blackwell, 1982).

Hayward, Susan, 'The City as Narrative: Corporeal Paris in Contemporary French Cinema (1952–1990s)', in Myrto Konstantarakos (ed.), *Spaces in European Cinema* (Exeter: Intellect, 2000), pp. 23–34.

———, 'Design at Work: Renoir's Costume Dramas of the 1950s', in Alastair Phillips and Ginette Vincendeau (eds), *A Companion to Jean Renoir* (London: Wiley-Blackwell, 2012), pp. 88–105.

———, 'Filming the (Post-)Colonial Landscape: Claire Denis' *Chocolat* (1988) and *Beau Travail* (1998)', in Graeme Harper and Jonathan Rayner (eds), *Cinema and Landscape: Film, Nation and Cultural Geography* (Bristol: Intellect, 2010), pp. 161–75.

———, *French Costume Drama of the 1950s: Fashioning Politics in Film* (Bristol: Intellect, 2010).

———, *French National Cinema* (London: Routledge, 1993).

Hewitt, Nicholas, 'Shifting Cultural Centres in Twentieth-century Paris', in Michael Sheringham (ed.), *Parisian Fields* (London: Reaktion, 1996), pp. 30–45.

Hodeir, Catherine and Michel Pierre, *L'Exposition coloniale, Paris 1931* (Brussels: Éditions Complexe, 1991).

Horne, John, 'Introduction', in John Horne (ed.), *A Companion to World War I* (Chichester: Wiley-Blackwell, 2012), pp. xvi–xxviii.

Howard, Michael, *The First World War: A Very Short Introduction* (Oxford: Oxford University Press, 2007).

Hussey, Andrew, *Paris: The Secret History*, 2nd edn (London: Penguin, [2006] 2017).

Jeancolas, Jean-Pierre, *Le Cinéma des Français: 15 ans d'années trente (1929–1944)*, 2nd edn (Paris: Nouveau Monde Éditions, [1983] 2005).

Junyk, Ihor, 'The Face of the Nation: State Fetishism and "Métissage" at the Exposition Internationale, Paris 1937', *Grey Room* 23 (2006), pp. 96–120.

Kracauer, Siegfried, *From Caligari to Hitler: A Psychological History of the German Film* (Princeton, NJ: Princeton University Press, 1966).

———, *Theory of Film: The Redemption of Physical Reality* (Princeton, NJ: Princeton University Press, [1960] 1997).

Kuhn, Annette, 'Classic Hollywood Narrative', in Pam Cook (ed.), *The Cinema Book* (London: BFI, [1985] 2007), pp. 45–6.

Leenhardt, Roger, 'Les Arts: *Les Bas-fonds*, Prix « Louis Delluc »', *Esprit* 53 (February 1937), pp. 833–4.

Lefebvre, Henri, *La Production de l'espace*, 4th edn ([1974] 2000).

Leutrat, Jean-Louis, *« La Chienne » de Jean Renoir* (Crisnée: Éditions Yellow Now, 1994).

Lourié, Eugène, *My Work in Films* (San Diego: Harcourt Brace Jovanovich, 1985).

Lury, Karen and Doreen Massey, 'Making Connections', *Screen* 40.3 (1999), pp. 229–38.

McCann, Ben, *Le Jour se lève* (London: I. B. Tauris, 2014).

———, *Ripping Open the Set: French Film Design, 1930–1939* (Oxford: Peter Lang, 2013).

Macdonald, Nicholas, *In Search of* La Grande Illusion (Jefferson: McFarland, 2013).

Marie, Laurent, 'Renoir and the French Communist Party: The Grand Disillusion', in Alastair Phillips and Ginette Vincendeau (eds), *A Companion to Jean Renoir* (London: Wiley-Blackwell, 2013), pp. 328–46.

Massey, Doreen, *For Space* (London: SAGE, 2005).

———, *Space, Place, and Gender* (Minneapolis: University of Minnesota Press, 1994).

Mérigeau, Pascal, *Jean Renoir* (Paris: Flammarion, 2012).

Mérimée, Prosper, 'La Carrosse du Saint-Sacrement' (1829), in *La Carrosse du Saint-Sacrement; Lettres d'Espagne; Carmen* (Paris: Larousse, 1927).

Mirbeau, Octave, *Le Journal d'une femme de chambre* (Paris: Gallimard, [1900] 1984).

Mouézy-Éon, André, *La Chienne: pièce en trois actes et quatorze tableaux* (Paris: Les Cahiers de Bravo, 1931).

Murdoch, Jonathan, 'Middle-class Territory? Some Remarks on the Use of Class Analysis in Rural Studies', in Richard Munton (ed.), *The Rural: Critical Essays in Human Geography* (London: Ashgate, 2005), pp. 359–76.

Narboni, Jean, Janine Bazin, and Claude Gauteur (eds), *Jean Renoir: entretiens et propos*, (Paris: Cahiers du Cinéma, [1986] 2005).

Nevin, Barry, 'Paris vs Providence: Framing the Crystalline City in Jean Renoir's *La Chienne* (1931)', *Journal of Urban Cultural Studies* 3.1 (2016), pp. 55–72.

———, '"Prochainement: Arizona Jim contre Cagoulard": Framing the Future of the Front Populaire in Jean Renoir's *Le Crime de Monsieur Lange* (1936)', *Studies in French Cinema* (forthcoming 2018), pp. 1–20.

———, '"What we have done is shameful": Interrogating the Relationship between France and Its *Algérie* in Jean Renoir's *Le Bled* (1929)', *Studies in French Cinema* 16.2 (2016), pp. 1–18.

Newby, Howard, 'Locality and Rurality: The Restructuring of Rural Social Relations', *Regional Studies* 20.3 (1986), pp. 209–15.

Nora, Pierre, 'Between Memory and History: *Les Lieux de Mémoire*', *Representations* 26 (1989), pp. 7–24.

Nowell-Smith, Geoffrey, 'Cities: Real and Imagined', in Mark Shiel and Tony Fitzmaurice (eds), *Cinema and the City: Film and Urban Societies in a Global Context* (Oxford: Blackwell, 2001), p. 99–108.

O'Brien, Charles, *Cinema's Conversion to Sound: Technology and Film Style in France and the U.S.* (Bloomington: Indiana University Press, 2005).

———, 'Relocating Renoir's Sound and Music', in Alastair Phillips and Ginette Vincendeau (eds), *A Companion to Jean Renoir* (Oxford: Wiley-Blackwell, 2013), pp. 35–52.

Ogle, Patrick L., 'Technological and Aesthetic Influences Upon the Development of Deep Focus Cinematography in the United States', *Screen* 13.1 (1972), pp. 45–72.

Ory, Pascal, 'De « Ciné-liberté » à *La Marseillaise*: Espoirs et limites d'un cinéma libéré (1936–1938)', *Le Mouvement social* 91 (1975), pp. 153–75.

O'Shaughnessy, Martin, 'Between the "I" and the "We": Jean Renoir's Films of the Popular Front Era', in Jessica Wardhaugh (ed.), *Politics and the Individual in France 1930–1950* (Oxford: Legenda, 2015), pp. 41–57.

———, 'Breaking the Circle: *Le Crime de Monsieur Lange* and the Contemporary Illegibility of the Radical Text', *South Central Review* 28.3 (2011), pp. 26–44.

———, *La Grande Illusion* (London: I. B. Tauris, 2009).

———, *Jean Renoir* (Manchester: Manchester University Press, 2000).

———, 'Shooting in Deep Time: The *Mise en Scène* of History in Renoir's Films of the 1930s', in Alastair Phillips and Ginette Vincendeau (eds), *A Companion to Jean Renoir* (Oxford: Wiley-Blackwell, 2013), pp. 16–34.

Ousselin, Edward, 'Film and the Popular Front: *La Belle Équipe* and *Le Crime de M. Lange*', *The French Review* 79.5 (2006), pp. 952–62.

Parry, D. L. L., 'Counter Revolution by Conspiracy, 1935–37', in Nicholas Atkin and Frank Tallett (eds), *The Right in France: From Revolution to Le Pen* (London: I. B. Tauris, 2003), pp. 161–81.

Perez, Gilberto, *The Material Ghost: Films and Their Medium* (Baltimore: Johns Hopkins University Press, 1998).

Pisters, Patricia, *The Matrix of Visual Culture: Working with Deleuze in Film Theory* (Stanford, CA: Stanford University Press, 2003).

Poulle, François, *Renoir 1938 ou Jean Renoir pour rien: enquête sur un cinéaste* (Paris: Éditions du Cerf, 1969).

Pratt, Geraldine and Rose Marie San Juan, *Film and Urban Space: Critical Possibilities* (Edinburgh: Edinburgh University Press, 2014).

Privitello, Lucio Angelo, 'The Incompassable Language of Natural Aristocracy: Deleuze's Misreading of Visconti's *The Leopard*', *Senses of Cinema* 37 (2005),

<http://sensesofcinema.com/2005/feature-articles/leopard/> (last accessed 20 August 2017).

Pulju, Rebecca J., *Women and Mass Consumer Society in Postwar France* (Cambridge: Cambridge University Press, 2011).

Reader, Keith, 'The Circular Ruins? Frontiers, Exile and the Nation in Renoir's *Le Crime de Monsieur Lange*', *French Studies* 54.3 (2000), pp. 287–97.

———, *La Règle du jeu* (London: I. B. Tauris, 2010).

———, 'Renoir's Popular Front Films in Context', in Ginette Vincendeau and Keith Reader (eds), *La Vie est à nous!: French Cinema of the Popular Front 1935–1938* (London: BFI, 1986), pp. 37–59.

———, '*Toni*: A Regional Melodrama of Failed Masculinity', in Alastair Phillips and Ginette Vincendeau (eds), *A Companion to Jean Renoir* (Hoboken, NJ: Wiley-Blackwell, 2013), pp. 444–53.

Renoir, Jean, *Correspondance (1913–1978)*, ed. David Thompson and Lorraine LoBianco (Paris: Plon, 1998).

———, *Écrits, 1926–1971*, ed. Claude Gauteur, 2nd edn (Paris: Ramsay, [1974] 2006).

———, 'Gorki en celluloïd: « Les Bas-fonds »', in Claude Gauteur (ed.), *Le Passé vivant* (Paris: Cahiers du cinéma, 1989), pp. 27–8.

———, *Ma vie et mes films*, 2nd edn (Paris: Flammarion, [1974] 2005).

———, *Œuvres de cinéma inédites*, ed. Claude Gauteur (Paris: Gallimard, 1981).

———, *Pierre-Auguste Renoir, mon père* (Paris: Gallimard, [1962] 1981).

———, 'Propos rompus', ed. Jean-Louis Noames, *Cahiers du cinéma* 155 (1964), pp. 22–30.

———, 'Souvenirs . . .' (1938), in André Bazin, *Jean Renoir*, ed. François Truffaut (Paris, Ivrea, [1971] 2005), pp. 143–53.

Rhode, Eric, *A History of the Cinema from Its Origins to 1970* (Harmondsworth: Penguin, 1978).

Rivette, Jacques and François Truffaut, 'Entretien avec Jean Renoir', *Cahiers du Cinéma* 34 (1954), pp. 3–22.

Rohmer, Éric, 'Le Cinéma, art de l'espace' (1948), in *Le Goût de la beauté*, ed. Jean Narboni, 2nd edn (Paris: Cahiers du Cinéma, [1989] 2004), pp. 41–55.

———, 'Les singes et Vénus', *Cahiers du Cinéma* 64 (1956), pp. 37–40.

Rushton, Richard, 'A Deleuzian Imaginary: The Films of Jean Renoir', *Deleuze Studies* 5.2 (2011), pp. 241–60.

Salt, Barry, *Film Style and Technology: History & Analysis*, 3rd edn (London: Starword, [1985] 2009).

Sarris, Andrew, *The American Cinema: Directors and Directions, 1929–1968* (Boston: Da Capo Press, [1968] 1996).

Sennett, Richard, *The Fall of Public Man: On the Social Psychology of Capitalism* (New York: Vintage, 1974).

Serceau, Daniel, *Jean Renoir: la sagesse du plaisir* (Paris: Éditions du Cerf, 1985).

———, *Jean Renoir, l'insurgé* (Paris: Le Sycomore, 1981).

Sesonske, Alexander, 'Jean Renoir as Moralist: *Le Crime de M. Lange*', *Journal of Aesthetic Education* 8.1 (1974), pp. 5–26.

———, *Jean Renoir, the French Films, 1924–1939* (Cambridge, MA: Harvard University Press, 1980).

———, 'The River Runs, The Round World Spins', *New Review of Film and Television Studies* 3.2 (2005), pp. 105–31.

Short, Brian, 'Idyllic Ruralities', in Paul Cloke, Terry Marsden, and Patrick Mooney (eds), *The Handbook of Rural Studies* (London: SAGE, 2006), pp. 133–48.

Singer, Irving, *Three Philosophical Filmmakers: Hitchcock, Welles, Renoir* (Cambridge, MA: MIT Press, 2004).

Slavin, David Henry, *Colonial Cinema and Imperial France, 1919–1939: White Blind Spots, Male Fantasies, Settler Myths* (Baltimore: Johns Hopkins University Press, 2001).

Sorlin, Pierre, 'France: The Silent Memory', in Michael Paris (ed.), *The First World War and Popular Cinema: 1914 to the Present* (New Brunswick, NJ: Rutgers University Press, 2000), pp. 115–37.

Strebel, Elizabeth Grottle, 'Jean Renoir and the Popular Front', in K. R. M. Short (ed.), *Feature Films as History* (Knoxville: University of Tennessee Press, 1981), pp. 76–93.

Tally, Robert T., *Spatiality* (London: Routledge, 2013).

Tesson, Charles, 'Jean Renoir et Luis Buñuel: autour du *Journal d'une femme de chambre*', in Frank Curot (ed.), *Jean Renoir: nouvelles approches* (Montpellier: Université Paul Valéry, 1995), pp. 39–62.

Thompson, Kristin, *Breaking the Glass Armor: Neoformalist Film Analysis* (Princeton, NJ: Princeton University Press, 1988).

Tifft, Stephen, 'Theatre in the Round: The Politics of Space in the Films of Jean Renoir', *Theatre Journal* 39.3 (1987), pp. 328–46.

Turim, Maureen, 'The Displacement of Architecture in Avant-Garde Films', *Iris* 12 (1991), pp. 25–38.

———, *Flashbacks in Film: Memory & History* (New York: Routledge, 1989).

Viry-Babel, Roger, 'Les Images de la femme dans l'œuvre de Jean Renoir', PhD dissertation (Université de Nancy II, 1988).

Vitanza, Elizabeth Ann, 'Rewriting the Rules of the Game: Jean Renoir in America, 1940–1947', PhD dissertation (University of Los Angeles, California, 2007).

Weinberg, Herman G., 'Lettre de New-York', *Cahiers du Cinéma* 24 (1953), pp. 35–7.

West-Pavlov, Russell, *Temporalities* (London: Routledge, 2012).

Williams, Christopher, 'The Deep Focus Question: Some Comments on Patrick Ogle's Article', *Screen* 13.1 (1972), pp. 73–9.

Williams, Raymond, *The Country and the City* (New York: Oxford University Press, 1973).

Wollen, Peter, *Signs and Meanings in the Cinema*, 5th edn (London: BFI, 2013).

Younger, Prakash, '*The River*: Beneath the Surface with André Bazin', in Alastair Phillips and Ginette Vincendeau (eds), *A Companion to Jean Renoir* (Chichester: Wiley-Blackwell, 2013), pp. 166–75.

Artwork

Renoir, Pierre-Auguste, *La Mosquée*, oil on canvas, 1881 (Musée d'Orsay, Paris).

Filmography

Only the works mentioned over the course of this book are listed here; see the Appendix for a list of Renoir's entire body of films. Details of DVDs used for screenshots are provided after production details of individual films where relevant.

Antonioni, Michelangelo, *Il deserto rosso/Red Desert*, 1964. France/Italy: Francoriz.
———, *L'Avventura*, 1960. Italy: Cino Del Duca.
Bresson, Robert, *Pickpocket*, 1959. France: Compagnie Cinématographique de France.
Browning, Tod, *The Unholy Three*, 1925. USA: Metro-Goldwyn-Mayer.
———, *The Unknown*, 1927. USA: Metro-Goldwyn-Mayer.
Carné, Marcel, *Le Jour se lève/Daybreak*, 1939. France: Tobis.
Chaplin, Charles, *Modern Times*, 1934. USA: Charles Chaplin Productions.
Clair, René, *À nous la liberté/Liberty Is Ours*, 1931. Paris: Tobis-France.
Dreyer, Carl Th., *La Passion de Jeanne d'Arc/The Passion of Joan of Arc*, 1928. France: Société Générale des Films.
Eisenstein, Sergei M., *Bronenosets Potemkin/Battleship Potemkin*, 1925. USSR: Mosfilm.
———, *Staroye i novoye/General Line*, 1929. USSR: Mosfilm.
Flaherty, Robert, *Nanook of the North*, 1922. USA: Pathé.
Griffith, D. W., *The Birth of a Nation*, 1915. USA: David W. Griffith Corporation.
———, *Intolerance: Love's Struggle Throughout the Ages*, 1916. USA: Triangle Film Corporation.
Kanin, Garson and Jean Renoir, *Salute to France*, 1944. USA: American Office of War Information.
Lang, Fritz, *Fury*, 1936. USA: Metro-Goldwyn-Mayer.
———, *Metropolis*, 1927. Germany: Ufa.
Mankiewicz, Joseph L., *All About Eve*, 1950. USA: 20th Century Fox.
Minnelli, Vincente, *The Pirate*, 1948. USA: Metro-Goldwyn-Mayer.
Murnau, F. W., *Sunrise: A Song of Two Humans*, 1927. USA: Fox Film Corporation.
Ophüls, Max, *Lola Montès*, 1955. France: Gamma.
Ozu, Yasujirō, *Banshun/Late Spring*, 1949. Japan: Shôchiku Eiga.

———, *Tôkyô monogatari/Tokyo Story*, 1953. Japan: Shôchiku Eiga.

Renoir, Jean, *Les Bas-fonds/The Lower Depths*, 1936. France: Albatros. DVD: Criterion, 2004.

———, *La Bête humaine/The Human Beast*, 1938. France: Paris Film.

———, *Le Bled/The Bush*, 1929. France/Algeria: Société des Films Historiques. DVD: Gaumont, 2012.

———, *Boudu sauvé des eaux/Boudu Saved from Drowning*, 1932. France: Les Films Michel Simon. DVD: Criterion, 2005.

———, *Le Caporal épinglé/The Elusive Corporal*, 1962. France: Films du Cyclope.

———, *La Chienne/The Bitch*, 1931. France: Braunberger-Richebé. DVD: Criterion, 2016.

———, *Le Crime de Monsieur Lange/The Crime of Mr Lange*, 1936. France: Obéron. DVD: StudioCanal, 2004.

———, *Le Déjeuner sur l'herbe/Picnic on the Grass*, 1959. France: Compagnie Jean Renoir.

———, *Diary of a Chambermaid*, 1946. USA: Camden. DVD: Olive Films, 2013.

———, *Eléna et les hommes/Eléna and Her Men*, 1956. France/England: Franco-London Films. DVD: Criterion, 2004.

———, *La Fille de l'eau/Whirlpool of Fate*, 1925. France: Les Films Jean Renoir.

———, *French Cancan*, 1954. France: Franco-London Films.

———, *The Golden Coach*, 1952. France/Italy: Panaria. DVD: Criterion, 2004.

———, *La Grande Illusion/Grand Illusion*, 1937. France: Réalisations d'Art Cinématographique. DVD: Criterion, 1999.

———, *La Marseillaise*, 1938. France: Société de Production et d'Exploitation du film *La Marseillaise*.

———, *Nana*, 1926. France: Les Films Jean Renoir.

———, *Partie de campagne/A Day in the Country*, 1936. France: Panthéon.

———, *La Petite Marchande d'allumettes/The Little Match Girl*, 1928. France: S.O.F.A.R.

———, *Le Petit Théâtre de Jean Renoir/The Little Theatre of Jean Renoir*, 1970. France/Italy: Office de Radiodiffusion Télévision Française/Son et Lumière/Radiotelevisione Italiana.

———, *La Règle du jeu*, 1939. France: Les Nouvelles Éditions Françaises. DVD: Criterion, 2004.

———, *The River*, 1951. USA/India: Oriental-International Films. DVD: BFI, 2006.

———, *The Southerner*, 1945. USA: United Artists. DVD: Kino, 2016.

———, *Sur un air de Charleston/Charleston*, 1927. France: Les Films Jean Renoir.

———, *Swamp Water*, 1941. USA: 20th Century Fox.

———, *Le Testament du Docteur Cordelier/Experiment in Evil*, 1959. France: Compagnie Jean Renoir/Radio-Télévision française/Société Financière de Radiodiffusion.

———, *This Land is Mine*, 1943. USA: RKO.

———, *Tire-au-flanc/The Sad Sack*, 1928. France: Néo-Film.

———, *Toni*, 1935. France: Les Films Marcel Pagnol.
———, *La Vie est à nous/Life Belongs to Us!*, 1936. France: Parti Communiste Français.
———, *Woman on the Beach*, 1947. USA: RKO.
Rossellini, Roberto, *Roma città aperta/Rome, Open City*, 1945. Italy: Minerva.
Sica, Vittorio de, *Ladri di biciclette/Bicycle Thieves*, 1948. Italy: Ente Nazionale Industrie Cinematografiche.
Stroheim, Erich von, *Foolish Wives*, 1922. USA: Universal.
———, *Greed*, 1924. USA: MGM.
Varda, Agnès, *Le Bonheur/Happiness*, 1965. France: Parc Film.
Visconti, Luchino, *La caduta degli dei/The Damned*, 1969. Italy: Eichberg.
———, *Il Gattopardo/The Leopard*, 1963. Italy: Titanus.
———, *Ludwig*, 1973. Italy/France: Cinétel/Mega.
Welles, Orson, *Citizen Kane*, 1941. USA: RKO.

Film Index

General Subject Index

CPSIA information can be obtained
at www.ICGtesting.com
Printed in the USA
BVHW061555300620
582685BV00003B/23

9 781474 426329